Ignite Your Parenting

Real life, heartfelt stories to help parents find balance and joy in raising happy children.

FOREWORD BY

Dr. Shefali Tsabary

Clinical Psychologist, Best-Selling Author

PRESENTED BY

Ana Sofia Orozco, Ashley Avinashi, Bippan Dhillon, Bonnie Chan, Catherine Malli-Dawson, Christy Yates, Elise Edmeades, Elysse Green, Faraaz Ãlì, Gina Ingram, Helle Simonsen, Helle Brodie, Hilary Cole, Ivana Antunović, Ana Cukrov, JB Owen, Jodi Law, Kara Ann Block, Madalina Petrescu, Michaela De Sapio-Yazar, Olivia M. Dam, Parth Nilawar, Phyllis Roberto, Saydee Short, Sally Daniels, Sara Feldman, Stacey Yates Sellar, Steven J. Posner, Shrreya Shah, Sunaina Vohra, Tanja Powell, Ulla Jovkovic, Uri Yeszerski, Virginia L Lehay, and Yendre Shen.

Published by Ignite Publishing and printed by JBO Global INC.

DEDICATION

This book is dedicated to anyone who is on the path of parenting and re-parenting themselves in a conscious way. We know that raising ourselves and our children can feel, at times, like a difficult road. Perhaps, this is due to the era of disconnection in which we find ourselves today.

Despite this reality, we have a tremendous opportunity to re-connect and experience the love that is available to us by working through the limiting beliefs and pain patterns that have held us back. When we can come into our vulnerability and trust the lessons and teachers along the way, we, alongside our children, can evolve to become the best and most beautiful versions of ourselves. We all deserve to live a life that is true to our own blueprint.

The authors profiled in this book have overcome many hindrances to reach their own greatness. By embracing the courage and wisdom within, they have triumphed. They share many moments that have propelled them into deeper compassion, joy, acceptance, patience, empowerment, learning, understanding and much more.

As you dive into the stories, we hope you are reminded that you are worthy of a beautifully ignited life and support along the way. Our hope is to spread encouragement to show up more fully in the beauty of our humanness, and by doing so, model for others what is possible.

Let's step into our greatness so that together, we can not only elevate our lives today but that for generations ahead.

Much love and gratitude for all that you are.

~ Ashley Avinashi, Founder of Raising Humanity

Krish Avinashi, age 5

Ignite Author's Testimonials

"I never thought that writing a story for the parenting book would have been so transformative. I changed how I engage with my son and how I show up as a father. Going through this process with the Ignite team and the community has been amazing. I loved the support and inspiration. I never thought of myself as a writer, having written the story, I now feel I am and it's inspired me to take writing more seriously and hopefully write more chapters and who knows maybe a book one day. Thank you JB and the team, you definitely Ignited my life."
~ Steven J Posner

"Moving through my story sharing my experience with the Ignite community was deeply impactful. It helped bring focus to where I could show up more fully for myself and others. Overall, the process itself was very empowering in helping me bring my voice and heart forward on paper." ~ Ashley Avinashi

"Writing my parenting story for the Ignite series has been an experience that surprised and restored me in ways I did not expect. I felt love and community among people who collectively want to contribute something good to the world. Recounting part of my life in this art form of the written word has been unexpectedly therapeutic and uplifting for me. I hope readers are touched by the heartfelt stories told in these pages." ~ Yendre Shen

"We embraced the possibility to become authors in this fabulous book series. Why did we decide to do it together? Being twins and raising five children each, we are blessed with the gifts of motherhood and constant mutual support. Working on this book made us even more aware of that, and in the process it made us both grow even more, personally and between us. We enjoyed waking up our creativity, exploring our own growing-up and parenting, sharing with readers what we learned along our way. Our message to parents of the world is to lean on each other, so the kids can grow and glow. For us, working with the Ignite editorial team was like that – supportive, joyful, professional and heart-warming. It was full of growing and glowing." ~ Ivana Sošić Antunović and Ana Cukrov

"I am so grateful to have birthed my first book with an incredibly supportive team. I could not have asked for a better experience. You all have been my doula in my emotional labor. It has been a truly healing and empowering experience."
~ Uri Yeszerski

Publisher's Note:

We are delighted to offer the third compilation book in the IGNITE series. Our mission is to produce inspiring, motivational and authentic real-life stories that will Ignite You in your life. This book contains 34 unique stories told by 35 exceptional authors. They are of the highest caliber to offer engaging, profound and life-changing examples that will impact the reader. Our mandate is to build a conscious, positive and supportive community through our books, speaking events, writing workshops, ignite experiences, podcasts, immersions and a product marketplace. We welcome new authors onto our platform and new book ideas. Should you desire to be published and featured in an Ignite book, please apply at www.igniteyou.life/apply or reach out to us at suppport@igniteyou.life.

Ignite Your Parenting

Shefali Tsabary and JB Owen

FOREWORD BY
SHEFALI TSABARY

Clinical Psychologist, Best-Selling Author, and International Speaker

"Life doesn't happen to us, but happens with us."

I am honored to acknowledge the true stories of conscious and awakened parenting being shared in this book. They are the real and raw reflections of the ebbs and flows in the process of raising another human being. It is in these stories that you will find courage, perseverance and tenacity. Along with unconditional love, overwhelming acceptance and deep, unwavering devotion. These are the many sides of conscious parenting. These are the stories of the shadows and the light. It is in looking at all sides that we are able to see the clarity and beauty. It is from sharing those authentic sides of ourselves that we find our parenting purpose. These stories reflect that and so much more. I commend the thirty-five individuals that committed their time and effort, (with children in the wings) to share their stories and inspire others. This book is truly a gift.

I wish for you the ever-present and all-encompassing joy of experiencing conscious parenthood. It is often said, "Life is to be experienced". Many have uttered these words and then left it at that, not fully qualifying or explaining more. I like to say, "Life is to be experienced, not fought against, run from, or engaged half-heartedly. Though we may wish to make changes in the future, to be conscious is to be with an experience as it is unfolding, rather than thinking about how we would like to change it."

Nowhere is that more relevant than when it comes to parenting. The parent is asked to both lean in and let go. To fully engage in the most exuberant ways, while detaching, standing back and at the same time, observing and always connecting. It is the most peripherally engaged, independently intertwined relationship in the world, and if you are reading this book then you fit into this category. You are loving both yourself and your child in the greatest role ever created.

What is new after centuries of raising children is a breed of parents fostering a co-collaborative and co-creative relationship. A new paradigm is emerging, which encourages our children to embrace their true light based on a blueprint that is unique to them; not a norm that is customary to society or past generations. Until now, the model of parenting has been turned outwards, onto our children. We have held them responsible for creating our experience of parenthood, rather than taking ownership to create the experience that exists within us. It is the parents' work to unwind the conditioning that keeps them tied to what no longer serves them. This is their responsibility while offering the child a clear path to living a life uniquely designed for them.

In this new conscious modality, parenting becomes an incredibly powerful co-created experience. We learn to raise our children outside of ourselves. We encourage their self-discovery while in turn discovering our own authentic selves. Parenting becomes one of the greatest portals towards self-awareness and transformation. Noticing the lessons as we journey alongside our children, rather than in front of them, we learn to intuitively teach and heal our own wounded inner child. We see our own immaturity and opportunities for growth. We heal our past wounds and reconnect with our awakened self. We happily relinquish the reins of control and conviction, so that wonderment can easily flourish.

What we see in the world today is children not having the freedom to be who they want to be. Instead, their light is dampened by fears their parents' project and the confines society imposes. As a result, children lose their own self-exploration and autonomy in a desire to meet their parent's unmet needs. They internalize and acquiesce trying to live out their parents' idyllic dream of how they thought parenting should be. This is a heavy burden for a child to carry and one we can absolve when we take responsibility to clear out our pain patterns and false beliefs as parents. When we shed the constructs of who they as children, and we as parents idealistically need to be, we freely enjoy our role as parent.

To Ignite your parenting, a shift must take place in you. A new version of your parenting dogma must emerge; void of the shackles that have enslaved you till now. A bright awareness must blossom honoring who the child is in you and in them. We were all born in our truest essence. Each one of us deserves to bask in that glory. Conscious parenting is a paradigm in which you realize that you are raising a spirit bursting forth with its own signature. A human being perfectly okay with their okay-ness. I have often said...

"My child isn't my easel to paint on Nor my diamond to polish My child isn't my trophy to share with the world Nor my badge of honor My child isn't an idea, an expectation, or a fantasy Nor my reflection or legacy My child isn't my puppet or a project Nor my striving or desire My child is here to fumble, stumble, try, and cry Learn and mess up Fail and try again Listen to the beat of a drum faint to our adult ears And dance to a song that revels in freedom My task is to step aside Stay in infinite possibility Heal my own wounds Fill my own bucket And let my child fly"

May you and your child fly high and soar far in your love and connection.
- Dr. Shefali Tsabary

AWAKENING TO PARENTING
BY JB OWEN FOUNDER OF IGNITE

I had the joy of meeting Dr. Shefali in Tallinn, Estonia at a conference on personal growth. She asked a few audience members to come up on stage and share some problems they were having with their kids in the hopes of discovering the underlying issues. Two brave souls and I stood in front of a thousand people and told the intimate and private troubles we were currently facing. One lady shared how she couldn't get her teenager to do anything she asked. The man beside me expressed how he felt he didn't belong at such a conference. His parenting didn't come close to what was expected and a part of him, he admitted, wanted to run and hide like a kid.

It isn't every day you get face-to-face time with one of the greatest minds in the parenting space. Her best selling books have changed the way millions of people parent. Her innovative ideas have transformed families around the world, and she is repeatedly shown on Oprah spreading her revolutionary message of conscious parenting. I wasn't going to pass up the chance to honestly share and get some insight into my parenting conundrums.

Coincidentally the day before, I had gotten into a bit of fray with my teenage son. He too was attending the conference along with my eleven-year-old daughter. We were on a one-month immersion for families where both the adults and kids learn personal development and self-improvement skills. I was feeling a bit off that day. My energy was low, my hormones jumbled. It was clear to me I was ovulating and I needed some quiet space. But like a bee to honey or a dog after a bone, my son was following me, pestering me, insisting he get maximum attention from my off-balanced self.

The interchange went on for a while. Each time I tried to nod in agreement or patiently say no to what he wanted, he ramped up the wattage and kept pushing. I am sure you can see where this is going. He kept insistently pushing and I lost my composure and eventually grabbed him by the ear and tugged on him to stop badgering me.

I have to laugh now telling the story. I never pull my son on the ear. But I believe the divine Universe had me do so I would get up on that stage and share candidly with Shefali what I had done. Telling a thousand people one of your not so proud mommy moments wasn't easy, but Shefali was gracious and dove deeply into the feelings and emotions behind the reasons we parents do what we do. After a lengthy and exposing conversation sat down; a bit splayed opened for the crowd but inspired by Shefali's conclusions.

When we returned to the lecture after the break, Shefali had invited all the young kids at the conference to join. She wanted to have the children speak up and the parents just listen. Her idea was to ask the kids what they needed and wanted from their parents without any filters. Except in a large room with so many adults, so many kids and an intimidating microphone, none of the children were volunteering any information. Shefali probed the audience of little faces all sitting up close to the stage. She asked them who would like to share something they need from their parents or take this opportunity to tell 'us parents' how kids really feel. After a long silence and awkward shyness, one brave little girl put up her hand.

She rose and took the microphone, cautiously telling the entire room how she wished her mom knew how much she was trying to make her happy. How she tries so hard to put a smile on her mom's face and it doesn't always happen. How she wished her mom didn't work so much and played with her more. Shefali happily used her examples to expand on some vital parenting concepts and kindly probed for more. The little girl let down her guard, tearing up due to the pressures she felt from her mother. After a lengthy conversation, the young girl felt better. Shefali had expertly persuaded her to share some deep intimate feelings and reveal some very personal family dynamics. It was a heartfelt and a moving conversation to see the inner pain of this young girl trying to bear the responsibility of making her mom happy and doing so much to be perfect.

When the conversation ended, Shefali thanked the little girl and asked very graciously for the mother of that articulate and brave child to stand up. I rose to my feet. That was my daughter revealing her anguish for everyone to see. Yes, the same parent who earlier had admitted pulling her son's ear. It wasn't my proudest mommy moment while I wiped the tears from my eyes. Shefali recognized me and tenderly explained a pattern forming in my interactions with my kids. She went on to use what my daughter and I shared to teach the entire room more about this common parenting dilemma.

I used the lunch break to connect with my daughter. She was afraid that I would be upset by her telling her truth. I kissed her repeatedly and told her how thankful I was for her sharing, for being so courageous to reveal her feelings and how important and grateful I was to hear them. It was a magical moment for both of us. Her unburdening her worries and me softening my expectations of her. It brought us so much closer and opened a deeper connection between us. We hugged tightly as the lecture resumed and my daughter ran back to the kids' room, leaving me in the conference hall.

This time Shefali had invited the teenagers to join the conversation. Just like before, she wanted to open the forum to have that age group share their feelings and express what they needed from their parents. Unlike the youngsters, it didn't take long for this generation to speak up. One by one, kids stood up to say a short sentence: my parents expect me to get top grades; my dad is so strict; my mom is too mothering. The peer pressure in the room was obvious and few were willing to say much more until one boy stood up, ready to talk. He engaged in a hearty debate with Shefali about the purpose of this entire conference. He felt it was all fine and dandy that we were talking about improving parenting, but would it amount to anything? Would all these parents easliy agree to what she was saying, but then revert back to their parenting styles after they returned home. Up for the challenge Shefali happily engaged, played out the scenario of what would happen if just a percentage improved, or if some parents made an effort and life got better, even a small amount, for some. This smart and tenacious young man was skeptical and Shefali used his willingness to share, to investigate what was beneath his doubt. She uncovered that he felt he worked so hard to please his mother, but it never seemed enough. He felt her endless need to 'make him responsible' was way too much. He voiced how he wanted to be a kid and felt he was being forced to grow up too fast. He became choked up as he painfully explained that he had shared his feelings with his mom and it didn't change how she treated him.

This was moving for Shefali as she used his examples to talk passionately about the roles of parents and the roles of children. She beautifully explained the many generational constructs we as parents adopt and how high expectations and pressure negatively impact children on the deepest level of their Being. After a long and heart-wrenching confession, she thanked the boy for digging so deep and being so raw with his emotions.

Like before, she kindly asked the parent of this sincere young man to stand up. And like before, I rose to my feet. It was my son who so candidly shared his pain and sorrow. The boy whose ear I had pulled because he wasn't acting how I wanted. Wiping tears from my eyes again, our family became the micro-example of families for everyone in the room. Shefali was kind as I was vulnerable, jokingly inviting the entire audience to my house since they all knew us so intimately. It got a sympathetic chuckle from the room at first, but when I looked into the eyes of everyone around me. I saw love and compassion. Every parent there could relate and connect to the challenges I was having. They could sympathize and identify with the idealistic way I was raising my kids. And they could feel what I was feeling because, at one point in their parenting, they had felt it, too.

To say it was a life-changing moment would be an understatement. It was my IGNITE parenting epiphany. All the things I thought I was doing to make strong, hard-working kids, was just a reflection of the hard-working life I had grown up in. I was repeating the cycle of how I was parented. Doing the same thing I rebelled against, instilling the same feelings of disconnect under the guise of achieving success.

That day at the end of the conference we did a lovely closing exercise to connect with our kids. Shefali led us through a sharing, releasing and forgiving process which profoundly moved me beyond my own parenting paradigm with my children. Yet, it also shed many of the things I had been holding onto since I was a kid. It was liberating and powerful, emotional yet exhilarating. I left transformed! The words of my two adoring children had awakened me and I knew I had to recreate my current style of parenting. I embarked on a 30-day experiment of non-parenting. Then moved to unparenting, mindful parenting, and re-parenting myself. I re-examined everything I was doing to my children and how ingrained my parenting patterns had become. That journey was fantastic. To tear down the habits and peel back the layers of why one parents the way one does was revealing. I dove so deep, I ended up writing a book called *Enjoying Parenting*. My idea was to help other parents dispel all the outdated systems and rules around parenting and instead find the joy. It was a miraculous exploration that has led to the most delightful new relationship with my kids. We still have our moments, but they are much more honest and a loving connection always ensues. It all started with one Ignite moment that has changed our family forever and I am eternally grateful.

IGNITE YOUR PARENTING

Ignite Your Parenting is a book designed to inspire parents across the globe. It is a diverse compilation of stories, told by parents on their journey towards a more rewarding and enjoyable experience of parenting. Each author, sharing their story is unique in where they live, the ages of their kids and the backgrounds they grew up in. Yet each is similar in their desire to do their best at parenting. They all have a wantingness to lead by example, speak their truth and let go of the parameters placed on them in their own childhoods. These parents want to be different by allowing both themselves and their children to flourish. Each one of the individuals in this book has made a clear choice to parent consciously. Not better, just wiser. Not perfect, just perfectly designed to fit their family and all its needs.

Many of the parents in this book have explored alternative parenting modalities. Most have abolished many of the "parenting rules". They have stepped beyond the typical and broke free of the past enforced on them by their own parents. They have worked to overcome their inner issues and freed the child within that may have be caged or wounded. These parents have embraced their journey; the windy road, with ups and downs. The crooked path with potholes and speed bumps, but a path no less, to the heart of themselves and their child.

As you turn the pages of this book, you will find each story begins with an inspiring *Power Quote*. It is a statement said with the intention to inspire. It is a mantra you can use to remind you just what you are after. It is a quote that pushes you to do even more and makes you think even deeper. It is what that motivational sticker would say on the back of your minivan. Each power quote is designed to remind you how you want to parent – ***amazingly***. Power quotes are that sentence or phrase that you say when the tears might be flowing both in hardship and in reward.

Then, you will read each parent's *Intentions*. These are the author's goals and aspirations of what they wish their story will do for you. It is a personal message, filled with meaning, and purpose. They want to Ignite YOU to begin parenting in your most exceptional way. Their intentions set the tone for their story and are designed to both awaken and inspire you. Use their intention to connect with them at the very beginning of the story.

Next is their IGNITE *Story*. It unfolds with them sharing a powerful time when their life was profoundly changed. It is a true account of a mother or father stepping into their divine role as parent; embracing the learning through growth. We all have Ignite moments in our lives that change us, define us and set us on a new path or trajectory. These stories are those moments, told in the most heartfelt and supportive way. They show that all of us have *those* moments and they not only define us but transform us.

Once you have finished their heartfelt stories, you will find an inspiring *Ignite Action Step* (or Steps). These are the tangible things they did to support and awaken themselves. Each author explains an easy-to-do, practical step for you to take so you can close the book and immediately implement. They are the processes and practices that worked in their lives. Each one is different and unique just like you are and proven to yield amazing results when done consistently.

We all know actions speak louder than words and never is that more accurate than with parenting. Those little eyes are always watching and their little ears hear everything. How we show up and communicate with them is vital. Yet, what we do is essential! Action IS the key. To truly move the needle forward in your parenting, we encourage you to try one new action step each and do it consecutively for thirty days. We know everyone has a unique family with all kinds of special needs. That is why we have offered you an assortment of different action steps to try. Each one is potentially the step that could change your family forever. Start with one. Pick something that calls to you and follow through. When you shift, everyone else shifts. You taking action, inspires others to do the same. Remember, your kids are looking to you for leadership. They are watching you first to see exactly what they should. So lead in a way they can emulate.

PARENT WITH LOVE

We know that many people read compilation books to be inspired. If you feel that your parenting story is still unfolding, or you're trying to figure it all out, we are with you. We have all been through our own parenting moments. And, likely we will continually go through them throughout our lives. Our stories are designed to show our mini-successes, amidst our learning. We still wobble and make mistakes, yet, we have, consciously decided to parent differently than how we once did. The learning will never stop. It will just become easier and more rewarding as we embrace a more conscious way.

We each support you and cheer you on as you find your flow in parenting. We all extend our hands should you need a bit of support, some advice or a shoulder to cry on. We offer ourselves should you ever want to reach out because something we said resonated or what we shared was exactly what you needed to hear. Please know we are all accessible and eager to connect so feel free to find us.

Raising kids is also about raising ourselves. We need to have compassion for our process as we grow and learn. We need to help each other along the way even if that means we don't always have an answer. For everyone in your family to benefit, you must not be afraid to ask for help, seek new options and try new things. In your quest for great parenting, you will be challenged and confronted, but if you are true to your inner knowing, those challenges will be met with the purest intentions. A parent is someone who selflessly supports, follows their heart and looks beyond the obstacles along the way. Give all you can to your expansion because you are worth it. Once you do that for yourself, your children with reap the benefits of a wonderful life enjoying you.

The stories you are about to embark on are all our stories. They supercede race, culture, age and even gender. They are the human story, the experience of being a parent on this earth. They touch at the very heart of belonging, connecting and sharing. They are raw, real and unrestricted... that's what makes them so amazingly engaging. They cut through all the 'stuff' we want people to see and shine a light directly on the heart of who we were born to be.

Ignite was created to ignite others and impact humanity. Our mandate is to do more, share more and spread a conscious positive message to as many people as possible. We believe in the human connection and that power comes from being heard, being seen and belonging to something greater than one's self. We invite you to Ignite others. To let your story be heard, share your experiences find your voice. We pride ourselves in bringing people together, offer a solution, give back and do something good for the planet. That is the mission and purpose behind IGNITE. There is power when one person touches the heart of another, and a spark begins. Be it inspiration, love, support, encouragement, compassion or belief. We all can be an amazing parent by in living a kind and gracious life.

May you have many ignite moments that transform your life into the amazing person you were meant to be. – JB Owen

ASHLEY AVINASHI

"The depth of connection to ourselves determines how meaningfully we can connect to others and a life of infinite possibility."

I encourage you through this story and through our commitment at *Raising Humanity* to live your most meaningful, connected life as a parent. Your choice to be vulnerable and reach out for support will invite connection in. You are worthy of the journey back into the greatness you were born with. It is when we own our greatness as parents, that our children have a chance to live in theirs.

THE RECONNECTION PROJECT

Completely disconnected from the emotions of my children, overlooking their every reaction to an unmet need. *I was that parent.* Staring at my child blank in the face many a time, simply having no bandwidth to share myself with anyone. *I was that parent.* Wrestling with my child to 'behave', hoping he'd finally comply with my wishes. *I was that parent.*

I was the parent I never thought I would be.

We all believe that we are going to raise the most perfect, resilient children. Until, one day we have children... and our fantasy world and reality collide.

It was an average night, hanging over my first son in an awkward contortion, attempting to breastfeed efficiently while staring into the dimmed screen of my phone. Night after night, this continued. Each time, my eyes grew to adjust, squinting at my numerous emails in all of the darkness that surrounded me. What was next on my to do list? My mind was foggy yet racing. As per usual, a deeper panic set in each time I felt I was lagging behind. Was my agenda within reach? How much could I tackle while putting him to bed again? His weaning coincided with my second pregnancy.

Soon I had a toddler and an infant, neither of whom slept consistently. Night after night, I felt like a complete failure. I would rush to them the moment they cried, in hopes of assisting an immediate return to their dream state. Going from room to room trying to settle them, my impatience would escalate. I managed no more than three fragmented hours of sleep most nights. The eldest had a tendency to awaken and call out for comfort routinely, every 20 to 45 minutes in fact. Though it felt shameful to admit it, something inside me knew that my own anxiety was running deep within them.

The pressure I put on myself to turn the situation around was not for the reasons you may expect – the logical answer being a desire for more sleep. My hope was to push through more work. Check more boxes. Yes, even through the night, I found myself bound to the illusory conviction that my productivity would pay off.

I was a perfectionist, a workaholic with multiple businesses, an explorer of life – dedicated to my physical health and social connection. This meant my calendar was jam-packed, with little room to breathe or even contemplate.

A 100-hour workweek was not foreign to me. After years in corporate and now real estate in one of the most active markets in North America, I had learned to build my life around what I identified with most – work. Though I had previously experienced burnout, I was still operating from an innate sense of responsibility to keep proving my worth. It became habitual to be running negotiations into the wee hours of the morning. My commitment to make myself readily available meant that strategic decisions could be made quickly, and I could stay the course as per my life prior to children.

Yet, despite the success on the outside, there was a gaping hole in my heart. The disconnect would often come out as impatience, emotional and physical exhaustion or even anger. My heart was begging me to take rest, like a cat curling up, enveloped in cushions, yet my mind would not give permission for it. The fear of letting go of what I knew best was terrifying. My entire identity was wrapped up in the hustle.

Despite the voices around me, urging me to slow down, I felt it was a valid choice to not take maternity leave. There was no giving up on this "dream life" I had created. The overwhelm only grew with time. My body spoke words to me I could not recognize, as I had become numb to my own needs. My cup, already in deficit prior to my second child, was now becoming further depleted. Looking for answers by doing more only led to continued dissatisfaction. I was grasping for relief, a way out, though I had no idea what that was. In fear of further discomfort, I stayed on the 'success' wheel.

The resistance would come up and then I would cleverly find a way to bury it – more work, another social event, another trip. I recall parties where I quite literally felt ill at the thought of expending energy on another surface-level conversation or watching people intoxicate themselves. I realized this wasn't my life anymore. But what defined me now? Who was I? I found myself making my way to the bathroom during more than one of those parties, falling to the floor in a heaping mess of confusion. Feeling completely alone without a single soul to witness my heart's cry. Not even my own self.

My identity outside of the home was not one of a mother – it was that of a successful business woman who could keep it all together, even with an infant and toddler at home. There was many a morning where I attempted to breastfeed prior to a full workday. I couldn't produce milk. The stress on my system had dried me out nearly completely. While out working, I would run into other moms with their babies at coffee shops. Connected. Alive. Present. I wanted to approach them but felt disconnected from my own motherhood journey. Ashamed of having nothing to share. So I continued to run off my feet, until it was time to race home when the nanny called. The call that always reminded me of the closeness I truly longed for.

Another morning arrived. I rushed out of bed, sloppily pulled my hair back after another unsuccessful night of little sleep and dressed in the same clothes I'd worn the day before. The simplest of tasks felt so laborious. Exhaustion was running at its peak through my every vein. Moving my two boys through their breakfast routine, my task list consumed my mind, like a raging river with neither a calm middle to swim in nor an end in sight. I rushed to tackle the day, as per usual.

I was irritable. The boys were eating so slowly, completely oblivious of my day ahead. Yes, completely oblivious of my scheduling constraints at the age of one, and two and a half. As I reached over the stove to inhale a few spoons of oatmeal from the pot, something unexplainable happened. The whole scene we were in froze.

My older son and I locked eyes. He was mute, quite literally, lifeless. There was an emptiness in the depths of his eyes that dropped me into a deep state of fear. These were the same eyes which had carried a bright sparkle at birth. He had completely shut himself down from his own expression in that moment. Intuitively, I could read his thoughts loud and clear, *"Mama, I don't want to put anything more on you than what is on your plate. So, I won't ask for anything I need. I will sit here with my lips sealed."*

Instead of blindly pushing through my usual tasks, I came into an unshakable sinking feeling. The beautiful life force had been pulled, not only out of me, but out from these two innocent children. My truest essence had been dying rapidly, and all along, impacting the well-being of my children. In that moment, it became real, life-altering real, just how disconnected I was from myself, from the children and from the world around me. How my whole life was running on autopilot, based on past paradigms. *You come last. Self-sacrifice is honorable. Self-care is overrated. Work tirelessly for all those around you and run yourself dry. You will survive. This is the way of motherhood.* My heart contracted further, realizing the sheer isolation I had been living in based on false beliefs, despite having a vibrant life on the outside.

The kitchen island between myself and my children represented the distance I had been creating from the connection I so deeply yearned for but feared. It was in that moment, I realized that I felt more unalive than I had ever felt before. Through my doubt and pain, I had learned to cover up my feelings. I had become so creative at distracting myself and running away from that which I feared. Yet now, whispers of truth demanded a voice.

The entire trajectory of how I approached the world shifted in that moment. I began to sit with the pain. For months thereafter, I embraced the confusion, the darkness and unknown. I explored who I was beyond the constraints of who I thought I had to be, to be loved and be seen. I connected with me – beyond the role of a mother, a daughter, a partner, a businesswoman. That *me* began to hit pause. My heart started speaking to me as I opened up to it, a voice that was unrecognizable at first.

Though I felt victim to my circumstances, I kept exploring. The little girl in me wanted to be released from the shackles that kept her living a life which was not her own. Those societal, cultural and familial shackles adopted as a child, felt like dead weight. It had been decades of shutting my true self down by playing into old stories that no longer served me. My children were being affected each and every day by my inability to see myself and therefore, them. The unwieldy impact of the previous patterns was clear.

My heart grew hungry for answers. I knew there had to be more – but what? What could possibly exist beyond what was visible to my own two eyes? It took being very honest with myself because a part of me had always known there was another way. In fact, I had experienced another way. My mother, who had been on a non-conforming parenting path for a number for decades, encouraged self-discovery in us. By way of good fortune, I had been exposed to transcendental practices and ancient wisdom. Perhaps that is why the resistance came up for me as strongly as it did. I knew there was more here than to go through the motions alongside my children. It had been too much of a cumbrous journey for me through years of miscarriages, pregnancies, breastfeeding, and sleepwalking through life, to believe that the experience of parenthood was limited to the roles and responsibilities that accompanied it. I was grateful for the life experiences I had had, but it was time for me to choose differently for myself.

I dove in. Pain was my guide. I was so motivated to find a way to break the cycle of disconnection and unfulfillment. First came books, talks, self-guided programs and then a step into a variety of healing communities. This was perhaps the first time in my life I reached out honestly. I was willing to be seen as I was and supported in all of my confusion, rage and pain. My well-masked vulnerability was finally ready to show itself.

I didn't trust this would lead me somewhere different, but it certainly could not feel more painful than what I had come to know. As I couldn't return to where I had been, I faced my deep-rooted beliefs head-on, and learned to embrace the unknown courageously. With so much coming to the surface, I was also fortunate to meet guides who had walked the path of coming into their own truth. Deep emotional exploration brought heightened awareness and gentle compassion to my own journey. Spending time with my authentic self brought me closer to my own equilibrium.

Venturing out beyond the mindset I had embraced in recent decades, I saw and experienced the opportunity which is before all of us—*the joy of being deeply connected with our true self and authentic heart. The turning point in my life was a decision to wholeheartedly invest in myself and my truth.* With that, I started guarding my time more. I took an intentional sabbatical from the busyness, relinquishing the attachments and identities I had built into my life. This space allowed me to see what really mattered for me – that I could lead and live by way of the heart. I experienced infinite possibility and endless beauty through my children's eyes. As I allowed life to unfold, I came into the lessons that had always been there.

I was no longer caught in the hustle. I was done sabotaging myself by way of guilt and anxiety. I no longer attempted to control every outcome of my life and that of my children. I began to love and accept myself no matter what I felt. I resigned from needing external validation to feel that I was enough. I developed deeper compassion for myself and those around me. *This was the way I was seeking.* This gradual awakening spoke to what I had been sensing from the depths of my soul but could not put words or meaning to. I saw that fear had been driving much of my life unknowingly.

It was through being seen for who I was in all of my messiness that I found the courage to dance with the unfamiliar. To then explore my truth beyond the known, and to continue to ask for help. This led me to see past my own blinders and embrace the parts of me I had been hiding away. My lens became clearer as I reclaimed more of my forgotten self.

Taking 100% responsibility of how I experienced life was the beginning of adulthood for me. Just as a wound becomes the place where light enters, the transformation of the beliefs I carried launched me into a greater life purpose. I grew very passionate about how we can raise children in today's world; facing the excessive demands of parenting with ease, confidence, and joy, rather than guilt, exhaustion and anxiety.

As I sat in parenting circles and joined forums across the globe, I witnessed countless others struggling in the modern-day parenting experience. They too were battling the epidemic of disconnection and unfulfillment. The learnings that arose on my path of studying as a coach and a therapist revealed the crucial role compassion has in helping us see what is not understood by the mind. All of this time I had wronged myself for what I didn't understand, in isolation and self-pity. The courage to step into honest conversation helped me discover that I wasn't alone in this. I came to see that we all want more for ourselves and for our children but struggle with the 'how.'

My own transformation and that of many others showed me just how it is that we can return to the greatness we were born with. But this requires moving beyond the control and certainty we seek, and the roles we play. Until we don't meet ourselves fully beyond the mind-based antics that bind us to our conditioned self, it is not possible to step into the heart and authentically love another for their true selves. My invitation into deep self-discovery only came when I could no longer pretend that I was fulfilled moving through life on autopilot.

Though my children proved to be my best teachers, there were many others who helped lead me into the most expansive and alive life I could have ever dreamed of by simply witnessing me in my humanness. It has been a significant and meaningful journey for me over the last six years, one that has required I step out of my comfort zone.

What I realized is that I too am an evolving being. That life is nonlinear, and we are not meant to stay status quo and love all of the things we once did. We have our own unique path to joy. We may grow into a new purpose as we step out more. We can decide to slow down in life and treasure quieter moments. We may be so impacted by the journey with our children that we decide we want nothing else than to grow with them and continue to learn from them.

I am experiencing what is available to me, even with two young children by my side. There is a sense of connection, purpose and freedom that has opened my life up to a state of limitlessness and only enhanced the way of my children. If you had asked me just two years prior, I couldn't have told you that I could ever anticipate finding my joy again. My own vulnerability was my starting point, and it's led to the most meaningful and fulfilling connection to self, others and this magical life we are in.

You are worth it. Choose yourself over and over and over again. The universe and all those around you will thank you for it.

IGNITE ACTION STEPS

*Accept** that a nonlinear path of self discovery is the cost of true liberation and joy. It may not be pretty or perfect, but it's worth the exploration.

*Slow down and listen.** The messages from within will come as we surrender our shoulds, coulds, woulds and have-to's. Trust your gut, and listen for warning signs. Any resistance could be an indication that the heart is not being heard, or you are getting ready to break out of the cocoon. Stay with it and face the discomfort.

*Allow for the shifts** to occur that need to take place. They will become more fluid as you become increasingly aligned with your truest version of self.

*Step into your vulnerability.** When you share your stories from this place, you will invite connection. Connection in turn nurtures greatness. When you experience your intrinsic greatness, you will feel safe to shine.

*Meaningful connection is our oxygen.** Make time with self and others count. Let go of what doesn't serve as it will drain you and your energy.

*If you want better, seek it out.** There are many ready to support you along the way.

Ashley Avinashi, Founder - Canada
Raising Humanity
www.raisinghumanity.com

STEVEN J. POSNER

"We raise our kids and our kids raise us."

We might not be aware of how, as parents, our attitudes and behaviors may negatively affect our kids. We might think we are acting in their best interest, but we may just be satisfying our ego, expectations, and even compensating for our insecurities. How we show up for our kids will shape who they become. I hope to help you find more self-awareness of how you are showing up for your kids.

SIR MAX – DEFENDER OF THE CASTLE

It's 3 AM. I hear my six-year-old son crying from the other side of the apartment. My immediate reaction is, "Oh No! Not again." I look over and see my wife asleep. I am grateful she is resting. We have both been dealing with a lot. Three months of sleep deprivation have kicked in and I am exhausted and frustrated. I thought the phase of midnight wake-ups had gone away with diapers. But no luck. I gather my strength, get out of bed and go to him. He needs me, but I'm not sure if I have the energy to show up.

Apart from exhaustion, I feel deep insecurity. Can I soothe him? Can I really help him? Why do I feel like I am failing as a father? How is it that my wonderful son is now like an overly demanding special-needs child? I ask, why is the Universe doing this to us?

I get to his room and he is out of control, crying incessantly and scratching himself to the point of making his skin bleed. He seems possessed by some evil being that kidnapped the son I knew leaving an uncontrollable child that only calms down with an iPad. Thank you, Steve Jobs.

This time I don't get the iPad. I take a deep breath, gather myself, put him on my lap, chest to chest, and hug him. Console him. I tell him it's going to be alright and that we are all in this together. We will get over this, although in my tired mind I don't know if we will. I calmed him down with tender massages and cold packs to soothe his inflamed skin. Two hours later, he falls asleep. It's now 5 AM. I just lay there beside him broken-hearted and wide awake. How can life be so unfair that my dear Max must suffer a condition that would drive any adult insane? No one told me that watching helplessly as your child suffers was the ultimate parenting challenge. If they did, it did not sink in.

Since my son, Max, was six months old, he was diagnosed with atopic dermatitis. Initially, it was not a severe case, but by the time he turned six, his condition got dramatically worse. There were patches of dry and red skin all over his body. He was scratching himself most of the day. The creases on his pinkies were cracking open as if the skin had been slit open with a knife. A full night's sleep was something that got left behind.

The dermatitis was also taking a toll on him psychologically; he was fearful of his own skin. When he'd see his body covered with scabs, cracked and flaking, he was convinced that it was going to fall off and he'd be left only with muscles and bones. In his own words, "my world is finished!" He would blame himself, as if he were responsible for his condition. He'd say, "I deserve this. I deserve to be punished..." as he was not able to control his own hands. I never thought it possible for a young child surrounded by love and comfort to be depressed and skew to a negative view of life; something that usually happens to adults if we are unable to overcome life's hardships.

The anxiety in me grows when I feel that there is nothing I can do to help or that even if it was my decision, unknowingly, that had created the suffering. Lost in the angst-ridden midnight scratching fits, I find it hard to see anything positive coming from this, but the optimist in me still thinks there must be something good.

There is no greater pain as a parent than to see your child suffer. As his father, I want to try to control everything to make Max's childhood as best as possible. I try to make sure he is happy, healthy, goes to good schools, has good friends, lives meaningful experiences and is exposed to positive, loving relationships that give richness to his life. But things don't always go as I would like and I am challenged. Clearly, all parents can name numerous instances when things don't go as planned. It's a regular occurrence in parenting, but when a situation is more extreme, like Max's dermatitis, the challenge is more significant.

Perhaps one of the darkest moments was last summer when Max, right before bath and upon seeing his skin, started crying hysterically. His levels of anxiety skyrocketed. He started picking at his skin and scratching all over his body. He tore away scabs and started bleeding again. He was in some sort of bizarre trance. The Dermatitis monster had taken over. He could not hear my words. My soothing was pointless. He would not stop. All he could do was look at me; I heard a piercing fear in his cries. He could not speak, but his tear-filled eyes were telling me, "I'm so scared! I'm sorry! I'm sorry!" He was lost, helpless and so was I.

Everything that had worked before was not working. I got angry, very angry. Something quite visceral took over me; something I had never experienced before. A strange voice deep inside told me, "Switch the source of fear. If he fears you instead of his skin, he will stop scratching." I don't know why, but I listened. I grabbed his hands forcibly, looked straight into his eyes and yelled at the top of my voice, "STOP SCRATCHING! I cannot let you scratch yourself like a crazy monkey. If I let you, you will scratch off all your skin and we'll end up in a hospital. Is that what you want?"

He froze. It worked. He was out of his scratching trance. After a few seconds of silence, he broke into tears, but this time it was different. There was still fear in his eyes, but it was fear of his dad. I had never seen that. If anything, I had always prided myself in helping him build up his self-esteem, confidence and self-reliance and never using fear as a tool. At that moment, I felt like a total failure. What semi-conscious father purposely tries to instill fear in his child? I did not recognize the person that, in the past, Max lovingly referred to as "Papi".

It took me a while to process my behavior. I was not proud of myself and having screamed that way to my child was my low point as a father. I still am not 100% sure where that visceral voice came from, but I did know that months of sleep deprivation had taken a toll. I was more irritable and my patience threshold was much lower. I was sick and tired of how Dermatitis was affecting him and all of our lives. It simply was not fair.

After deep reflection, I realized that, under the guise of trying to help, I was very selfish. Max was not living up to my expectations of how he should be managing his skin condition. He was not using the different tools I taught him to control the flare-ups. We had worked on deep breathing, switching attention to distract the brain, using flat hands to rub instead of nails to scratch, etc. He was failing to apply my lessons. He had let me down. That is partially why I got angry. I was also upset at him for all the sleepless nights, ruined family vacations and tensions Dermatitis created in the family. My yelling was also a venting of my own frustration – my inability to control the situation I was in. Ironically, we were in the same boat. And I thought it was all him.

As I realized that, I felt horrified. That is not the father or person that I thought I was, yet it was me. The slow wearing down had taken its toll and I had not noticed how it was affecting me. Most adults would struggle to manage a condition similar to Max's and there I was demanding that a 6-year-old boy have the maturity, self-awareness and self-regulation skills to control himself. I suddenly understood the fear in his eyes. It wasn't because I had yelled at him. It was because he let me down; in a big way. It would come to no surprise that later he would say that he "was not enough" and even that perhaps "it was better to be dead." Those words drove a sword into my heart. I was not helping him, I was damaging his self-esteem and that could leave a lifelong scar.

On top of my failings as a father, I was also full of deep-seated guilt. What if our decisions had been a critical factor in his suffering? After years of following the advice of leading pediatric dermatologists, my wife and I started to question the "evidence-based" path to healing. Endless coats of cortisone creams and steroid-based treatments were not helping. When the last dermatologist suggested that it was time to inject Max with immunosuppressants, we knew we needed a different approach.

My wife and I had started to read about the gut-skin connection and how dermatitis was not a skin disease, but rather a symptom of chronic inflammation that manifests in the skin. Rather than trying to fix the problem from the outside-in with topical creams, it was necessary to heal the body from the inside-out. That approach compelled us. We took an alternative path, trepidatious, since both of us like the reassurance of science and "real" doctors to make health-related decisions. We consulted with healers, naturopaths, bioenergetic doctors and microbiome experts. We embarked on an uncharted journey of radically changing Max's diet, adding natural supplements, probiotics and other nutrients. We also started testing all sorts of natural skin hydration and soothing treatments, some of which involved covering his body in coconut oil, smothering his wounds with fresh aloe vera which we then wrapped in saran wrap and taking baths with leaves from a supposedly magical healing tree in Guatemala.

Max was our petri dish as we experimented with endless treatments. He was a real trooper. Not only did we cut out sugar, dairy and wheat which were the core ingredients of many of his favorite foods, but imposed all sorts of odd treatments and foul tasting concoctions that theoretically would improve his condition. It was not easy, but we all pushed along and Max, as an unwilling passenger, had to follow our lead. He had no choice. Any resistance to the treatments was answered with further imposition. "You have to do this if you want to get better. Sorry son." We made him powerless.

So when things would get bad, I would feel tremendous guilt. Have we made a massive mistake taking an alternative route? Are we following the advice of witch-doctors versus skin experts? Are we experimenting with our son at the expense of his well being? Were all questions that haunted me.

There was some progress, but it was slow and uncertain. We needed more options. My step-father had an article that mentioned some very successful water treatments of kids' dermatitis in a specialized center in Avene, France. My wife and I decided we would skip three weeks of school and give the treatment a chance.

My wife courageously took the first turn in the first half of the three-week treatment. Halfway through, we saw his skin get better. The Avene waters were working their magic. Emotionally he seemed to improve, but he was still depressed and apathetic most of the time. His preference was to watch the iPad instead of playing. The distraction of the cartoon fantasy worlds was way better than his life.

When I arrived to switch places with my wife, I was cautiously optimistic. He was better, but his innate childhood joy was still missing. I knew the Dermatitis monster was not easily going to give me back my son, so I planned many exciting adventures to bring him joy. Then there was a magical moment. We had gone to have lunch in a beautiful medieval walled town. In a store, I bought Max a wooden sword and a shield. He was quite excited about the new toy. I hadn't seen that delight in a very long time. As we walked through the main square, he ran towards the town's castle door. There he stood in a triumphant posture. He was 'Sir Max – Defender of the Castle'.

Tears welled up in my eyes. I had not seen him use his imagination in months. Dermatitis was giving way and letting the son I knew, come back to life. There was joy, laughter and imagination. His childhood was back. He was my hero, the defender of *my* castle and my heart. Deep inside, I was finally feeling the reassurance that we had made the right choice in the path we had taken.

We returned home and Max went back to school. Things were not perfect, but the improvement in all areas was constant. As the year ended and we rolled into the early spring, the progress was tremendous. We had been successful in turning away from the toxic approach of traditional dermatology and were healing Max's skin through natural means. *The best part?* – psychologically, it seemed 'Sir Max' was back for good.

Unfortunately, as spring progressed, his skin started to get bad again. My wife and I knew that there was no way we could repeat the hell we all lived the summer before. We had to get ahead of the curve. So once again, we took Max to the Avene center in France, but this time the healing was not as successful.

As I write these words, we're still on an uncertain and often unnerving healing path. We don't yet have a happy ending to this story yet, this time it's different. Max has taught me many lessons on this journey. Perhaps the most fundamental is that even during the most challenging, dark parenting moments, there are gifts for growth to make us better parents, if only we give ourselves the time and permission to hear and learn the lessons. When I realized it was my ego and not me that was challenged when dealing with Max's outbursts, I found a pathway open up that would allow me to show up as a much more supporting and caring Dad. If I was going to be there to soothe and help him, I needed to put my needs to the side and give support without expectation.

In the same way that we are wired to love our kids, our kids are wired to seek our love and acceptance. When things get tough, it's very easy to let our shadows take over and show up with control as a strategy. They will respond to that, they have no choice, but it does not empower them to take on more responsibility for their lives and their actions. It might serve us in the short term, but in the long-term, we could leave deep self-esteem wounds that will condition how they live out their lives.

There is another path that requires letting go of the expectations of how we want our kids to be and how we *should* be acting as parents. When we let go, we open the door for real love to flow and connect at a deeper level. Ironically, we may end up getting to where we would have wanted to go with ease and so much more fulfillment.

This change in my mindset has been tremendously empowering. I no longer judge Max for his skin condition. It's not his fault. He is not his skin. He still often wakes up in the middle of the night and now I know how to show up. When I am there, I am there for him. I am his guide and his coach, but I follow his lead. That is empowering for him.

I am raising Max, and Max is raising me. He takes me to a much higher level when I understand the lessons he is teaching me during good times and bad. When your child is not acting as you would like, ask yourself, what is the lesson in it for you. It could change everything.

IGNITE ACTION STEPS

We are not born with all essential parenting skills. While intuition can guide us frequently, we are better served in developing skills to help us manage the complicated situation that our kids can throw our way. These are some of my favorites:

*Heart Coherence Breathing—This practice entails 5 minutes for slow breathing through the nose. The trick is 5 seconds of inhale and 5 seconds of exhale for six breaths per minute. Physiologically this type of breathing activates the relaxation response in the nervous system and reduces stress. It allows us to gather ourselves and be in a better place when we have to deal with a challenging situation

*Validating and playing back our child's emotions regardless of what they are – It's very natural for parents to tell their children what to feel, "Don't be angry. Don't be sad." It's much more effective first to play back their emotions, "You're angry. You're sad." Then the child feels understood. With that understanding, it then becomes easier to steer the conversation to find a constructive solution.

*Forgiveness meditation—Be aware of the emotional charge that lingers after a challenging situation with a child. Going through a guided forgiveness meditation on the their behavior will help you release negative emotions and put you in a better place to deal with future events. This does not mean "excusing" the child for what they did, but is meant as a release of negative emotions, freeing you to see the situation from your child's perspective and build greater empathy. It's also a powerful practice to run on ourselves when we have not shown up as the parent we would like to be.

*Check your ego at the door—When dealing with a challenging situation, imagine that the doorway you need to go through to get to where your child is, has magical powers. It allows you to "check our ego at the door." Take a few seconds before going through. Take a few breaths; say to yourself, "This is not about me. It's about him/her."

Steven J. Posner - Spain
Entrepreneur, advisor, part-time biohacker and father
@SJPosner

STACEY YATES SELLAR

"I don't want to be afraid of parenting badly.
I want to be conscious of parenting well."

My wish is that you, the reader will read my story with an open mind. My hope is that you turn off the judgment reflex. My intention is that you finish this chapter knowing that none of us are perfect, none of our children are perfect (despite what it looks like on social media!) and that we are all just "learning parents". We are doing our best with the knowledge and beliefs we have. Imagine what a magical world we would live in if we could eliminate judging ourselves and fearing judgment from others.

THE WORST PARENT EVER!

I am the WORST parent ever! Well… according to my five-year-old who declared this after I refused to carry him on our short walk to the park. My eight-year-old nominated me as well recently when I wouldn't buy him the inappropriate gaming t-shirt that he HAD to have. That was also, by his assessment, the worst DAY ever as well. And to think… I wasn't even sure I would be a parent.

I didn't meet and marry "the one", Barry, until I was 40. Before the wedding, he and I went to see my doctor to tell her we would try to get pregnant soon and to discuss prenatal care. Her anxiety about the risks of my age drove her to insist we start right away (and when I mean right away, I actually thought she was going to lock us in that room then and there).

After a year of no success using the usual fertility tools; timing, temperature, books, acupuncture, supplements and even I.U.I., we started looking into I.V.F. Not only did we find out it was incredibly expensive in the United States but we also found out my reproduction levels reflected that of a 90-year-old.

When I turned 42, we had been trying to get pregnant for two years and every 28 days my body said, "Nope. Not happening." By September, we decided to jump off the fertility treadmill and wait until January to reassess our options. In November, my aunt arrived for dinner with her new puppy named Dash. I asked where she came up with that name and found out it was after the author Dashiell Hammet. I said, "Dashiel", with a smile, "that's going to be my son's name." I was pregnant a week later.

But before we get back to how I became a parent (and the WORST one at that), I need to take you back a few years, to my own childhood. I was number four of five children and my mother was ALWAYS nervous. She had a horror story for everything! She was never separated by more than three degrees from someone who died doing anything. Don't hang your arm out of the window while driving because she knows a kid whose arm was ripped off by a passing car. Going on a trip? She can narrate a detailed story of someone that was injured, impaled, stranded, robbed, kidnapped or even trampled by a water buffalo. Everything in your house is dangerous if it isn't nailed in place and she has a Rolodex of tragedies involving dangerous household objects. Don't tell her if you want to bungee jump! Her optometrist told her that someone's retina detached from their eyeball when they jumped on holiday. Don't leave your toothbrush near a toilet, don't drink alcohol in a hot-tub, don't wear overalls because they make you easier to kidnap. I couldn't sleep with a necklace on as a child because it might choke me to death in my sleep. Halloween candy likely had a razor blade hidden in it or was poisoned (which, did take some of the fun out of the holiday). If you don't cover your drink at a bar you will wake up the next morning in a bathtub full of ice and your kidneys will have been taken to be sold on the black market. I haven't been able to lick an envelope since she told me what was in the glue. I can never drive near trucks with big wheels because a driver was decapitated by a wheel blow out. It's a miracle that I leave my house and no wonder that I have had extreme anxiety for as long as I can remember. On the bright side, her bedtime stories about kids who died from trying drugs just one time did keep me puritanical (*mostly*).

You can imagine the level of anxiety I had about having a baby! Pregnancy always brings out the worst near-death labor stories and tales of babies being forgotten in the back seats of cars. Then there are thousands of books about what you should be doing prenatally to optimize the womb experience and increase Ivy League college acceptances. I was not the mother that played opera music via headphones perched on belly nor did I read the complete works of Shakespeare in four languages and I only made it to prenatal yoga once. I agonized over the theme of the bedroom as if the perfect bedding would lead to a Nobel prize and the wrong color palette would lead to a life of crime.

Regardless of fear, babies come anyway. And to my great relief, a healthy Dashiel William Bradshaw Sellar arrived late July 2011. But it was not the magical experience I anticipated. Because my age made me "high risk", he had to come out the sunroof (C-section). I knew that the first few minutes were the most critical for bonding and I mentally rehearsed placing his bare skin on mine immediately. I couldn't wait to see his soft face; his divine eyes, his tiny nose and bitty ears and to count his delicate fingers and little toes. I couldn't imagine a greater, more miraculous moment in life than seeing and touching my child for the very first time.

But it didn't go like that.

Firstly, with a history of panic attacks (refer to aforementioned mom + death stories), I didn't turn down the offer of anti-anxiety medication. Second, I wasn't getting numb below the waist (rather important when slicing and removing a small human from my belly) so they kept pumping me with numbing agents. Then I had to dissolve some chalk-like substance in my mouth to reduce the effects of all the other medications, so by the time the baby did appear at my cheek, I barely knew where I was, much less who he was. They whisked him off for his ingress protocol and my husband followed and made sure he didn't let the baby out of his sight – because, as mom convinced us, babies get switched all the time and we didn't want to end up in an agonizing news story 20 years from now.

My husband leaves with our newborn and I wake up in another area enclosed by those annoyingly imperfect sliding hospital curtains. Everything is blurry and I see a nurse at my side who happily asks, "Do you want me to bring the baby to you now?" I can barely hold my eyes open or my head up so I can't imagine holding my newborn baby. I realize I have missed the most important moment of bonding and just before I can freak out, I pass out. I come to minutes later (it feels like hours later), grab the nurse's hand

and ask, "I'm dying, aren't I?" And pass out again. I come to and see my dad in a chair in the corner reading a gossip magazine, seemingly oblivious to the fact that I am dying.

My doctor is now by my side.

"You can tell me, I'm dying aren't I?"

"No," she says with a smile, "you are just recovering from all of th…"

I pass out again.

It was probably 30 minutes but it felt like 30 hours of going in and out of consciousness (or maybe it was just sleep). When I finally woke up and unstuck my dehydrated tongue from the roof of my parched mouth, I confirmed with my doctor, "I'm not dying?" And just then, Barry walked in with the most gorgeous, cherubic baby I had ever seen. He laid him on my chest. Dashiel and I finally met and bonded.

Seeing how distraught and worried I was, my doctor asked if I needed more medication.

If I thought medication would eliminate the worry, I would have asked for a double.

I couldn't believe they let us go home with this tiny, fragile, innocent, pure and perfect mini human with no more than a few pamphlets and the handful of swaddling cloths I stole. I was terrified of everything, from not holding him correctly to S.I.D.S, from not making enough milk to misreading the colors of poop. We slept with him in our bed – despite my mom informing about a mother who rolled over on her baby while she was sleeping and suffocated him. The good news is that all that worry gave me no time for postpartum depression.

I 'bought' (not to be misinterpreted as read) every book about newborns and what I should and shouldn't do. The problem with all those books, aside from contradicting each other, was that my baby wasn't reading them also. Every baby is different, every parent is different and clearly there was no one "right way" for every baby. If I had studied and executed it all perfectly, I would have been an expert in the nuances and meanings of each cry, handmade all his food from organic fruits and vegetables, got him on a sleep and feeding schedule immediately, introduced him to the great artists and musicians from the last few centuries, spoken to him in a second language and he would have been asking "another glass of milk, please mama" via sign language. But I didn't do anything perfectly.

Luckily for Dashiel and I, Barry was a calm, patient, un-worried father who could quiet the concerns. He never forced me to feed or sleep or dress or train our baby one way or another. He let me work my way through my waves of obsessions and just stood by with life preserver at the ready.

I just wanted Dashiel to be safe and happy and for it to be easy. But he wasn't. Well, he was happy but he wasn't easy. He had colic, which is just a fancy word for "cries all the time for apparently no reason so parents lose sleep and sanity". He cried so much I would look at him and swear there must be a nail impaling him somewhere I couldn't see! Barry and I would spend hours every night rocking and shushing and singing and bouncing and even driving in efforts to get him to sleep.

Other parents recommended we hire a sleep trainer; someone who coaches you to let the baby "cry it out". On the first night, within minutes of Dashiel crying from his crib in another room, I dissolved into an ugly cry. My maternal, biological, primal instinct to pick up and soothe my distraught baby was so strong that in every scream I could hear the disappointment of generations of ancestors who knew how to get their babies to sleep. The sleep trainer looked at Barry with a mixture of concern and annoyance and asked, "Is she going to be o.k.? I know the baby will be fine but I am not sure she will." Sleep training worked until it didn't and then I never went back.

This is when I decided I needed to turn down all the noise of how I *should* do it, and embrace all the ways I could do it. There were too many opinions, fears and judgments ruling my head and I needed to rule from my heart. Do you know there are places in the world where they never put their baby down? Or cultures where having a family bed is believed to be healthiest for the child? Do you know there are countries where children don't start to learn to read until they are seven and others where they simply feed on demand as opposed to schedule? We needed to focus more on the end goal and less on the means. I needed to come to terms with the reality that there is NO perfect parenting, program, training, ritual or schedule. What worked for others, even thousands of others, may not work for us. I needed to get above the turbulence of my internal criticism and fear of doing it "wrong". Barry and I needed to develop a compass based on our most deeply held beliefs, values and reverse engineer happy adults. While we would try to sneak in more broccoli, reduce electronics and encourage more flossing, building their character and confidence was our true north.

We became conscious about building a dynamic relationship that included being curious about the world from Dashiel's perspective. So when he unrolled a mega roll of toilet paper throughout the house, I didn't get mad. I got into his present mind and saw how fascinating that experience must be for him. We had fun as we wrapped furniture and saw how far we could roll it down the hall. Then we cleaned it up together.

When Dashiel was three years old, he got a new baby brother, Declan James Page Sellar (also naturally conceived, thank you) and it was also the beginning of Dash's learning delays. He was diagnosed with a myriad of labels that would imply it may be hard for him to fit into school – but lucky for him, his parents aren't tied to the outdated beliefs, models and modalities. But that is for another book at another time.

For now, our practice of Positive Psychology, our willingness to go to couples coaching when life gets crunchy, our open-mindedness to new learning and focus on our true north, all turn the volume down on our fears and we lean further into conscious parenting. The boys are now eight and five as I write this and I have never given them a time-out. That is not because they are perfect, or that we are perfect parents – and you may not even agree with the way we parent (I question it at times myself). We are conscious, beginner, learning parents who use these approaches below to help us maneuver through the clutter of parenting information I have hoarded.

IGNITE ACTION STEPS

*Connect & communicate. First, we connect with them by seeing every situation from their perspective. Young children live in the immediate present. They can't think about the consequences their actions from today will have on anyone three days from now. Once we see it from their perspective with compassion and appreciation, we let them know we understand how they feel. Example: When we want to walk in and turn off their television show right before the climax, we imagine someone doing that to us with our favorite show. And we further imagine they do that because we need to do an hour of math that we aren't interested in or because someone else said it was time to go to sleep even though we don't feel tired. Instead, we kindly communicate what needs to happen and why.

*Coaching doesn't involve shame, fear or pain. If they aren't immediately compliant (lol, we have two hyper boys so "immediately compliant" is rare unless there is ice cream involved) we coach. We don't yell (ok sometimes we yell but that's when we are tired or grumpy). We see it from their perspective and then offer more effective ways to proceed. We believe that every behavior is a communication and sometimes their "communication" is not appropriate. Our job as parents is to coach on more effective and encouraging ways to deliver their feelings. Example: Using words works better (and more socially acceptable) than hitting. Asking for help brings you closer to success than destroying something in frustration. Taking deep breaths helps calm the engine when it's getting hot. Asking for what you want with good reasoning is more effective than demanding it. Every interaction is an opportunity to coach.

*Consequences. There are natural consequences that are just as powerful as threats and time outs and help teach responsibility for behavior rather than compliance out of fear. Example: When Declan splashes water all over the bathroom (because he is living in the moment and splashing water is fun), the natural consequence is that he needs to clean it up. If Dasheil doesn't want to get dressed for school, then he can go to school in his pajamas and change there when he is ready (but WE have to not care about what the other parents will think when we follow through).

Every interaction we have with our children is a lesson in how to behave. So our north star is to strive for interactions that model and develop strong interrelationship skills and emotional intelligence including personal responsibility, self-control, kindness, reasoning and respect. Children repeat what we DO, not what we say.

If new parents ask for advice, mine wouldn't be about feeding schedules or sleep strategies. It would be to have patience with the child and themselves. Build in extra time with everything to allow for patience. We get stressed when we are late or have expectations that aren't being met and if we have time to be curious, understanding and kind, we are more likely to be more conscious parents who raise great kids.

Despite the many times I cringe about and judge my own parenting mistakes, mishaps and missteps, I am very confident that I am NOT the worst parent in the world. I remind myself that I am not trying to be better than you or to be as good as the mom that *seems* to do it all right. I, like every parent, land somewhere on a scale from good to bad, best to worst, perfect to imperfect, terrified to calm and my concern is just to be a better mom and person than I was yesterday. It's a constant abacus in my head sliding beads back and forth, adding and subtracting and forever hoping that the parenting choices I make help them grow into confident, brave, mindful, kind, resilient adults who learned more from my consciousness than my fear. Stay tuned...

Stacey Yates Sellar - USA
Happiness Coach
happierbytheminute.com

ANA CUKROV & IVANA SOŠIĆ ANTUNOVIĆ

"When parents support each other in unity,
we evolve as a community."

Our mission is to remind you that we all need love and support as parents in order to give our best to the next generation. Look inside yourself for Divine guidance. Reach out for constant support and settle for no less than full acceptance and total appreciation. Parenting is a chance to tremendously grow and learn from our children. We can all step above the ordinary and be our best. Be the parent that Grows and Glows. Ignite your parenting with Love.

GROW AND GLOW

Parenting. It is a chance to care for another human being. To be responsible for their happiness. To give our children all we have so they can flourish. But it is also a call to explore your own feelings, desires, memories, struggles, relationships, goals, fears, passions and most sacred values. That is precisely what you will give to your child. Willingly or not, they will get it; both the conscious and unconscious parts. The best gift we give our children is our self-acceptance and continuous work on self-awareness. If we accept and cherish ourselves and accept and nourish our children, everything else is minor. To love them freely and fully – that is the parent's calling. Then, when we have laid our bases on solid ground, all experiences that come to life are welcome lessons. One of the most important truths in parenthood is this: Living beside children we learn immensely; as they learn about life from us, we learn about life, just watching them be.

Having five marvelous children each, we have truly been blessed with the gift of motherhood. Continuously raising all ten of our kids, constantly supporting each other, we have been a lifeline to one another. But that is not all. We share the gift of being identical twins. Twinship gives a unique perspective on closeness and connection. From the womb on, you know you are not alone, because you share not only your space, but your whole self with someone who is always there; someone who you trust, fully and unconditionally. You have the innate and recurring experience of being supported. It comes so naturally to you to openly witness each others' joy, laughter, pain, learning and growing. From very early on, we both knew that the unitedness of people is actually a default state. We grew as perfect playmates and friends, understanding each other without many words. Everywhere we went together, people could see how Love was spreading around us, more strongly than with other people. They were attracted to us, warming their souls on our heavenly connection which was so obviously nurtured between us. It was a huge gift, one we were not even aware of. Today we know – it is our calling to say out loud to the world: we are *all* supposed to live harmonious, close, intimate, loving, supporting relationships. Life is meant to be lived in *(comm)unity*.

On the other side, we were challenged with difficulties during childhood, adolescence and adulthood. Our parents had us young, they were still college students and were surprised when two babies arrived. Our grandparents helped raise us, pouring love, compassion and peace on us in enormous amounts, enough to last a lifetime. That made us aware of the importance of the first years of life and of a stable environment for instilling basic security in children.

At preschool age, we left our maternal grandparents' home and moved in with our parents, who struggled with the responsibilities of adult life. Soon they divorced. When confronted with that decision, our whole world collapsed. We felt tremendous pain, the spinning in our little heads, hearts aching, legs shaking. We held hands, relying on each other. But that wasn't all. The pain had just begun. For ten long years, they did not speak to each other. We often moved from mother to father, not being able to fully develop a sense of belonging, missing the security we had with our grandparents. Our childhood experiences made us fiercely determined to avoid divorce when imagining our own marriages. We had to deal with residual feelings of not being enough, guilt, fear and rejection. We eventually dealt with that later in life. Our parents couldn't help us cope better, they did not get enough support themselves. Over time we forgave them.

Thirty-seven years after their divorce and not communicating with each other, during the writing of this story, we all met and enjoyed a beautiful cup of coffee together. It was a warm moment with many of our children present. How important and healing it was for us to see our parents together again! How powerful for our children to have both of their grandparents present after never seeing them this way. All of us could feel it…we were drawing in the possibility of forgiveness and togetherness after so many years. It was a moment of forging bridges between the generations and full of healing lessons for us all.

Although struggling with their own issues, our parents gave us many gifts. Many of their values are alive in our own parenting today. Amongst them, the gifts of being humorous, creative and brave, we get from our mother. Although being a naval architect meant she often traveled, we knew she was there for us, either intuitively supporting us or being physically present at important moments like exams, performances, celebrations and personal struggles. She encouraged our intelligence and playfulness, often introducing new games (cards, crosswords, puzzles, mind-games) and taking us on cruises and fieldtrips. Fun and learning were her priorities.

Our father taught us balance, responsibility, consistency and a love for nature. He would plan everyday life such as chores and finances, and outings like diving, Nordic skiing and picking mushrooms. His masculine Spartan approach has built resistance and warrior survival skills in us. He taught us to catch our own fish, then gut and clean them by the age of ten. We even had our own harpoons and diving gear. It all required growing our endurance muscles. This was all crucial during childbirth when we had to persevere without food and endure long labors. He was also gentle, hugging us, talking to us, being present. Stability and exploring were his priorities. They both spent quality time with us, igniting in us a love for life and science.

At school, we both performed very well, longing for extrinsic acknowledgment through achievement in studying (high grades) and other different areas like sports, music, and dance. But, trying hard to live up to high standards does not make a child feel appreciated and fulfilled, as our western society often falsely promises. If only we knew how precious we are just by being here. So, we kept looking for answers. After high school, we both enrolled in university to study psychology. Obviously, it was due to the unconscious urge to understand how life works, to cope with unpleasant personal history and to resolve our own issues. Also, there was this innate need to help other people grow and to support them to become their better selves. During our studies we received an excellent scientific education. But something was missing.

After the civil war in ex-Yugoslavia and the fall of socialism, we finally discovered the missing part – spirituality. It was a beautiful adventure. Personally meeting Jesus Christ confirmed what we intuitively knew - there **is** a divine *(comm)unity* designed and meant for all of us. There is Love beyond all human capabilities to love. Already adults, we both entered the Catholic Church freely, asking questions and correlating spiritual answers with our scientific background and knowledge. Through Catholicism, discovering its treasures bit by bit, we both slowly and intensively grew more and more aware of both our shadows (dark sides) and our divine nature. Every person is both a saint and a sinner. In everyday life, we witness that as individuals but also as partners and parents. We are all capable of mistakes as well as divine deeds. It's important to be aware of that. Growth always goes hand in hand with awareness.

The more challenges life brought to us, the more we learned. The more we mastered and enjoyed life. It gradually became clear, through suffering we get to know ourselves and build self-acceptance; through coping, we developed skills we needed later on. We both married and started families. Children came along.

We both agree, having the possibility to witness the miracle of life is awesome. Pregnancy. The thrill of a new life inside. Preparing and expecting to meet the beautiful person who is given to you to cherish, nurture and love is outstanding. Giving birth was the greatest moment ever. Nursing a newborn baby, the bliss of their smell, the feelings of fulfilment and pride to have been a co-maker to a creation of a new person are the most beautiful parts of parenting, and if all goes well, it is the honeymoon time – sweet and innocent.

Each phase the baby grows into is a fabulous and intensive period for a parent. First, there is an immense amount of joy and bliss by seeing your child make a new sound or new move. Connecting to another soul that closely, is a miracle and that bond is forever. The beauty of breastfeeding. Baby learns to sit, turn over, crawl. First step. First word. First everything. You don't want to miss a thing! The list goes on… tooth comes out… a new tooth comes in... first drawing… first homework… first love. With every child you have, the joy and fascination with life developing in front of you is immeasurable. It is a completely new and unique experience, as every person brings to this world their own unique touch. Each time a son, a daughter, a nephew or a niece came, all of us grew. Each brought a lesson of significant importance. And this is what it looked like:

November 2000. Ana gives birth to her first child, Marko. We are all astonished with perfection, beauty, heavenly face-expressions and the loveliness of this tiny but so perfect person. We all learn from scratch. The whole family rejoices. *From him, we learned about: wisdom, generosity, softness, intuition and eternity.*

June 2001. Ivana gives birth to twins Luka and Lucija. Double the blessing, double the challenge. Precious moments like seeing them taking each other's little hand while nursing them simultaneously, were unforgettable. They developed a beautiful attachment not only to us parents but also to each other, empathizing from very early on and taking care of each other in the sweetest way. *From them, we learned about: gentleness, closeness, cooperation, respecting differences, acceptance and intelligence.*

October 2002. Ana gives birth to her daughter Lina. Oh, so precious and delicate she was! Although being a second child, she was strong and deliberate from the start. Perceptive to every detail, she explored the world fiercely and loved creating. *From her we learned about: autonomy, self-care, arts, colorfulness, poeticness and beauty.*

March 2006. Ana gives birth to her third child Peter, a beautiful boy. Always smiling, gentle and simple, he brought a new fragrance to our lives. Mild, yet strong and humorous, he was the glue to stick us all together again. *From him we learned about: strength, bravery, music, sportiness and tenderness.*

August 2006. Ivana gives birth to her second set of twins, Matija and Niko. Two strong loving boys, significantly different in personality and needing a well-organized environment as boys often do. It was beautiful to watch the older twins loving the younger ones. *From them we learned about: individuality, bonds, temperaments, uniqueness and courage.*

December 2008. Ana gives birth to Klara. Born in the bathtub, clean as a drop of water, she was an open book, mere honesty and pure courage. Unstoppable in energy and curiosity, a crib-scientist joined the crew. *From her we learned about: determination, enoughness, honesty and joyfulness.*

March 2012. Ana gives birth to Dora, the cutest candy. As her name suggests, she brought sunlight to all of us. As steady as all seasons, she was a new beginning, a reminder of the circle of life. Wise and quiet, ready to process things slowly and oh, so ready to eat. She got us to focus on the basics though she loves her cookies and milk. *From her, we learned about: safety, coziness, balance and awareness.*

March 2013. Ivana gives birth to Filip, the sweetest bubble. Peaceful and kind, he brought harmony to the family. A real singer and a dancer and makes us all smile. *From him we learned about: love, amusement, connectedness, unity and peace.*

Look how lucky we are! We got the opportunity to witness that for all ten of our wonderful children. They got lucky, too. Being in a crew of 14 (parents included), our children had different opportunities to form the way they are thinking, feeling and reacting, while learning how to treat themselves and others; how to cope and how to deal with different situations. The beauty of it all is in the phenomena we could call a *kaleidoscope effect*. Each of us learns from the other and we reflect on each other, forming beautiful and unique patterns, every time new and thrilling.

Our IGNITE moment is one real life situation that lit a candle of awareness in us. Awareness of how important it is to have a close person around while taking care of your children and yourself. Our stubbornness and commitment to always being there for each other was the wick to our candle. We hope you can find someone close and committed to keeping your candle alight as well.

It's summer 2013. We are on vacation in Poreč, Croatia, our husbands are working, and all of our kids are with us. Days go by, we sleep, breastfeed, shop, cook, play, go to the beach, read to children, organize their time in age groups...no incident happens. It's early afternoon. Four teenagers, after having participated in making lunch, relax in their own way (boys read or play the console, girls engage in some craftwork in their room). The youngest toddlers are asleep for their second nap. Three 7-year-olds play with LEGOs on the balcony in the shade. A 5-year old girl plays with a dollhouse. The IGNITE moment happens... and the magic lasts. The two of us sit with a cup of coffee looking at the family photo albums. We talk, relax, nothing in our way. We can even afford to play a game of Quirkle. All of the needs met, our ten loving, gorgeous children giggling around the apartment, we realize that having a reliable person around, one who truly sees and respects you (and vice versa) is enough to make miracles. For us, that means coming closer to the image of the Holy Family, the vision of Mary, loving and educating Jesus, living in simplicity and humbleness. If we were to sing it, the phrase would sound like, "When I hold your back and you hold mine, parenting is Divine."

There is nothing comparable to LIFE! We believe that every child of today is the responsibility of us all. We can evolve as humanity if we see and act with the utmost love and compassion to every child we meet. That way all the children (adults-to-be) including us, as parents, individuals and humanity may Glow and Grow.

IGNITE ACTION STEPS

* **Be** open to life. Life as a gift of God. Life as a wonder. Life as a chance to be, to grow, to serve. Life as a responsibility. Life as a promise.

* **Renounce** the perfect-parent ideal. Parents also make mistakes.

* **Raise** your personal and parenting awareness every day. Become extraordinary.

* **Commit** yourself to your child from the first moment. The early years are the most important, the first three vitally matter.

* **Give** them what they need. You can't spoil your child with too much love. If your child cries, take them in your arms. Nurture them. Hold them. Talk and sing positive words.

* **Pay** attention to your children, teach them self-trust. Acknowledge their uniqueness. They are the biggest experts about themselves.

* **Bring** joy and light in your everyday life. Take trips. Explore. Play. Laugh. Tickle. Run.

* **Base** your relationship with your child on the principle of equal dignity. You are two people, equally valuable, growing and learning together interdependently. Parenting should always be in the best interest of both the parent and the child.

* **Reinforce** your child's social-emotional development; the basis of important life skills. Accept their emotions, show kids how to cope, respecting themselves and others.

* **Discover** your child's dominant language of love.

* **Boost** your child's self-esteem. Praise their effort, not result, don't criticize. Focus on your child's strengths, not weaknesses.

* **Let** your child practice personal responsibility at age-appropriate levels.

* **Support** yourself and your partners in child-rearing (spouse, sister, mother, teacher, trainer…) by encouraging four aspects. *Spiritual:* pray, take a walk in nature, meditate. *Emotional:* show compassion, talk, spend quality time. *Intellectual:* read, journal, learn. *Physical:* exercise, eat healthy, dance, do sports.

* **Look** for support, rely on significant adults in emotional and instrumental ways. You are not alone. When parenting demands you expand - expand your parenting!

Ana Cukrov & Ivana Sošić Antunović - Croatia

SHRREYA SHAH

"I get one life to live. Either I live it as a warning of what not to be or I live it as an inspiration of what to be. It's my choice."

I wish for every parent to understand that we are the creator of our own moods and our own world. When I get stressed, have a sleepless night or experience tensions, I then look at my children smiling and laughing. I ponder: children fight, they fall, they forgive and by the end of the day, they sleep peacefully. I ponder further, who is more wise?

I AM REBORN AS A MOTHER

Sitting in the counselling room, the bright yellow and white paint had no power to help me lighten the energy of loss in the room. Her child had just been stillborn. No accident, no fall, no medical complications but still the baby was delivered, not breathing, no life to resuscitate. Both parents were crying when they later came to me. Waiting out their grief, then listening to their story, we slowly moved into the future. "Let's start fresh," I suggested. "We need to be knowledgeable, fit, aware and at the same time be cognizant of any alarming signs in a future pregnancy." By the time this book goes to print, she will be a mother of a healthy baby as we have monitored throughout her new pregnancy. They have followed every guideline shared in my class. Her husband has encouraged her caringly, even insisting, she do her exercises every day.

That same day, another couple came to the hospital to abort their child of an unplanned conception. They reach the hospital and saw one expectant mother walking with a big belly and something within urged them, "Let's have this baby." I still remember the way we all three had tears in our eyes when the first scan showed it was twins. As a doula, it's such a super feeling to see a woman having a normal delivery and this one was extra special with the twins. She was able to breastfeed them both.

Such a huge contrast: one couple whose baby is no more and one couple who came to the hospital so they could end their pregnancy. Experiences like these have taught me that the story of parenting does not start when we have kids. It starts from the time we plan to have children. I got married at the age of 22. I was still studying and was very clear that I didn't wish to be a parent soon. I always felt, I will think about becoming pregnant when I feel I am completely ready. Similar to my saying, "I can hypothesize on the theory of swimming, but I will never learn the techniques till I enter the water."

As a childbirth educator and counselor, working with expectant mothers and fathers, I keep telling them, "Parenthood is not a status; it's a responsibility." Some stories are cute. Some are funny. Many, especially those I encountered personally from my work in a hospital, can be heartbreaking. More than once, I have cried with a few expectant parents while walking with them on their path.

I have always felt once I became a parent, the journey will be even more special.

My first child Siya was born when I was 26. As she grew, I was excited to apply some of my counselling training to my own parenting. But I started observing my child being unhappy and sulky. It became difficult to accept her feelings. Then my introspection of our relationship stopped me in my tracks. I was confused; my eyes moist. A lingering question bothered me, "Am I doing a good job or do I need to change my perspectives?" This question left me both stunned and inspired, promising myself to strive to be better from then on.

You as a parent might not have had a day in which you snapped at your child as much as I did on the day of which I speak above. But you may have had a hard day being a parent. Even just a difficult hour before bedtime when maybe you weren't quite the mom or dad you wanted to be. I had that day. When I went to check on her before I went to bed. She was peaceful, happy, angelic, beautiful… and I was struck with a pang of guilt? A thought haunted me, "Have I missed this day with her? I know that I have."

That night I sat down to write a letter to my daughter, Siya. I don't know if it was to confess a few things to her or correct myself as a parent. It was my chance to tell her, "Thank you so much for gifting me with motherhood."

There are things I was thinking, Siya: "I have been cross with you.

When I came to your bed to wake you up for school you just asked for five minutes to wake up slowly. I raised my voice, saying you promised me you will cooperate – now get up fast and get ready for school.

I scolded you as you were dressing for school because you gave your face merely a dab with a towel. I took you to task for not cleaning your shoes. I called out angrily when you threw some of your things on the floor. I rushed you to leave as the school bus had already arrived. I did not allow you to share your pop-up thought with me and spoke roughly that you should not waste time when you might be late.

At breakfast, I found fault in you, too. You spilled things. You gulped down your food. You got lost in your thoughts. You ate a few things without holding your plate to avoid dropping crumbs. As you started off to your school bus, you turned and waved a hand and called, "Goodbye, mumma! Have a great day." You wanted to hug me but I frowned, and said in reply, "Leave now, the rest of these things we can manage in the evening. Hold your bag properly!"

Then it began all over again in the evening. I reminded you that you did not convey thank you for a pair of books that I bought. They were expensive – I spoke in a tone which made your eyes moist! You must carry gratitude Siya, next time I am not getting you anything!

Do you remember, later, when I was working on a presentation, how you came in timidly, with a sort of hurt look in your eyes? When I glanced up over my screen, impatient at the interruption, you hesitated at the door. 'What is it you want?' I snapped.

You said – missing you and you ran across within a moment, and threw your arms around my neck and kissed me. Your small arms tightened with an affection that God had set blooming in your heart and which even neglect could not wither. Then you released me, puttering in our room, me back focussing on the screen.

You wanted me to sleep next to you, read a story for you. I got busy replying on my mobile to all unread messages. You said, 'Mumma, you keep telling me no technology when we are sleeping.'

I angrily replied, 'Mumma has got important things to respond to so go to sleep now. I am too tired to read anything.'

Well, Siya, it was shortly afterwards that my thoughts slipped from my mind and an unexpected reflection came over me. 'What have my habits been doing to me? The habit of 'finding fault' as a parent and showing I am superior in our relationship. I am teetering on the edge of planting guilt in you for almost everything. This was my reward to you for being my daughter. It was not that I did not love you; it was that I expected too much for your age. I was measuring you by the yardstick of my own years and the way I have been parented.'

There is so much that is good and fine and innocent and true in your character. The little heart of you is as big as the dawn itself over the wide hills. This was shown by your spontaneous impulse to rush in, hug and kiss me goodnight. Nothing else matters tonight, my little angel. I come to you reflecting in the darkness. I kneel here, ashamed!

It is a feeble atonement; I know you would not understand these things if I told them to you during your waking hours. But tomorrow I will be a real mumma! I will laugh with you, I will dance with you, I will read things to you. As I know soon the time will come when you will be independent unto yourself. I will miss you, my little princess, when that happens. But until then. I will bite my tongue when I am impatient; swallowing the words that make you feel guilty before they leave my throat. I will keep saying as if it were a ritual: "She is nothing but little – a little angel! With an absolute blank slate. I can play a role as a parent so that she can discover the best version of herself."

I am afraid I have visualized you as an adult. Yet as I see you now, Siya, crumpled and weary in my thoughts, I see that you are still a baby. Yesterday you were in my womb, then in my arms, your head on my shoulder. I have asked too much, far too much."

I realize as I reflect and recognize my flaws it helps me to authentically connect with my child. I can not change the world, but yes, I can change myself to change my world. It will help me to accept my child as the gift she is to me. This was my my *dvija* moment, the sanskrit expression for 'being reborn as a mother'. It was clear that I can make a new beginning once I decide. It opened up hundreds of doorways and opportunities as I was moved to accept new thoughts, new emotions, new expressions and yes, rediscover my passion working with expectant mothers.

I, as an adult, have had decades of life experience. I am allowed to make mistakes, to act out at times, to learn and move on, then what about the little ones? They are going through all of this for the first time, without my history and without understanding of themselves to draw upon. They must certainly be allowed some leeway.

My second daughter Saachi had arrived in my life by this time. She has helped me move further in my goals to be kind and patient. My journey with her was different; I felt more mature as I moved beyond possible blunders and 'experiments' with my elder daughter. My self-correction time has reduced drastically. Even at the thought level, I could see when I was going in the wrong direction. My younger one is proactive. She will always convey, "Mumma, I will only listen to you if you talk to me with love." Her approach made us actually sit and communicate about each unbalanced interaction and get things sorted out in the moment.

I realize: **Communication is the key for stronger bonding with children.**

In the process of becoming kinder and more patient with my children, my new outlook reflected in all the relationships in my life. I was happier as a wife, as a daughter-in-law, and as a daughter. I was better at accepting people around me the way they are. My husband is super-organised in thoughts and in actions. I am like a pile of clothes crumpled and unorganised. None of us is perfect. I need him in my life to get myself organised and at times, he needs me to think out of the box. I reside in a house with a joint family of four generations. The great grandparents in the house wonder, "Why do you need to parent like you do? Your kids will just grow as our kids have grown." Grandparents believe, "Being strict with kids will make them more stubborn; this is the only age to enjoy life. Let them be a bird without proper direction." There was a constant war within me to defend myself as a parent. Better to realize, accept and let them believe what they think is right as I continue to play my role that fits for me.

I realize: **All that can be achieved through hatred and frowning can definitely be achieved through love and smiles.** Patience is the key.

When I was able to keep this realization in mind, I naturally gravitated towards patience, resilience and love. To keep myself aligned, I created brain-tattoos for myself which help me to be peaceful and on-track. Let me share a few key brain-tattoos I use.

***Redefining parenting – be what my children want me to be.
Be what they need me to be.**

There are times that my child might misbehave or give me attitude. Still, I need to keep my cool and respond calmly in the way that I really want. But then, as the attitude keeps coming, sometimes I am at my last nerve and *just done with it*. I snap. My voice is raised. Tempers flare, maybe tears fall, but my child gives in. I have won. But have I?

I realize my approach ended the problem at that moment. But more relevant is, my child walks away with a lesson I didn't want to teach: getting angry is the way to solve problems.

I didn't want to be artificial in my approach as that would be inhuman. But it's easy to treat each little infraction, each interaction, as a one-off battle for us to win... without looking at the overall mission of raising kids. When we can keep the big picture in mind – that we are teaching kids to be good human beings – then we naturally gravitate from negative to positive connections.

*I can neither undo my actions nor take back my words. I need to understand my child learns more observing me than from what I say.

When I am raising my voice, I start asking myself is it for their good or for mine?

Hey, this whole parenting thing isn't easy. It's not a formula to be applied step by step to raise a champion. I need to figure out my own life and encounter my own professional, practical and emotional challenges each and every day. I have got to understand and remember that every interaction with my child is potentially providing a lifelong lesson – and the thing is, I have no idea which interaction is going to have the most impact. One of my biggest learnings over this period has been:

*Attitudes don't care where they are shaped, but once they get shaped, they will remain for a lifetime.

I realized I need to take care of myself so that I can better take care of my little ones. I am not part of a competition called parenting to prove and portray a picture that is not me. My parenting journey is diminished when I see myself more superior than my child. I feel ignited as a parent, when I see them as a bundle of potential.

*There is no place for guilt trips in this journey.

The pangs of guilt that hit me as I stood next to my sleeping child's bed felt terrible. It's easy to be overcome with a spiral of destructive thoughts that I am not a good parent; that I am harming my little one. But I have let these realizations guide me to make productive changes in my parenting journey.

Luckily, each tomorrow is a new day, a new opportunity, to be the person that I want to be and build the relationship I want with my children. Of course, I can't let a day slip by before I without paying attention to what I am doing.

Today my two daughters are eight and five years old. I still slip at times. But now I am back on track faster with a clear understanding.

Tonight, my fellow parent, when you stand next to your child's bed, or right now as you read this – choose to make this moment – the moment when you can get started on a completely new track. The one that leads you to being the parent you want to be for your children.

IGNITE ACTION STEPS

Here are some pointers that might help you make your own plan of action in your parenting journey.

* **Respect your child** as you respect an adult.
*Take **responsibility** for your actions.
*No **guilt trips** in the journey of parenting.
*Make **small changes**, they will automatically lead to big differences.
*Remember **a child learns from observing** rather than listening.
*Tonight **sit back, take out a pen and paper.** Give a handwritten letter to your child.

Shrreya Shah - India
Childbirth Educator
www.mydvija.com

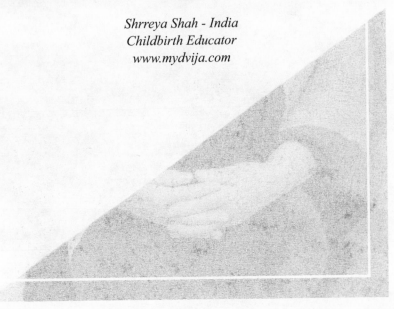

PHYLLIS ROBERTO

"If the path has been traveled it belongs to someone else. Our children are meant to blaze a trail of their own. We as parents are meant to provide the freedom for them to do so."

Open communication can be uncomfortable. We don't always want to hear what our children need to share. Sometimes we don't want to know the risks they are taking, the pain they feel, or the fears that haunt them. In knowing, we have to battle our dread on their behalf – knowing that we cannot save them or protect them or even assuage their worries. I believe parents actively listening to their children from the earliest of times, with no topic taboo or too boring for their attention, will keep communication open. Then even in teen years, parents will be the trusted adults their children can confide in.

LET'S TALK ABOUT IT

"Why do I have to wear a shirt?" Nine-year-old me argued. "It isn't fair – the boys don't have to!" I was outraged at the injustice. Unbeknownst to me, my breasts were starting to 'bud' in a noticeable way. Under protest I put on a shirt.

A couple of years later, "Mom, when I wake up my panties are sticky. Am I okay?"

"You're just growing up dear." This was the sum total of 'The Talk' which led me into puberty and adulthood. In grade six, girls were given a pamphlet containing pictures of ovaries, fallopian tubes, and floating eggs, explaining menstruation. My only other resource was a misinformed older brother who apparently never got much of 'The Talk' either.

The topics of sex and reproduction were not initiated by myself, my siblings or my parents. Pregnancy, labor, and post-delivery recuperation were too private to be discussed with anyone but the doctor. I don't know when my mother went through menopause or what her experience was like. Our bodies were kept a mystery.

It was a confusing time, being a teenager in the 60's. Hippies, long hair, bare feet, love beads and rock and roll were all in direct contrast to the values of my parents' generation. 'Make love not war' was the motto in my generation, along with protesting the war in Viet Nam and supporting sexual freedom with the invention of 'the pill'. Camping with friends at 14, I saw my first naked adult, a man from a nearby hippy commune running down the beach, nude. I was fascinated, embarrassed and amused at the same time.

Taking curiosity into my own hands, I borrowed a smut book from a guy friend in junior high. It was a very explicit read and only opened in the dead of night via flashlight. Two days later, I found the book in my garbage can, ripped up. My alarm at being unable to return the book momentarily outweighed my fear of Mom's reprisal. When confronted, my mother had no concern for my dilemma. She stated, "That book is filth. It's where it belongs. Your so-called 'friend' should be ashamed of himself for having such a book." There was no alternative offered to satisfy my curiosity.

Books being my go-to led me to 'The Happy Hooker' by Xavier Hollander, a memoir of a former call girl and madam. Now better at hiding things, *The Happy Hooker* became my sexuality encyclopedia.

At 16, wanting to have sex with my long-term boyfriend of a whole six months, I went to see Dr. Chen. "I will prescribe birth control pills but I prefer to have parental consent," he advised. "Parents will ensure pills are taken on schedule." The idea of talking to my parents about sex and contraception was terrifying. I wanted to be open and honest with Mom and Dad, but how would I bring up such a subject?

In the living room after supper, I dug deep and took a huge risk. After a couple of false starts, I told them I'd been to the doctor. It was a short conversation. Mom, obviously upset, said she did not approve of premarital sex and would not condone birth control pills. Dad said even less.

Later that night I found a long letter from my mother on my pillow. Twenty pages of handwriting told me how devastated she was. Mom was heartbroken, the moral values she held so strongly made sex permissable only within the sanctity of marriage. It was not a value I held. I don't remember all her reasoning within the multitude of pages. Certainly there was a lot about the church and its rules that said premarital sex was a sin. There were arguments and advice around relationships and the sacred union between husband and wife. The gift of virginity could only be given once and should be given with great care and consideration. Using a letter to convey such deep feelings avoided possible confrontation with a headstrong teenager and left me confused and bewildered. There was no room for questions or discussion. Her case was stated. She did not want to hear anything I had to say. I obviously wasn't going to get the support and approval which I desperately wanted.

Dad being more practical, poked his head into my bedroom. "I'd rather have you on the pill than pregnant." End of conversation. The door I'd opened with such apprehension was firmly shut, the subject not to come up again. As a young girl, I was making a huge personal decision and I felt like I was out on a limb alone. Mom never knew my father had given permission. After she passed on, I read in her diary of her deep hurt and despair. Having daughters who did not live by her creed meant failure as a mother. I cried because she was ashamed of me.

It was no surprise, I was married by 19. I could hardly wait to be a mother. My first daughter was born before I was 21. Three more daughters and a son followed. I resolved to have open communication with my children. I was especially determined my daughters would not be as ignorant of the female body as I had been. They would know their bodies and have a more natural view of sensuality, nudity and sexuality. They would have accurate information and feel free to bring up any topic they chose.

One day, kneeling at the edge of the garden preparing to plant, I noticed my three year old daughter sifting her hands through the fluffy softness of the freshly tilled soil. She was totally engrossed. Not wanting to disturb her I watched out of the corner of my eye, loving how she was reveling in the sensations. After a few seconds, I went back to my task. Moments later I again glanced her way. A neat little pile of clothes was stacked on the grass and she, skin bare, smile wide, was on her back rolling back and forth in the dirt as freely and as naturally as the horses in the field. I understood her rapture, as I too was mesmerized by the living, breathing earth. On her cue, I took a moment to delightedly sink my arms into the rich smelling, sun kissed soil.

It was important to me that my children knew what a woman looked like, what a body that had given birth looked like. I didn't flaunt nakedness but neither did I hide it. It was not unusual to have a child sit on the edge of the tub to visit while I soaked. One day my youngest daughter, then about eight, came in to chat. After a moment or two she scanned my naked body, then commented, "Mommy you have really young feet."

I knew it was a risk but I had to ask. "Do you see anything else young?" She looked up and down. Up and down. A few more seconds of silence passed, then up and down again. Finally, she answered, "Well, your eyes are young, but everybody's eyes are young." Not the ego boost I had hoped for. Still, I was thrilled to have such a natural interaction and a good laugh.

Being a parent motivated me to learn more and more. First in simple areas. When my children became accomplished swimmers, I knew I needed to learn to swim better so my fear and lack of skill wouldn't keep me from allowing them the freedom to swim in deep water.

Their developing bodies dictated I learn more about sexuality and the issues that applied to teens in their generation. I wanted to be an adult they could trust to give them accurate information. I did not want my own lack of knowledge to keep me from being open and honest with them.

When my oldest turned 13, I volunteered as a leader for local sexuality workshops created for teens 13-18. Teen leaders joined adults for extensive training, to create awareness and fill in the gaps within sex education. Although it was a struggle with embarrassment for me to be so open, it was essential to hold space for the teens attending the program. It was incredible to be trusted with both shocking and heart-wrenching conversations. For example: girls who were not aware that urine and babies did not come from the same opening, a 13-year-old girl beating herself up because she didn't know how to perform sexually to her 16-year-old boyfriend's satisfaction, and a 15-year old-boy who was forcing himself to date girls, afraid his friends and family would find out he was gay.

All the teens started out reluctant to talk to each other and across genders. It was always a surprise for them to find out others felt the same. We had two days to build rapport with the teens and to provide a safe space for them to share and build the confidence to talk with their parents.

On Friday nights the parents were taken through a mini version of what the teens would be doing. The intention was to give families a common language and understanding which would open doors to ongoing communication. I discovered most of the parents while growing up, had similar experiences to my own. The men were more familiar with the female body than the women, most of whom had never taken a mirror to look at themselves. In many cases, female orgasm was by 'accident' rather than intention and for some, not experienced at all. The clitoris was a mystery – in location and function. As adults and parents, many knew little about how the opposite sex thought, felt or functioned sexually. It was a brave trek these parents were taking in the hope of supporting their children through the hormonal minefield of the teen years.

I was in charge of creating props for our sessions. Poster boards, 2ft x 3ft, were taken home to make pictures of female and male anatomy. As the whole family sat around the kitchen table coloring different parts of sexual and reproductive organs, the conversation flowed with ease. Questions were asked and answered amongst various other causal topics. My daughters' experience was definitely different than my own.

When my son was about 10, his older sister brought a Playboy magazine home which featured Chyna, a female wrestling star. His sister was learning to draw and wanted to use the photos as examples of female anatomy. As we passed the magazine around the table a respectful discussion ensued with comments on how beautiful her body was. As her muscles were admired, we talked about her modelling and wrestling careers, and how strong she must be. My hope was that a comfortable easy conversation with a boy coming into puberty would lead him to ask questions and talk openly whenever necessary.

As the years went by and dating with sexual intimacy became a part of my childrens' lives, I heard more than I had ever hoped to and was asked questions I had never imagined. Many conversations included a little voice in my head, "Do not react. Do not react. Do not react." It was repeated over and over to ensure my comments, opinions, or fears would not deter any future conversations.

A few years ago, the local radio station had a Mother's Day Contest. The entries were to be Mother's Pearls of Wisdom. My oldest daughter entered this tongue-in-cheek advice, "When I was a young woman and being a bit promiscuous, my mother told me, 'You are only given so much sex in your life. At the rate you are going, yours will be used up in no time'." I won the gift basket.

Later on, I won far more than a gift basket. I received a call from my second daughter who was soon to become a mother. "Mom, will you be in the delivery room with me?" she asked. I was speechless. Such an idea had never occurred to me. In my day it was debatable if the father would be allowed in the room. If so, he was off in a corner out of the way. For me, the delivery was set up for the doctor's convenience. I was flat on my back on a table as uncomfortable and firm as a board, legs up, and feet strapped into stirrups. It was all very sterile and clinical. It never entered my mind to invite my mother into the room, feet up and all. What an exceptional privilege to be asked to be present for the birth of my first grandson.

The room was spacious, with my daughter able to walk around, lie down, sit or whatever suited her. The birthing bed, soft and comfortable could be maneuvered as need be. Doctors, nurses, father-to-be and myself chatted amiably with relaxed anticipation. As the time drew near I was given one task, to note the time the baby was born. When I saw him, I got so excited I totally forgot to look at the clock. His birth time had to be estimated. After a few moments of celebration I stepped out to give the new parents time with their freshly born son. Noticing the excited father leaving to make announcement phone calls, I returned to the birthing room and found Mama also taken elsewhere. Alone with my beautiful new grandson, I immediately scooped him up and settled into the rocking chair next to his wee bed. We gazed into each other's eyes. Overwhelmed with love, I was filled with gratitude to have such an open relationship with my daughter that she not only felt comfortable having me with her, but wanted me to share the birth experience. I marveled at how times had changed.

Although I know my parents did the best they could with what they knew, I had wanted to do 'better.' I had the intention to communicate openly so my children would be comfortable in their sexuality. In truth, it's my children who have made me comfortable and accepting of my own. I am my most authentic self with my children. They have seen me at my best and known me at my weakest and my worst. I can trust them to be open and honest in the most kind, loving, supportive ways possible. They have become a source of companionship, friendship and wisdom. They are my most treasured friends and teachers.

You may not want to be as open about sexuality as I chose to be. Still, the way can be paved so children turn to their parents in times of trouble, discord, curiosity, or need. We can practice communicating with them in meaningful ways from the day they are born. Your connection will grow when you share not just your words but an open heart and your honest truth.

Ignite Action Steps

Children know when they don't have our full attention. Practice putting everything else aside and giving them the same focus you would a significant adult. Really hear them, reading between the lines to understand what is important. Be fully present, attentive, calm, and relaxed even when you don't like what you are hearing. Surefire ways to dissuade conversation are being distracted, uninterested, angry, impatient, or frustrated.

BE CURIOUS: **What can I learn from my child in this moment?** Notice when you feel impatient or want to interrupt. Ask yourself why? Notice what emotions you are feeling – empowering or disempowering? Notice when you want to advise. Is this an opportunity for your child to learn from experience – even if it means making a mistake?

ASK YOURSELF: **What is making this conversation difficult?** Am I wanting things my way? Is it necessary to be the one in control? Am I fearful – worried for their well-being or am I afraid of the unknown? Am I uncomfortable or embarrassed with the subject matter? Why? Am I avoiding topics because I think I need to have all the answers? Am I willing to say "I don't know," and help find the solution?

IDEAS TO ENHANCE COMMUNICATION:
*Journal your thoughts.** Discuss them with your children. Jot down their responses.
*Set aside one-on-one time**, such as bedtime with small children, giving them the opportunity to say what's on their mind.
*Talk with older children or teens in the car.** When driving, eye contact is not required and it is more comfortable to bring up sensitive subjects.
*One-on-one lunch dates, after school and snack times** are other great opportunities to share.

In our busy, overactive lives, it is easy to ignore or minimize the importance of what children have to say. If we communicate with them well in small things, we will have the same opportunity when life-changing decisions are being made. By putting aside our own turmoil we can show support and offer guidance that gives our young people the confidence to direct their own journey. In the process, our path is revealed as well.

Phyllis L. Roberto - Canada
Personal Development Facilitator and Coach, Speaker and Author
Prairie Rose Wellness

FARAAZ RISHAD ÃLÌ

"Transforming intentions into reality feels better when you show
up with a big smile and a heart full of love."

I welcome you to create parenting life by your own design. I wish to share with you my experience featuring tools and opportunities, rather than rules and obligations. My goal is to empower you by sharing ideas. Parenting has its challenges but if you approach it with a winning mentality, it does not need to be difficult. The joyous moments exist in abundance. Let us strive together towards excellence.

THE THREE MINDSHIFTS IN MY PARENTAL JOURNEY

My two years and nine months of parenting experience, plus the eight and a half months of pregnancy is best described through three phases: analysis and acknowledgment of becoming a father, acceptance of and adaptation to becoming a parent and finally, advancing and appreciating being a guardian. I had to learn and act fast before evolving to the next level. Each phase had its challenges and helped me get to my parental A-Game faster.

Analysis & Acknowledgement:

"I am way too young to have a child!" this was my reply to my wife, Maria, when we were having that conversation about the two of us becoming three. I was thirty-two years old and my reply was designed to protect me from a world that scared me. The stories of parenthood being difficult, with life changing drastically, living the suburban life and driving a family van, were some of the resistance blocks in my decision making. These stories I had heard or seen but never researched to validate, created my premise to oppose the idea of parenthood. As a consequence, they armed me with the answers to why I shouldn't have a child?, for the future conversations on this topic with Maria, our parents, friends and strangers. It seemed like an inescapable cultural-set dialogue, where it was okay to constantly ask married couples when the first baby was coming. Entertaining the parental idea was further put off when my mom thought it was a good idea to talk about my aging sperm on our weekly Skype calls.

Maria and I traveled a lot so adding a baby would reduce our options. This was my selfish excuse that I hung onto creating a smokescreen of reasons to protect my truth. Delaying the process made me feel like I would have that extra year to continue exploring exotic locations around the world with Maria and friends. My rebellious outlook meant a never-ending honeymoon. I was made for continuous celebrations. Every day was a celebration for me. Having an active social life was important, so a lot of our honeymoon trips became buddymoons. Traveling the world with buddies creating lifelong memories was an amazing opportunity that I was grateful for and addicted to.

Every vacation reminded me that family was inevitable as I interacted with couples with children, seeing the smile on parent's faces as they played and hearing the child's laughter fill the room. Every joyous moment witnessed was a lesson that helped me grow past my internal blocks. Growing up, I had younger cousins that I had to look after when they were babies. I was naturally good with kids and had no struggles with entertaining them. It took me almost three years from the time Maria and I started talking about having a child, to acknowledge that I would make a good father. Being a late starter for most of my life, at thirty-five I told Maria that I was ready to plant the seed. We acknowledged that conceiving could be a complex process and may take up to a year or more. In my menspective, this simply meant a lot of sex and the masculine energy within me was ready to take on this responsibility.

One week! That is how long it took for the process of scoring a goal as we say in impregnating terms. In my mind I had mapped out a fantasy process stretching over six-plus sensual months, however, the reality was the magic went down within a week of trying while we were in the jungles of Luang Prabang, Laos. We only found out about the success of the jungle boogie while we were in Oslo, Norway back from our six weeks of buddymooning in south-east Asia.

I remember that moment when Maria approached me with the news that she had missed her period and decided to try the pregnancy test, which came out positive. As the words, "I'm pregnant," registered in my mind, I recall feeling that explosion of energy and my body froze. My facial emotions paused as I breathed very lightly, my muscles hardly flinching as I became a statue externally. Internally my thoughts were celebrating the news that I was going to be a father, drifting into questions like: Is it a boy or girl? What if it is twins? What do I need to do to prepare? Am I ready? When shall I tell the world? How amazing is this? Wow, is this really happening? Detaching from the physical moment and going deep into my thoughts meant a few too many seconds passed, with Maria looking for an emotional reaction. She snapped her fingers to pull me back to the present moment. I looked liked I'd seen a ghost. Trust me, this is not the reaction you want to portray on hearing baby news. I eventually got to express my happiness with the news, overjoyed with this feeling of ecstasy that we would soon be welcoming a child.

The next eight months were made up of doctor's appointments and baby scans. Finding out it was a girl was great. I wanted a daughter. Every scan and every kick from the belly assisted me in acknowledging I was going to be an awesome father. I was motivated to learn everything about babies so I would excel in this role. However truth be told, the information on the market is full of contradicting content. Showing up with love and a big smile to support Maria in welcoming our daughter was all I needed to avoid drowning in all the information.

The official baby news was met with delight by our family and friends. However, the news that we were going to India for our 'Babymoon' when Maria was at four months was met with fear and skepticism. This was my first introduction to the fear culture around parenting. Although babies exist in India, a lot of the advice we received painted India as a dangerous place for pregnant women. Don't go there! This advice even came from people who were not parents or been to India themselves.

Acceptance & Adaptation:

In early December I was preparing to host Maria's baby shower. We were two weeks out from the due date and this was the best weekend to squeeze in a party before all the friends dispersed for the Christmas holidays. I did a great job getting the place ready for a party, while trying to ensure Maria had no work to do. However, being a little impatient and stubborn, Maria decided to lift some small boxes to get things done faster. I was against this but a note to all men: pregnancy and hormones means be careful with what you say, so I chose silence as I had learnt my lessons over the past eight months.

Perhaps the lifting exercise was a factor but that evening around midnight, she went into labor. The hours that followed were the standard procedure of checking the contractions, calling the maternity team and trying to get some sleep (this part did not work out). Early in the morning, we checked in at the maternity ward, preparing for the big moment. The baby shower had to be canceled and in hindsight, we should have known our daughter was a party animal and coming two weeks early was her first expression of FOMO. (Fear of Missing Out)

From midnight to the afternoon, I was on autopilot trying to support Maria and get some vertical sleep on a sofa chair at the hospital. When the delivery part came, I thought I was ready. Sleep-deprived but smiling and filled with love, I had pictured in my mind, a process that was similar to most movies, where I held Maria's hand coaching her while she pushes, shortly after, a baby comes out and I cut the umbilical cord. The reality was more complicated as I had to assist the midwife and nurse. Swapping my wife-side seat to the medical team's front-row delivery view caught me off guard. I am not a fan of blood and Maria told me a few months earlier, *"Please do not pass out as I will need medical attention. Don't steal the resources."* Soldiering on helping the medical team for the next few hours, I was shook up seeing things that cannot be unseen.

Witnessing Maria in pain and being unable to help was a tough feeling. Finally, my daughter Nicola came out and was placed on my chest. In the moments prior to this, I was still processing the fact that the baby was covered in slime and blood. I thought I was supposed to fall in love with my daughter as soon as she came out but none of that happened as the whole scene reminded me of a horror movie. However, something did happen that I can't explain in words, when she was placed on my chest with her little fingers grasping my skin, our warmth melted into each other. I could hear her faint breaths and I dared not breathe too heavily to disturb her. I felt this paternal bond igniting between us, as I stared at her feeling proud and grateful. She was finally here. Then her grey eyes opened and that is when we first met. The explosion of energy that went through me... right then was extraordinary. My face lit up with a big smile. My love was now amplified to a whole new level. Tears flowed down my cheeks as I enjoyed that moment of oneness. My acceptance of this beautiful little human gazing back at me was uplifting, creating a human connection I had never experienced before. This was my creation. The power of life. My chance to be a guardian angel to my daughter. This was my acceptance that becoming a father was never about me, it was about us.

Appreciation & Advancement:

The first three months of Nicola's life flew by. The adaptation process was challenging. I would often find myself walking Nicola to sleep in knee-deep snow pushing a pram, snowflakes blowing into my face and her resting comfortably in her pram. Change was hard in the beginning but we adapted to the new situation. In this hibernation period, I enjoyed every smile and new gesture from Nicola, learning her needs and finding the best way to keep her entertained. My friends did say I had become an overprotective grizzly bear. I guess that was my natural fatherly instincts. Nicola had all her necessary vaccinations done within these three months and we were finally ready to travel, starting a new trend called familymooning. Traveling with a baby had mixed viewpoints from around the world, with the majority of information feeding into the huge fear culture that deemed it dangerous. Forums on the topic of traveling while pregnant or with a baby were populated with negative advice. I felt it all inaccurate. There were babies born in all the countries I was going to and the majority of them had babies growing up healthily.

The next eight months were filled with adventure and exploration. It was a simple plan to enjoy the parental leave and work remotely. We started off with a short trip to England to test out Nicola's comfort levels while airborne. Once we knew she was comfortable in planes we put our parental adventures in high gear visiting Asia, Europe and Oceania. What did these adventures teach me? The fear culture associated with traveling with children was inaccurate. It was a lot of work carrying the luggage; suitcases, the car seat, the pram, the baby backpack and most importantly the baby in one hand while going through customs, airports, planes, boats and trains. It was worth it as Nicola was met with so much love in every city. Hotel and restaurant staff could not get enough of her and she enjoyed being around so many people from different cultures.

We met many wonderful people in our travels and were reminded of how much we all have in common and that love unites us. I met people who didn't speak the same language but there is something about adults, they light up with love when toddlers are around. Some of the people I met did not have the easiest lives but they had the biggest hearts and this was a gentle reminder of my humble beginnings in Fiji, where a big smile and love is the first step to any action. A bonus to having so many volunteer babysitters was that it allowed Maria and I to have quality couple time.

The sleeping routine was the biggest casualty in our travels. The change in time zones was challenging for everyone. The constant excitement and interactions for Nicola meant she developed a case of FOMO. Sometimes she would fall asleep in a car and wake up on a boat, or fall asleep in a plane and wake up in a hotel room. She tried to stay awake to keep up with the changes. That meant I had to walk her to sleep or drive around in a golf-cart till she fell asleep. The walking to sleep was something I continued to do once we got back to Norway. A lot of advice was around placing the child in a bedroom and letting them cry to sleep. I simply could not do this, as a child has no real understanding of bedtime. They fall asleep when fatigued. The emotional trauma of being left in a room screaming, waiting and crying in fear, feeling that you are not good enough, hence no one is coming, is not something any child should go through. Maria mentioned that this was common practice in her culture and this led to one of the few clashes we have had on parenting techniques. I could not stand hearing Nicola screaming and alone, so I continued our evening walks where she fell asleep while enjoying time with her dad. Some nights took longer than others but it was a sacrifice I needed to make to ensure she fell asleep feeling acknowledged.

As we progressed with our parenting routines, Nicola moved out of our bed and into her own. She did not need to be walked in the evening at a certain point and just needed a bedtime story or light entertainment. Doing things different than traditional methods meant creating an environment for her that was absent from fear and judgment.

My parenting journey has been one where I had to get comfortable with the idea of being a father before I became a father. During fatherhood, there have been struggles where I have reached breaking point and cried. Trying to be an awesome father has many challenges. God knows how many times I fail each day but I am aware of my failures and consistently work on delivering the best version of myself to my daughter. My experience has taught me that there are substantial gaps in parenting today. The information we have inherited from different decades is outdated. As a parent we have the choice to people-please or we can choose to nourish our child's needs by being present physically and emotionally. The biggest shift I have experienced as a parent has been seeing myself in my daughter. My traits of being impatient, stubborn and disobedient are reflected in her attitude. She is like a mirror to my soul and for that I am grateful as it has made me improve and be a better example. Our parent-child relationship is one that interchanges as student and teacher, where personal growth happens at the intersection of curiosity and courage.

My journey into parenthood has been one where I choose not to people-please or fit into a world of mass instructions. You are the master of your life, so choose your terms for parenting and your child will adapt and thrive. The parenting rulebook is changing and adapting to new information from today, so don't let historical societal rulebooks hold you back from enjoying the modern parent life. Your dreams should never be put on hold because of children, the dream must continue as a family and as a team.

IGNITE ACTION STEPS

*Be Present: Being present means putting your devices away when you are with your child. Make time to be there completely, with no distractions. This will make them feel they are good enough for you and not competing against a device. Set time in your schedule for dedicated quality time.

*Be Non-Judgemental: Passing judgement on right and wrong, good or bad, creates a spectrum for your child where negative words create the *I am not good enough* feeling and set up expectations of people-pleasing, which eventually affects their self-esteem. Do not lash out at the child with judgment, instead discuss things in a logical manner breaking down the WHY he/she did those actions and understanding WHAT was the consequence, and HOW we can fix it.

*Be Conscious: In non-verbal communication, your facial gestures and body language speak volumes. Your external voice and energy is your child's internal voice and energy; it shapes their being so you have a big responsibility to be aware of what you say and do. Being conscious is a tool we all need to embrace.

*Be Seen: Children love to do what they see, rather than do what they are told. Be the example you want your child to see and be. Use the three C's in Be-Seen: Courage, Curiosity and Compassion.

*Be Adventurous: Small steps of courageous actions create small gains towards unleashing the explorer within you. Do things that bring you closer as a family and always allow for unpredictability, to help you grow individually and as a team.

Faraaz Rishad Ãlì - Norway
Chief Empowerment Officer, Speaker and Explorer
www.faraazali.com

JB Owen

"It isn't what you have, it is what you give."

The greatest gift you can give, is the gift of you. Children only want the purest part of their parents: their love. It is my deepest desire my story encourages you to give the riches and treasures of you. Let your children delightfully enjoy all your splendor and glory and be the person who inspires you and them.

Having It All

I remember my seventh birthday. The table was beautifully set with party plates and birthday hats. In the center lay a large custom-cake of Big Bird with his Sesame Street friends. Outside in the pool, floaty toys bobbled in the water amidst party streamers and goofy games. Everything was poised immaculately for a group of young girls to enjoy on a June day in the sun. As my playmates arrived, we ran through the house. Up to my room with its designer wallpaper, into the game room, den, living room, dining room and even the laundry room that could fit us all. I remember one of my playmates flopping down our custom-made couch after all the chasing.

"Wow!" she proclaimed as she looked around. "You have EVERYTHING!"

The house we lived in did have it all. Grand rooms, great furnishing, and unique features facing a swimming pool and expansive backyard. The decked-out arcade room, curvy slide and diving board made our house the "fun-est" in the neighborhood. Most of my birthdays consisted of cannonballs and pirouettes into the pool. We played Foosball and took turns on the two authentic pinball machines in our oversized rumpus room. Lots of food spread across our massive kitchen, and a game of hide-and-seek could last for hours. We had a big house with lots of space and my parents did their utmost to provide 'the best' for both my older sister and me. To an outsider looking in, it did appear we had it all.

My young friend's comment affected me. It made me see my life through her eyes. Indeed, we did have a plethora of items. There were lots of toys, spacious rooms and cupboards full of food and treats. However, there wasn't a lot of affection or one-on-one connection. My parents were entrepreneurs, business owners, and workaholics. That meant 24/7 on the job, on the phone and always being busy. I had a lot of "things" but none of the important things I wanted. Despite my friend's opinion that we "had it all," we lacked the connection and closeness I was craving.

I didn't know the trampoline, motorbikes, two Pomeranian puppies and every board game Hasbro ever made were mainly for distraction. They kept my sister and I amused while my parents were busy doing their work. I learned quickly that "things" brought me attention. My top-of-the-line skis were envied by my friends. The new convertible car I drove to school made me "super-cool" at 16. Trips to Hawaii at Christmas labeled me the luckiest kid. No one realized the lamp in the hotel room was our Christmas tree, and my sister and I watched TV alone while my parents ate dinner in the restaurant downstairs. Somehow Santa and his festive sleigh never made it to Hawaii. There were no traditions, little merriment, and few boisterous hugs from receiving the best presents ever!

To the outside world I appeared privileged, inside my world, I felt lonely. Everyone expected me to be happy, for some reason, I wasn't. I didn't feel like I "had it all." I felt like I just had stuff. I painted a smile on my face and stuck out my chin, hiding my desire for affection. I let the attention of my friends become what mattered; their admiration falsely filled the sadness in my heart. I eventually stopped trying to get my parent's attention and switched to getting their approval through working.

I did what most children do. I followed in my parents' footsteps and became a budding, outgoing entrepreneur. For most of my adult life, I sat diligently working from my desk, crafting my skills. Business became my life. I loved the thrill of creating things and the excitement of being my own boss. "Earn to spend" was my motto. Make more so you can spend more was the way I thought. I filled my world with items, instead of filling it with what mattered in my heart.

When my two children blessed my life, I worked harder to give them everything! I did exactly what my parents had done. I bought them the biggest toys and the coolest presents. I went over the top providing the "things" I thought would make them happy. If I was away on a business trip, I'd walk in the door with a life-sized stuffie. If I missed snuggling with them at bedtime, there would be a little present outside their door when they woke up. To keep them from missing me while I worked, I bought them gifts to show how much I cared. That resulted in me needing to make even more. The "earn more to spend more" philosophy engulfed me in the same 24/7 life my parents had: on the job, on the phone and always, always busy.

Like many moms, business owners, and parents, I stressfully juggled life at home and life at the office. *I glossed over the need to be there with the need to provide.* I gave things to my children yet, gave less of my time. I was repeating the behavior of my parents, and their lifestyle; sending the message work is more important than family connections.

When my children were eight and 11, my years of excessive working finally caught up to me. I was divorced, raising them alone, overweight, unhealthy and utterly burned-out, mentally exhausted and feeling empty. Life had become a process, not an enjoyment. We had lots of things, but not the deep connection I craved. Working became hollow and my passion for doing "more" diminished. The private schools and expensive lessons taxed my spirit. Gifts stop meaning anything; the desire to give them became nil. Conversely, the kids were constantly asking for "something". It seemed as if they never had enough. They were used to my mommy guilt yielding them a present, or those long hours on the computer resulting in an overcompensating trip to the mall. Without realizing it, I had recreated my childhood experience of having it all yet, having so little of what truly mattered. Somehow I missed the important parenting road signs. I took a right when I should have gone left. I turn on cruise control and then forget to turn it off. I roared right past a roadblock, drove through the red lights, thinking they should be green. I concentrated on the miles behind me, instead of mapping out the route ahead.

I remember one day sitting in silence; questioning what was I actually doing to create a strong connection with my kids. I ask myself critically, what wrong turns did I make? Did I even know what was ahead of me? Most importantly…what path did I need to take to get to where I wanted to be? I thought I could intellectualize those answers; figure it out by working harder. Except on that day, my heart spoke loudly. It refused to be ignored any longer. It wanted to be heard. To be recognized. After years of disregarding it, I knew it was time I listen.

I had come to a place where my ideas, values and needs had fundamentally changed. Working and making money needed to take a back seat to raising a family and building a life. I wondered what I would do if life didn't revolve around earning money, what would fill my heart. What nurtured my soul? What would bring me real happiness? Sitting in the stillness that day, I gave myself the freedom to uncover the powerful answers not from my head, but most importantly from my heart. Truly seeking the answer, I asked myself, if money was not a concern, what would be my deepest desire?

Surprisingly, the answer came to me in seconds! "Take your kids out of school and go traveling." A faint smile spread across my lips. I had considered that idea a few times in passing; I even joked about it with a friend. Until then, it had only been a notion dancing around in my head, not an inner wanting. But that day those words were not spoken in jest. They were *told* to me loud and clear. I felt a passion behind them--a conviction! My inner voice was shouting out what I had not been willing to hear. I knew that **being** with my children, and truly connecting was the most important thing I needed to do.

With this new idea floating around in my head I found myself daydreaming about ways to make it possible. I used my skills in business to see how I could execute such an endeavor. In my mind, I planned the logistics, mapped the places and rehearsed an answer to the skeptical questions it would raise. Exhilaration flowed through me imaging such a trip and the joy on my kids' faces having unlimited time together. Believing they would be excited, I probed them the next day while driving to school, I asked them what would make them truly happy if they could do anything; if life had unlimited possibilities, what would make their hearts sing? Only... I took it one step further, "It can't be an object and we can't buy it." I wanted to break the cycle of happiness coming from material things. I told them it had come from their hearts and be something they could do rather than have.

My son sharply said as he stared out the window, "Not go to school!" My daughter snickered and agreed. It was 7:15 A.M. and we were already in traffic to get to their elite school, thirty minutes from our house. I probed a little further, agreeing if no school, then what? My amazing daughter became excited and said she'd like to help save the baby turtles who need protection and clean beaches. My compassionate son added he'd like to earn money to give to the refugees he'd seen in the news having to flee their homes. The two of them began listing initiatives and organizations they could support. They knew from social studies the Great Barrier Reef was dying, and a previous trip to Mexico had shown them the many orphans and homeless children needing sponsors.

Before I knew it, they listed a dozen charities they could support and the different countries those charities were in. Because children imitate their parents, mine started strategizing about how they could work hard to raise money to make a bigger impact. It was electrifying how excited they became about helping others and giving back. It was more encouraging to see they connected 'doing' to having fun and touching hearts.

Waiting at a red light, I was deep in thought about the ideas they were creating. In my mind, I could vividly see us traveling to those countries, making a difference and helping others. My soul sensed the impact we could make and the purpose we could form as a family. Lost in my daydream, my daughter asked, energized by our conversation "Mama, do you think we can go all these places and help them ourselves?" Before my mind had fully registered the question, my mouth answered her, "Of course we can."

It was as if a lightning bolt had shot through the roof of the car, hit me right on the top of my head and speared directly to my heart. It felt as if my chest had burst open and the darkness that was there had been filled with light. I heard my inner voice screaming, "of course you can," while my intellectual brain was stuttering to catch up. An inner celebration began happening in my spirit flooded with positive emotions. It felt euphoric, to say 'yes' to a dream. At that moment, without knowing how, I knew we were going to do it. The path had just been laid out before us, and without any hesitation, my whole Being agreed to put it into motion.

Over the next two months, the three of us mapped out a plan to travel to 12 countries in 12 months. Our goal was to raise awareness and funds for various charities in each place. I let my kids pick where they wanted to visit and the organizations they wished to support. They were excited to have a purpose and felt inspired about the difference they could make. They began a charity campaign called JUST GIVE TODAY. My youngest felt if we all gave a little, we'd all have a lot. My oldest felt if money wasn't an option, people could easily give time, support and effort because that is free. They wanted to show people you can "just give" hugs, smiles and joy to make the world a better place. They felt they could teach others some of the best things in life come from the heart and don't cost anything.

It was an ambitious endeavor, but a heartfelt one. We didn't know exactly how it was all going to unfold, but we knew we had a mission to serve as many people as possible. As I packed my house into storage and pulled my kids out of school, the naysayers arrived in droves. "Are you crazy? You can't do that!" "A woman traveling alone with two kids? What about school?" It was painful to hear their negativity and dissuasion. To have so many people doubt and put down your idea was disheartening. However, I kept listening to my inner voice and stayed connected to my desire and the enthusiasm radiating from my children. Their hearts and souls were focused on the good we could do and the lives we would help.

For the next 12 months, my two children and I visited nine countries, working and raising funds for charity. We bought food and school supplies for the kids in the Dominican Republic. We painted murals with inspiring sayings at a children's community center in Mexico. Then we funded the building of a much-needed bathroom there. We helped dozens of baby turtles make it to the ocean's shore in Costa Rica. Then we supported the rescue hospital for monkeys injured while climbing on the powerlines. We taught English in foreign primary schools, picked up garbage off congested beaches, spent time with the elderly, and delivered basic items to refugees across Italy, Greece and Turkey. Wherever we went it was with a purpose: to be in service. We wanted to give more of ourselves to others. We hugged, laughed and made friendships with people and saw how true gifts never cost a penny.

Naturally, there were a few harrowing moments. Tarantulas invaded our jungle treehouse in the Dominican Republic. We experienced mass floods that filled the streets and a tropical hurricane that diverted us to another country. One day we were lost on the subway; another day we were stranded on a dirt road with no one in sight. Many difficult yet beautiful moments now color any conversation my kids have--with a stranger on a plane, or cousins at a family dinner. They recount those memories with joy and personal satisfaction.

The best part is they learned to use their innate "super-powers" of intuition, problem-solving and courage. Not speaking the language, not knowing the way, or having to cook food in the dark gave them life skills and helped them find their inner strength. Despite mosquito bites, hungry tummies and rain-dripping moments, we all grew in character through those 12 months. We worked not for money, but for enjoyment. The three of us became a team, loving, appreciating and connecting with one another. Having "*things*" was the last thing on our minds.

I will forever remember watching beautiful blush sunsets with both kids lying content in my arms. Giggling uncontrollably while licking our fingers after eating the biggest, ripest peaches; juice dripping down our arms. Locked in my memory is the wind blowing through our hair as we played Captain Hook sailing on a rickety old boat while boisterously singing Disney songs. Looking up at millions of stars on a crystal-clear night, laughing until our stomachs hurt. I will cherish holding hands with my son while walking through the street markets and teaching my daughter side-by-side how to dive into the crystal blue sea. Those moments had no price tag and they're the 'things' that mean everything to me.

Even though a carton of eggs and a bag of rice was often our meals for a week, we were happy. Sometimes the three of us had to share one banana or finding a ripe avocado was a treat. We lived humbly, modestly with nothing but what we could carry. Things became irrelevant. Moments became everything. To see them smile, hear their laughter, then cuddle before bedtime became my measurements of success. We had "nothing," but in fact, we had everything, because we had each other.

For the first time in my life, I "had it all." The love and connection I had been striving for blossomed. The peace and contentment which had eluded me finally enveloped me. Having it all wasn't a bobble or shiny object. Nor was not in accolades from a colleague, and it certainly was not numbers on a bank statement! The love we had created made me feel much more complete.

I am reminded daily in the eyes of my children how important it is to take time to enjoy what is right in front of you. How vital connection and family togetherness truly is. Their smiles, warm hugs and continued devotion is what I work for now. What matters in life is free: love, companionship, support, compassion, kindness, and acceptance. These are the currency of love and joy. They cost nothing, and yet they mean so much. Have those, and you can truly say you HAVE IT ALL.

IGNITE ACTION STEPS

*Make a list of 10 things you can DO with your kids that don't cost money.

*Pick a time each day to stop everything to connect with your child. Between **breakfast or bedtime, assign a time when you both know it is all yours.**

*Be silly, have fun and be a kid yourself. Adults like to hang out with adults, kids like to be with kids. If you want to spend time with your child, bring out the child in you.

*Hugs, smiles, and joy. If you are looking for the currency of success with your kids, hugs often, smile whenever you can and create joy in your interactions. it is both free and worth millions.

JB Owen - Canada
Founder of Ignite, World-class Speaker, Best-selling Author
www.igniteyou.life

BONNIE CHAN

"If you change your lens, you can change your life."

My wish is to show you that by simply looking at things from a different perspective, you can empower yourself and your family to learn, grow and thrive. The purpose of this chapter is simply to share with you some perspectives from my own journey in parenting. I hope that you take any ideas that inspire, empower or light you up and discard whatever doesn't fit.

LOOKING THROUGH A KALEIDOSCOPE

The kids were late for school and they weren't listening to a thing I was saying. I was angry, I was fuming...and I was screaming at my four year-old son Jaden, "YOU BETTER STOP THAT NOW OR ELSE!"

In an effort to save his brother, my brave eight-year-old son Lucas pointed to the wall and interrupted, "Mommy, you're not following house rules." The only house rule running through my mind at that moment was that you had better listen to your mother or else. However, when I glanced at Lucas, he was pointing to a hanging wall-art in their room that read, HOUSE RULES: Hug often, Be nice & play fair. Help each other. Do your best. Forgive quickly. Be generous.

This interruption quickly shifted my perception from "My kids aren't listening to me," to "My kids are learning from everything and even teaching me."

It was an Ignite moment that snapped me out of anger and filled me with joy and pride at yet another opportunity for my boys to teach me to be a better person. I apologized, hugged them and basked in the moment.

Perspectives on Being a Parent. When you ask a parent how it's going, I'm guilty myself to have said and have heard responses from others such as, "My kids are driving me crazy," or "I don't have a life of my own anymore," or "Having kids cost too much," or "They are little monsters." Or maybe you've heard the following sentence: "Before I had kids I used to *(fill in the blank)*. Now I'm just a professional chauffeur."

I'd like you to stop and think about this for a second ...How would you like to be a child and hear this coming out of your parent's mouth? Even if you are joking, the unconscious doesn't know the difference and you may unknowingly plant an unwanted seed in your child's unconscious mind. What are your perspectives on being a parent? For me, I've taken on parenting as a privilege and an opportunity for an expanded life, personal growth and contribution to society.

Were you ready to be a parent? Ask any parent (before they had kids) this question and often the answer is, "No Way!" You don't get an instruction manual, you don't get a learner's license and there is no co-op program. One day you go to the hospital, and the next thing you know... a doctor hands you a baby and says, "Congratulations and Good luck!"

Before becoming a parent, I remember hanging out with Sarah and John, one of the first couples in our circle to become parents. As we sat on their rooftop balcony watching their toddler wobble from side to side as he pushed along a walking toy, Sarah said, "The experience of being a parent is like the best personal growth program out there."

Before that, I was nervous about starting a family but after hearing Sarah's comment it shifted something in me. I had already started on my personal development journey and if having a baby was just an extension of the transformation and growth that I was already experiencing, I thought I could handle it. It was an Ignite moment for me to get that **new perspective**.

A little bit about me. The impact of having a large extended family (eight siblings on each of my mother and father's sides) with most of them living in the same city was a constant feeling of support and a wide variety of viewpoints to learn from. Out of all my family members, the most influential to me was my paternal grandma.

During my childhood, she would round up the grandkids and go with us to the beach to play and dig for clams, go fishing at the lake and pick wild berries along the roadside. Then she would teach us how to make jam and seafood dishes. Grandma was always excited for an adventure together.

Although she grew up poor and uneducated, she taught herself essential skills such as reading and swimming. As a senior she suffered through multiple strokes but continued to retrain her brain to speak and walk. It was only at her funeral a few years ago, that I really grasped the impact she had on our family. Her commitment to doing things together created a lifetime of memories that we all cherish.

My Grandma taught us that, "Doing things together is better." If you typically resist doing things with others and are the *lone-ranger* type, this is an opportunity to explore for personal growth. For me, since I already had the *together is better* mindset, when I moved to a different city away from my family (in my late 20's) I actively searched out new friends and communities to be a part of. It was in this process that my journey into self-development and leadership flourished as I met unique individuals and was introduced to new perspectives on business, success, health and spirituality.

If you are already comfortable doing things together with other people, the next challenge is to do so with a variety of people. I've experienced that doing different things with people of different backgrounds is even more rewarding.

As a parent, wouldn't you like your child to be comfortable meeting new people, making meaningful connections and having access to more experiences and possibilities?

Parenting starts with setting an Intention. Here's mine: *We are a guide for you to become the best version of yourself and we are here to grow with you.*

Who do you listen to? and Trusting yourself. Often, whether due to laziness, habit or ignorance, we simply rely on whatever we are being told by others who supposedly know better than us. In my case, it was my doctor. He had been an OB-GYN for 25 years and I don't doubt he has *seen it all*. However, when I came into my appointment and mentioned a *natural* birth plan, he dismissed it completely and told me the pain would be too much to endure and I would be asking for an epidural. Certainly, he was very knowledgeable but he didn't know me better than I know myself.

I educated myself, enrolled in a hypno-birthing class, hired a doula and powerfully came to my own conclusion, "A completely natural birth was best for me." Both my boys were born naturally with no medication and the experiences were positive. For my first son, I even declared the exact day that I wanted to give birth (my doctor rolled his eyes at this). My son arrived on that very day.

One point of view I grew up with is that I shouldn't disagree with those in a position of authority, but rather, just listen to them. Here's the perspective shift—keep learning to be a better student. It is healthy to learn, debate, check in with myself and choose what is best for me.

My rule of thumb is whenever I have an important decision to make in an area that I'm not educated on, I do my best to stay open and seek out at least three recommendations. This includes things like choosing a healthcare practitioner, financial planner, renovation contractor, coach, etc. I would evaluate the researched data and check-in with my gut feeling to see if there's alignment with my heart and then come up with my answers.

This mindset and practice is something I want to instill in my kids. When we are kids we get all sorts of advice just like we do as adults. Recently, I was with parent friends sitting by the pool—the kids were in the water. One of the girls saw an inflatable toy that she wanted to play with. She started going towards it and her mother said sternly, "That's not yours, you're not allowed to play with it. Don't touch it." Then our other friend, responded, "I think it's okay, take it, play with it and apologize or say, thank you later." And then, I responded with, "Why don't you go find the owner and ask if you can borrow it first?"

She received three completely different responses. This is like the situation I described around my birth plan. We seek advice from people who we know to be authorities, in this case, all the adults. None of these are a RIGHT response, they are just different approaches. As parents, we can intentionally use situations like these to reflect with our children. It's good to look at the different options and address what you want, work it out and look at the impact on everyone else who is involved.

Do you feed your children with healthy habits? What do they see? What do they hear? What are they feeling? Do they see you living your potential and making the best use of the resources you have? Or do they see you blaming others instead of taking responsibility? "Monkey see, monkey do."

Accountability for self-love and self-care. Serious self-care started when we found out that we were expecting our first baby. I rigorously looked after my body – extra vitamins, proper rest, regular exercise, monitoring my stress level and playing classical music. I even reviewed one of my personal development courses so that the baby could start learning in the womb.

Being responsible for another human being, it was my job to care for him. Caring carries over into other areas of my life. If there's another person involved, I am more responsible – kind of like keeping an important appointment versus keeping an appointment with myself. Now that I'm a parent, this has been a wonderful context to help me take on becoming the best version of me in the same way that I am accountable to my boys to be the best mother and role model for them.

They indeed are mirrors. My mother, who was the eldest Auntie for all my cousins, had this reputation of being the 'strict' Aunt. No one ever messed with her. If you didn't listen or behave, she would put on her infamous 'don't mess with me' stare... all the kids would quiet down and behave better. One day, during one of my angry mothering moments, Lucas broke out that exact stare! I then realized that I had it on my face and he was completely copying me. I burst out laughing because he did such a good job of mimicking me – he had the exact same expression as my mother.

It was a funny but not funny moment.

So, an important exercise for me, is to think about the type of people I want my kids to be, then internalize how I can be the best mirror for them: someone who is kind, generous, compassionate, courageous and strong. Then continually practice being all of that for all of us.

Take advantage of the sponge effect. Have you ever heard the analogy, *children are like sponges*? I have found that to be true and I've experienced that they are listening all the time, especially when you don't want them to—or least expect it. For instance, I was blown away one day, when my three-year-old son Lucas walked into my bedroom one day, saw me sitting crossed legged with my eyes closed and asked me "Are you meditating?" I certainly did not teach him that word, but I was meditating and then he sat beside me and joined in.

As for my other son Jaden, on a beautiful July afternoon, he and I were off to the local shopping mall to get him ready for his first soccer season. As I pulled into a parking spot, I said out loud, "Hmm... I'm not sure if we will find cleats and shin pads in your size here." Jaden, four years old and still strapped in his car seat, looked me in my eyes through the rear-view mirror and recited one of my favorite quotes, "Mommy, if you can believe it and can conceive it, you can achieve it." I almost cried with joy.

As a passion project, my husband and I have written and published a children's books series about an Octopus named Oliver. The intention of these books is to introduce life success principles taught by Napoleon Hill (author of the book Think & Grow Rich). The kids were always around when we are working on the project and Jaden clearly absorbed that lesson. We roamed that mall with so much belief that walking out with a pair of soccer cleats and shin pads was a foregone conclusion and we did!

They don't only mirror the parents; they also mirror everyone else they are surrounded by. One of the primary factors in the growth and development of a child is the environment they are in. Our children's values, beliefs, language, actions and outcome will be shaped by their major influences including their extended family, friends, daycare, teachers and other educators. With this in mind, I have curated an environment around myself and my kids with people who are encouraging, energetic, loving, passionate, open-minded and supportive.

Importance of Date Nights. Have you ever heard these lines from your peers who are parents around the topic of Date Nights? "Having children means the end of date nights." Alternate variations could be, "There's no time for dates" or "We can't afford to go on dates." Another way to look at it is, "You can't afford NOT to go on dates with your spouse." or, "What is possible if you created regular quality date nights for you and your partner?"

Since we read *The 5 Love Languages* by Gary Chapman, we recognized "Quality Time" is a core love language. Thinking of our marriage as a tree and the love languages as the water, sun and nutrients, we saw we needed to spend more quality time together. With this in mind, my husband and I made weekly date nights a priority. It wasn't easy but it has been a blessing.

Here are some ideas that we've tried ourselves, for childcare if you don't have extended family or a regular babysitter: *Find another couple with the same constraints and arrange play-date barters. *Find a gym that has a 'child-minding' center. Then go to a fitness class together or connect while walking side-by-side on a treadmill. The benefit is two-fold; on top of getting quality time together, we are both feeding our minds and bodies as a couple.

Here are some other fun ideas for dates that we've been doing: *Take turns choosing date night activities, as you and your spouse will likely have different ideas of fun. *Invite another couple out on a double-date. The benefits are that you influence your friends and that they will add a friendly dynamic to the date. *Go hiking or on walks at the local park. There is something calming and rejuvenating about being in nature.

The journey of being a parent is sometimes tough, hard, fun, crazy, exhausting, blissful, rewarding, joyful, a blessing, a privilege, etc.. Good News - looking at things with an empowered perspective can alter your life and increase your satisfaction, joy and fulfillment.

Bad news (or better depending on how you look at it)—Changing your perspective may require stepping back and taking a good look at yourself, your past and even the future you are creating. This could be a joyous opportunity to let the inner child in you come out to play.

As we look through the parenting kaleidoscope, with open minds and good intentions, let us all continue to enjoy our journey! Try seeing your and your children's lives through this new lens and savor the adventures before you.

Ignite Action Steps

Here are six ways for you to explore your parenting style with a new lens:

*Set an intention for all your family goals including parenting.

*Practice asking new questions to look at various situations from different view points.

*Audit your own calendar. Ensure Self-Love and Self-Care practices are included.

*Assess where you are doing things alone and bring along a 'team' to support you.

*Reflect on your personal lessons out loud with your kids by sharing stories.

*Brainstorm ways to make regular and meaningful date nights happen.

Bonnie Chan - Canada
Life Coach
www.BonnieChan.ca

CATHERINE
MALLI-DAWSON

"Letting go of your child when they're suffering is never easy, but sometimes it's the right thing to do for them and for you."

My intention in sharing this story is to shed a compassionate light on a societal stigma that is often misunderstood, misdiagnosed, and mostly ignored. I want to help people understand that mental illness is not a symptom or result of bad parenting. It is a part of the human condition which many people needlessly suffer with quietly, alone, and without support.

SILENT SUFFERING

As my son Bryce slowly closed the door, I stared into his eyes and saw the pain and suffering he couldn't seem to express to me. I couldn't help wondering if this was the last time I would look into his soulful, green eyes. I knew he was hurting. I knew he was hiding. I also knew there was nothing I could do to help unless he asked. He was only 17 years old and it was his second year of university. Was I pushing him too hard I wondered? Was this all too much for him to handle at such a young age? I knew he was mature for his age and when I asked him about it, his response was in his classic dismissive fashion, "Mom, I survived boarding school, I can survive dorm-life at Arizona State University."

Untypical for Phoenix, it was raining that day I dropped him off at his university dorm. Driving home, I felt the grey world around me reflected my sadness, desperation, and fear. I had watched Bryce gently close the dorm door with such resignation; I felt a door within my soul close at the same moment. When I arrived home, I collapsed on my bed, drew my knees to my chest and sobbed. I didn't understand all the pain I was feeling, only that I had this overwhelming fear of losing him. I felt his pain and anguish deep inside me, but I didn't know if I was projecting my own parental fears of letting go of my baby or if it was my frustration at feeling helpless from his lack of communication.

I thought about the letter I had received from his boarding school in his third year. He had stayed in England when I moved back to the states and finished his education at Wycliffe Preparatory School. The Headmaster informed me he had put my son on suicide watch. I was shocked and ready to jump on the first plane back to England. However, when I questioned Bryce about it, he played it off as stupid and them overreacting due to a story he had written for English class. He said the crazy thing was that the story had won an award and been submitted into a young writers' recognition program. So, he didn't understand what all the worry and fuss was about. When he sent the story to me to read, I felt it was extremely well written and really pulled at your emotional heart strings. It dealt with some very deep emotions that most boys his age (13-yrs-old) wouldn't normally be able to share so profoundly. I could sympathize and understand why the school felt compelled to place him under close watch. Fortunately, nothing came of it and the heightened concern didn't last long, so we all moved on.

The thought of suicide took me back to a walk along a river when I was four months pregnant, on my own with little support. I worked full-time and had a few close friends, but all my family lived in another city. My baby's father had decided if I didn't want to marry him, he didn't want anything to do with either of us. I was about to embark on parenting alone. I remember waking up early one day with a heavy feeling in my heart and the need to walk and think. Leaving my house, I made my way toward a large park nearby to sit by the river's edge. Walking along the embankment, watching the swirling waters below rushing past, I found myself heading for a jetty. Reaching the end, I leaned against the railing feeling lost, alone, abandoned and overwhelmed with fear. Who was I kidding thinking I can raise a child on my own. I could barely take care of myself.

I was mesmerized by the hypnotic rhythm of the river rushing past me. A conversation with my father a year earlier echoed through my mind as I contemplated my future. He was trying to do the fatherly thing and give me important advice. "You know young lady, (he called me that when he was trying to be endearing) you're not getting any younger. You should start thinking about settling down, finding a man, having a family of your own… you can't just keep playing at life forever."

"Dad, really?" I moaned. "I don't know why you're so worried about me. I'm only 23 for goodness sake." I didn't really want to hear the ensuing lecture so I cut him off before he could start, "Look Dad, in all likelihood, I'm either going to have a child and never get married or get married and never have kids. Preferably the latter," I stated, hoping this would get him off my back.

A year later, one proclamation had come into reality. I hadn't planned on getting pregnant. I was lazy and forgot to use my birth control. The funny thing was, my dad was delighted when I told him he was going to be a grandpa. Most likely, after our earlier conversation, he never thought he'd get a grand-baby out of me, so this was his chance. But for me, I was conflicted with excitement and fear at what kind of mother I would be to my child. Especially since I had no intention of marrying the father.

These thoughts ran through my mind as I stared at the murky grey water reflecting my despondent mood. Another thought crept into my mind… what if I just jumped? That would certainly take care of the *situation*. Would anyone really care? The river is known for powerful undercurrents and many drowned here every year. It would solve two problems: end my pathetic life and stop me from bringing a child into the world I had no business parenting.

Growing up I was convinced I never wanted kids. Mainly, I didn't want another child to go through what I did growing up… but that's another story. However, when I found out I was pregnant with my son, I was elated. I never doubted that I should keep him. It was like some magic switch had flipped, and from the moment I knew I was going to be a mother, I instantly started thinking about my baby. I changed my diet, exercised, slept when needed and planned for his arrival. Yet, over time the loneliness crept in, the disagreements with the baby's father arose. The fear of being able to provide a good life for the child and the worry of what kind of parent I would be, heightened my insecurities. For a moment, suicide seemed like a reprieve from all of life's burdens.

Fortunately, the desire to become a parent overrode the dark thoughts when my baby gave me a kick like never before. One powerful little foot jabbed into my ribs and brought me back from the edge. This made me realize that the child growing inside me wanted to live and had chosen me to be his parent. We were on this journey together; ending it wouldn't be fair or right for either of us. With tears of gratitude streaming down my face I walked back to my house with a renewed desire for this life and a vow to be the best mother I could possibly be for him.

Laying in my bed sobbing, I thought about my decision from 17 years before to become a parent rather than commit suicide. Did those thoughts somehow affect my son's thinking? What was happening in him that was making me afraid I might never see him again? Call it mother's intuition—I knew something was amiss. I had tried talking to him during the school break, but he was walled up and impenetrable. Normally, I could get him to converse with me; this time he withdrew and became moody. I needed to figure out what proverbial 'kick' I could give him to get re-engage with me.

After my tears dried, I sat up on the bed and prepared to meditate. I asked the Universe, God, my spirit guides—pretty much any entity I thought might listen—What do I do? Why is my son suffering? Had I done something to cause this pain he was experiencing? What can I do to help him?

The response I received was very clear. I had done nothing wrong. This wasn't about me. I had done everything I could to raise him and be the best possible parent. This journey was his, not mine. Bryce is a strong, highly intuitive soul, and will find his way through this darkness he is experiencing. If I try to control it, I will push him away and rob him of the opportunity to grow and work through it himself. I must trust that I've given him all the tools he needs and now it's up to him to implement them and build his own tools and life skills.

It is a parent's natural instinct, when they see their child suffering, to want to step in and help. Yet, there comes a time in a child's life when they are on the brink of adulthood, they need to work through things on their own. Without you. In their own way. I released the situation to the Universe and trusted. I trusted Bryce would be guided to make the best decision. I believed that when he was ready, he would reach out. I knew deep within my heart, I would be able to handle whatever he shared with me.

I phoned him the next day to check-in and see if he needed anything else before classes resumed. He sounded tired and I made a point to let him know that I loved him and that if he needed anything to please let me know. He said he would and hung up. While I was still unnerved by my fears, I trusted he would reach out before he succumbed to the darkness that I felt settling around him.

About a month later he phoned, asking about medical insurance to see a psychiatrist. While I wasn't thrilled about the prospect of psychiatric treatment, I was overjoyed he finally reached out for help. Putting my misgivings aside, I helped him find a therapist who felt like a good fit. He was soon diagnosed with bi-polar depression. I felt relieved yet concerned. Having a label does not mean the issues are easily resolved. After several sessions, he seemed brighter, however, the first step was to prescribe medication. Not being a proponent for the over-medicated society we now live in, I cautioned him about taking them and asked him to monitor how they made him feel.

He confided in me the first medication made him feel like a zombie. While he didn't want to feel the anxiety, not feeling anything was worse. He went back and asked for something different. His doctor prescribed a second medication which made his left arm tingle. While he thought that was a side effect he could live with, I encouraged him to speak with the doctor about it. Result three, another prescription. This one evened things out for him, however it made him extremely hungry and he gained weight.

Mental health is one of those things that we don't like to talk about. We whisper about old, crazy Aunt Betty or scary cousin Jessie. I think it's because there is nothing physical to see. Symptoms can be random and are usually attributed to moodiness, hormones or just being immature. Recognizing the signs without any training or experience is quite difficult. I believe the psychiatrist was well meaning when they prescribed pills to balance out his brain chemistry. However, I was hoping they would focus on Bryce as a whole person and not just treat the symptoms. I wanted them to evaluate his environment including his nutrition and how it was affecting him. Instead they focused on administering pills and analyzing his past. I would have preferred they had included me in his treatment as a part of it rather than a subject of his symptoms.

As I thought about Bryce's childhood, searching my memory for any indication, there didn't seem to be any telltale signs of mental disorder. Never having experienced anything as severe as what Bryce was dealing with, I wasn't sure exactly how to handle the situation or support him. My mother had been depressed for as long as I could remember, so I knew what depression looked like. I had not noticed anything even remotely similar with my son. How had I missed this in him, I asked myself many times. He was a happy child, never too moody and rarely ill. He was smart, likeable and quick-witted. Our biggest conflicts were around completing homework. Had I been more aware, I would have realized his aversion to conflict was a sign of something not quite in alignment. Tension and anxiety other people release easily dragged him down. I realized he was highly intelligent, and highly sensitive to others' thoughts and feelings. As a child he withdrew into a world of Legos and video games. As an adult, he recently shared how being forced to interact in the world was often overwhelming for him.

Over the years since his diagnosis, I have seen him struggle from time to time. I hold on to my belief that he has the right tools and coping skills to work through any dark times. I also trust that if he were to get too far down the hole, he would reach out to me for help. Some of the things we've found most effective are meditation, conscious breathing and a significant change in nutrition. He learned that his diet of Ramen noodles may have filled him up, but it did not nourish his body or his brain.

During my research on mental health disorders, I found there's a strong relationship to food and mental stability. New research comes daily showing that changing a patient's diet, produces a measurable reduction in mental instability or episodes of depression. I helped Bryce navigate these uncertain times and did the best I could as a parent and a friend. I shared everything I learned and helped him make the best decisions for himself.

There comes a point in the parenting journey when we transition from parent to mentor. It may not come easy to establish this kind of relationship with your children, but when it does happen, something magical begins to grow between you. I believe this transition typically happens at a later age. For Bryce and me, it was the recognition of his struggles and his trust in me when he reached out for help. His maturity combined with my openness helped us recognize the opportunity to connect in a different way.

I was fortunate in my journey. Not only is my son wise beyond his years, I was ready to move into a new phase of my parenting. When the day came and I knew I had to let go and trust, I did. It was one of the hardest decisions I've ever made in my life. I give thanks every day for my son kicking my ribs to re-engage me and I am grateful I was able to be there when he needed me most.

As a parent we want all the best for our children. We want to make sure they have the best experience we can give them. We want them to have great friends and all the best opportunities. What we don't want is to see them suffer or feel pain of any kind. They say the first six years of life are the formative years. What we don't always realize is that during puberty there is another major transition and this is often when hormonal imbalances can reveal mental health issues. Through my journey of discovery, I learned many things, a few of which I share with you below in the hopes they help you build a stronger relationship with your child and a better understanding of mental health issues should they occur in your child or family.

IGNITE ACTION STEPS

Advocacy - Be your child's advocate. You know him or her better than any person with multiple Degrees and expensive equipment. Beware of white-coat authorities.

* Educate yourself. When a prescription is given, research the usage and side effects.

* Speak up. Ask questions about the treatment plan and how you can help implement it.

* Communicate. Discuss with your child what they are experiencing.

* Help them advocate for themselves. Especially if they are at that pre-adult age where it is a grey area regarding parental involvement.

Check the diet - Research is revealing the direct connection between cognitive function and gut function. How we nourish our bodies will contribute positively or negatively to our physical and mental health.

* Eat plenty of green leafy vegetables; eat good quality protein.

* Stay hydrated.

* Avoid sugar and all its variations.

*Eat seasonally and cycle fruits and vegetables.

Learn to let go/trust and when to intervene - One of the hardest lessons I had to learn was to let go and trust my son's ability to care for himself. This was not done lightly and I used several tools to help me through the process.

* Meditate and tap into your higher wisdom.

* Ask for help or guidance from a trusted friend or family member.

* Trust your instincts.

* Depending on how old your child is, provide advice, guidance and space for them to process information and make their own decisions.

Catherine Malli-Dawson - USA
Founder & CEO of LifeWhys LLC and Mother
www.lifewhysllc.com

CHRISTY YATES

"We have a chance and a choice to pass along
a legacy of love in how we parent."

My intention is that you come to consider children are always learning. As adults and parents, being aware and conscious of what we are teaching in everyday incidental moments is how we build a legacy of love.

BUILD A LEGACY OF LOVE

It was a Sunday evening and my family had once again picked up my parents from their apartment in a memory care facility and taken them to church. Since they would miss the community dinner, we generally took them out or had them over to our house for a homemade meal. This night, I had planned ahead to have a special dinner of cracked crab, sourdough french bread and tossed green salad. Cracking crab was a favorite treat from my childhood and I thought my parents would love it. It would be a comforting meal and memory.

I covered the kitchen table with newspapers, laid out the bowls for the crab shells, set each place with a crab fork in addition to the regular silverware, and placed nutcrackers in the center for everyone to share. All set, just like I remembered from my childhood.

When we returned from church, my son helped me get my father out of the car and into his transport wheelchair which had become necessary We moved him into the house as my daughter walked with my mother. My husband followed us in and helped get the crab out of the fridge and onto the table.

My son, 18, graduating from high school in a few months, and my daughter,15, finishing her freshman year, were both great with my parents. My dad had several physical ailments including vascular dementia. This manifested in slower response time, difficulty with conversation, and definitely some loss of social filters. Over the years he had grown into a classic curmudgeon. He would often say things a bit off-color, prompting giddy laughter and embarrassed titters from my kids, triggering me to say, "Dad!" with exasperation. My mom was in the early stages of Alzheimer's disease. She maintained surprising acuity with long term memories of her childhood, but she couldn't remember what she said five minutes before. My kids were both amazing at answering the same question as if it were asked for the first time. I was always grateful for how much they now doted on the two grandparents who had doted on them in their earlier years.

Maybe because my kids were one generation away and only knew my parents as older adults, they seemed to have deeper levels of patience. They easily forgave lapses of memory, slow, laborious movements, and so many other niggling little habits that frustrated me.

I hated seeing my parents in decline. It tore my heart out. My father, for instance, had a major stroke before I met my husband. Once a super quick-witted, dry and glib jokester, he lost his edge from the stroke. With speech therapy and other interventions, he was able to regain a lot, but he struggled with finding words at times. He had also lost his ability to calculate figures in his mind at rapid speed, which had always been his forte. He retained his wit and charm for many years, but now was slowly fading away. Sometimes I feel sad that my husband and children hadn't known him as the clever, sharp and humorous father I loved.

While my mom struggled with recalling recent events, she was still charming and happy. She retained her social skills and greeted people she thought she had never met with a smile even though she may have been introduced to them yesterday. She had little phrases of social etiquette that pulled her through conversations and gatherings, but recently she was becoming easily confused. Her world shrunk to the small apartment she shared with my dad and a few other locales. I missed being able to go places with her or have her attend events at my kids' schools, which had always been a favorite thing for her as a former teacher. These events, now outside her comfort zone, were confounding and disorienting. I missed her easy ways and love of life terribly.

As we all sat down for crab dinner, I found my Dad no longer had the dexterity to crack the legs or bodies of the crab and dig for the sweet meat, a chore that had always been half the fun when I was a kid. Now I had to do it for him. First, he had difficulty managing a fork, so I tried a big spoon, and that was still too hard. Finally, I fed him as he couldn't manage that either. I became frustrated and distressed, mostly because I felt shocked witnessing this rapid decline. My words became clipped. My eyes teared up and I acted out my frustration. I couldn't sit down to eat my own meal. I was visibly upset, scowling and petulant, and it showed up as an adult-sized temper tantrum. Not my best day by any means.

I looked up to see my children's faces filled with horror, not for my father's difficulties, but with my behavior toward him. It was a cold slap in the face and I suddenly felt small and mean. The look on their faces stopped me. I felt so ashamed. I became aware of the monster in me created by my grief and despair. I looked at my father, his hand trembled when trying to hold the spoon, his head bent down. This had to be so hard for him. My son said, "Mom, it's okay, take it easy. Sit down and eat your food." He offered to dig out the crabmeat for my dad. My daughter engaged my mom in conversation distracting her from me. I took a deep breath and slowed my furious hands and went to work on another crab leg, recognizing that my kids had just provided my mother, father, and me the gentle support we each needed to move through that moment.

When the meal was over my son came to me and gave me a long, loving hug. He then helped my dad to the couch and sat with him. My daughter cuddled with my mom. They talked with them and kept them company while I tried desperately not to cry as I cleared the table.

My husband took them both home. After my son helped them to the car, he came back to give me more hugs and help clean the kitchen. He and my daughter listened as I told them how hard it was to see my dad so unable to manage himself. Both of them encouraged me to be more patient. "He can't help it, Mom. We know it's hard for you. It will be okay," they consoled me.

It was this tender understanding that later brought a flood of tears—acknowledging their maturity and gentleness. I know I hadn't shown my parents much care or love at that evening meal, but somehow, my children knew I needed compassion. Looking at it now from the perspective of time, I can see a legacy of love from one generation to another. My children had learned more about compassion than I could have predicted. They didn't learn it that night, but somewhere in their past, they had felt it, internalized it, and that night used it. The fact that they were able to shower me with so much love made my heart swell.

In my family, my parents were very committed to my brother, sister, and me. It showed in how they spoke to us, cared for us, and treated us. They also took an active interest in who we were. There was a time when my dad chose to forego membership in a golf club so that he could spend each Saturday one-on-one with us. It was our special day with him since he worked during the week, and he didn't want to miss out on spending time with us. My mom also shared her time with us. She was the one who joined the PTA, volunteered for school committees, and any other sort of activity we joined.

I knew they were my parents and not my best friends, which was comforting in so many ways. I experienced their dependability, strength, and guidance. They were there as our mentors.

My husband and I took this one step further to curate parenting tips, techniques, philosophies, and theories with our kids. We both had good experiences with our parents which was a great starting point.

I went from developing homeless services programs to getting credentialed as a school psychologist. The importance of parenting continued to be a strong thread in my professional life. Many of the people I worked with were homeless, emotionally scarred, and some even had physical scars from abusive parenting. In fact, one of the case managers I supervised often spoke of "re-parenting" some of our "guests." Case managers and therapists had to walk a tough line of consistency, integrity, boundaries, and compassion in order to help others help themselves. Our clients deserved to know what healthy relationships felt like; we were positioned to do that.

We all deserve to know what healthy relationships feel like. I learned that from my parents and so did my husband. Our families were not perfect. In many ways, I was the troubled one in my family. I pushed the limits, yet my parents never gave up on me. They accepted and adapted. Our little family of four is not perfect either. At times, both of my kids have pushed the limits. Somehow I knew – perhaps because my parents adapted to me as I grew and challenged them – my job wasn't to mold my children into someone, but rather to simply allow them to be and develop, free of expectations. I came to know my job wasn't to race ahead in the jungles of life before them, clearing a path with my machete, but to walk beside them, cheer or comfort when needed, allowing them to clear their own path.

I am by no means a perfect mother...my behavior over a crab dinner speaks to that fact. I continue to stumble as a parent to this day. I've learned self-reflection is the key to clarity. Ignite moments—like mine over a crab dinner—have taught me so much as both a parent and a daughter. I've learned in those small, incidental moments, transformation occurs when we stop to realize what is behind our intense emotions. It is in those moments, we seem to grow the most.

I had another Ignite Moment just the other day. Our son, now graduated from college, had been home visiting and was headed back to a city he fell in love with 2000 miles away. He'd been offered a wonderful position that suited him very well. I realized when he left, he was no longer tethered to us financially or legally. Now we are tethered to one another by love and respect which had been built over the years, including those years our family cared for my aging parents.

I felt the magic of our connection when our son was getting on a plane to go home like he had many times during college. I knew this parting was different. It was bittersweet. He would no longer depend on us for support, shelter, tuition, or gas for his car. As a grown man, he would now connect with us by choice and mutual admiration.

My daughter is also independent. She's still in college and making most of her decisions for herself, and stretching her wings. Yet she texts me with her excitement over what she's doing and shares tidbits about her joy in discovering new ideas. We raised our kids to be individuals. We encouraged them to blossom and allowed them to fall and get up again. We strived to be role models and demonstrated kindness and acceptance. In spite of my behavior one night over a crab dinner, both my children have reflected those characteristics back to me.

I know when my husband and I were first preparing for our family we talked a lot about who we wanted to be as parents. What were the lessons we learned? What did we appreciate, or perhaps see now as necessary and valuable even if we didn't like it as children? What behaviors or ideas did our parents have which we were determined to jettison to the history books? The huge gift we felt we could bring to our parenting was that we felt both loved and liked by our parents.

Over the last year, I spent a lot of time thinking about all of this, especially the unique challenges of living in the "Sandwich Generation": the time when one is raising one's own children while also caring for an aging parent. It made me ponder on how we come to know just how to parent... what behaviors and experiences do we pass along? What family legacy are we creating through our parenting? What talents do we encourage our children to carry on?

In my work with schools, I see many parenting styles. Some parents think it's fairly simple, and that you just do it. But it's more than that. Children are always learning. They watch us even when we aren't aware. Raising a child is more than providing food, water, shelter, and education. It's a profound opportunity to build a legacy of love for their future. We get chances in many little moments of life like a Saturday spent with a child, a special family dinner, or a bittersweet goodbye at the airport. When we take the time to make thoughtful choices rather than reacting, we help our kids feel safe and loved, and we model healthy habits, which are all part of the true legacy of love.

I hope in your parenting experience you are able to stop and savor the beautiful moments while sharing a true and honest connection. When you're triggered, step back and reflect on any extreme emotions. Be gentle with yourself. We all are learning our parenting role. We are human. I also hope that you see all those incidental times with your child as valuable and precious. May you have magical moments with them, and forge a relationship based on love and respect so that you can grow together, learn together, and pass on a genuine legacy of love.

IGNITE ACTION STEPS

Looking back now, I can see how I approached parenthood like I did many other things in my life: I looked for good examples. I had them in my parents, friends, and colleagues. I asked questions and I sought opportunities to learn. I also instinctively knew that parenting requires different things at different times, but it has to start with a strong foundation. Here are some building blocks that worked for us:

*Self-Reflection is the key to clarity and change. When you find you have very strong emotions (fear, anger, sadness, guilt) triggered by interactions with children, partner or family, stop to think, "Why am I making this about me? Why do I feel this way? Have I felt like this before?" It's not about the other person. We can only change ourselves and we can't do that until we take time to reflect. This is an ongoing practice.

*Live what you want children to learn. Whatever values you want to instill can be lived in action. Honesty? Ask for it and give it. Compassion? Show it and teach it. Kindness? Give it to everyone, kids learn through overhearing and seeing you interact with others.

*The family is the first community. Everyone in the family can contribute. Contribution feeds positive self-regard. I loved when my children said, "Let me do it!" From toddlers on up, children like to help. They appreciate knowing their efforts make us happy and it counts. Examples are helping with meals, daily chores, remembering setting expectations that making a mess is okay, but clean-up is included. It can be just as fun.

*Family dinners are like glue. The dinner or breakfast table is a great place and time to process, to talk to one another, support one another, and to share ideas. Make it device free! Include a check-in ritual such as everyone share: one thing that was great today, one thing that was hard and how did you handle it, and one thing to be grateful for today.

*Presence over presents. Physical presence and emotional presence can't be beat!. Rather than celebrating with gifts and tangible items, consider celebrating with special time together. Sometimes showing up for sports, school events and other activities are the most important ways to demonstrate presence.

*Spiritual practice. Believing in something bigger than ourselves and grasping that we are all connected on a spiritual level was important to us as parents. Consider how you might involve kids in some form of gratitude practice, mindfulness practice, or the faith of your family if that is a tradition. These practices are also wonderful opportunities for togetherness.

*Apologize and Forgive. One way to build a legacy of love (and build resilience) is to own your human faults and admit them. We all screw up! It may be counterproductive and harmful to force an apology. However, modeling an apology for children is powerful. We can do this by apologizing to our children when we may have made a mistake that impacts them. We can take it one step further by asking for forgiveness. "I'm sorry I did that. Will you please forgive me?" Children often feel bad for making a mistake or hurting someone but they may not yet have the words to offer an apology. While we can't make them feel something, we can teach them the words to use.

Christy Byrne Yates - USA
Licensed Educational Psychologist, High-Performance Coach
www.christyyates.com

ELISE EDMEADES

"Parenthood is a team sport. Pick your team carefully!"

My hope is that I can inspire you to have the best possible birth experience, to give your baby a great start, and to begin your parenting journey with all the help you need.

MY FIRST CHILDREN WERE TWINS: A PAIR OF TURTLES

To have a child or not to have a child… that was the question. A question I had been asking for as long as I could remember. For most of my friends, this wasn't a question. They just knew. Some were *yes*, and some were *no*. But I was a solid 'I don't know.'

My uncertainty stemmed from my very challenging birth and difficult childhood. I am not complaining, as you will see in this story, and I am also aware that I am not alone. Now, as my daughter approaches three, I can see the challenges I faced as a child were blessings that have served me and my daughter well.

Another reason for my uncertainty was that I had proof I would be a terrible mother. I was forced to give my first two children (Mable and Oscar) up for adoption. Luckily, they were terrapins, fresh-water turtles. On my ninth Christmas, my grandmother gave me two adorable terrapins. I was thrilled. My mother sat me down and gave me the. 'terrapins-are-not-just-for-Christmas' lecture. I agreed I would be 100% responsible.

Everything started off well. I fed them. I cleaned their tank. I spoke and sang to them. I even cuddled them. The first time my mother had to help was not a big deal. Neither was the second. But within a few months – in order to ensure their survival – my mother had become their primary caregiver and was not happy about it at all. In the end, my mother gave them up for adoption to a couple that really wanted terrapins. They adopted Mable and Oscar who did, fortunately, live happily ever after. While this may seem silly, my failure to care for Mable and Oscar would haunt me and cause me to doubt my abilities as a mother.

My husband, Eric, frustrated with my *to-ing* and *fro-ing* on the parental issue, finally told me that I had to want a baby for 30 consecutive days. In truth, I think he just wanted me to get through an entire menstrual cycle without me changing my mind.

So we started counting my I-want-to-have-a-baby days. Sometimes I would get to 10 or 15 days and then I would see a screaming baby in the supermarket and change my mind. I once got to 20 days and then I visited one of my mum-friends and saw her house, her kids, and her hair and I changed my mind, again.

Then it happened; I made it through 30 full days with a strong desire to be a mother. So, as we prepared for one of Eric's business events in Europe, a friend asked me what plans we had for the evening and I jokingly said, "We're gonna make a baby."

And we did. That night.

Three weeks later a test confirmed it. I was both incredibly excited and, when I thought of Mable and Oscar, terrified and nervous. It also didn't help when my mother-in-law pointed out to me that what was now the size of a sesame seed would, before I had to give birth, grow to the size of a watermelon!

I have another admission for you: Eric says I am a bit obsessive. When my curiosity is activated, I go all in. For instance, I didn't just go to Bikram Yoga, I became *The Bikram Yoga Lady*. Now that I was pregnant, I became *The Natural Childbirth Lady*.

Why? Because sometimes difficult things happen to us for a reason. My own birth was one of those things; it was traumatic for both my mother and me. After being promised an epidural, after 24 hours of labor, they could not give her one. Instead, she ended up with an episiotomy, which might not sound as scary as it really is: cutting the vagina wide open to make more room for the baby to come out. After making the excruciating incision, the doctor pulled me out using forceps clamped around my head. My mother never really recovered from this and experienced dreadful postpartum depression.

Knowing this, I was incredibly motivated to give my baby and me the very best birthing experience possible. Thus, before conceiving, Eric and I cleaned up our diet, exercised and prepared ourselves. Once pregnant, I turned my attention toward natural childbirth and, in so doing, made one major mistake.

To explain my mistake, I have to take you to Mt Kilimanjaro. Eric and I used to run leadership programs which involved taking people to the summit of the tallest free-standing mountain in the world. The first time we did it, we learned a powerful lesson. We prepared ourselves and our clients, physically, mentally and psychologically, for reaching the summit. But we forgot to prepare for the descent. We were all so focused on getting to the top that once there, we were out of energy. Getting down the mountain was incredibly difficult. We learned that we had to prepare ourselves and our clients for the entire journey – to the summit and back down the mountain.

The natural childbirth mistake I made was the same: I put all my thoughts, research and energy into creating the best possible childbirth experience I could, but that was only the summit; I had not prepared for what was next, being a mother.

I discovered this a few days before giving birth, while having tea with my doula. She asked me what my plans were for the first few months as a mother. I was speechless. All my focus had been on the birthing process. She reminded me that my labor might last anywhere from a few hours to a day or two and after that I would be fully responsible for my little girl for years to come. Suddenly, I thought about Mable and Oscar and wondered how they were doing with their adoptive family?

Sitting at home, reflecting on my conversation with my doula, all of my doubts surfaced and took over my mind. Would I, like my mother, experience painful postpartum depression? Would I find being a mother as difficult as she had? Would I love my little girl? What if I didn't? What if I lost interest in my baby like I lost interest in my terrapins? Further, what was I thinking? I had no idea how to hold, feed or even change a baby.

Suddenly, I found myself wondering how *they* could let this happen to me. Seriously, why wasn't there an interview or vetting process? Didn't *they* know that I had no idea what I had gotten myself into or how I was going to handle it? It takes more screening and evaluations to get a dog!!!

Until my doula started questioning my plans – mere days before my delivery – I thought I had it all under control. I had some cloth diapers, a 'trendy' carrier and some baby blankets, a few baby clothes and, of course, a baby monitor because I thought I might have some time to myself every now and again. Little did I know, the tea I was having with my doula would be the last warm cup I would drink for years to come.

I also thought I had professionally prepared myself by informing my clients that I would be off for a week or two. A week or two!? Clearly, I believed I was completely ready. In reality, I had no idea what I was in for.

With the childbirth research done, our apartment prepared, I thought I had two weeks to research being a mother. Even though my due date was around the corner, my midwife told me that I was probably going to be a week or two late, so she tempted fate by driving home, three hours away.

That very evening, Eric went out to a late-night yoga class. With my midwife three hours away and my husband gone, I felt something very unusual happen in my body. A contraction. I was thinking this can't be it. Where is everyone? Luckily, when Eric arrived at his yoga class he found it had been cancelled and so, minutes after my third contraction, he returned to the apartment. I told him I was in labor and I don't think he believed me, he was just too calm. "How far apart are the contractions?" He asked.

"Five minutes," I announced. His calmness faded slightly, he started filling the birthing pool, and lighting the locally-made beeswax candles I had specifically chosen. What followed next was my dream delivery.

Even so, it wasn't easy. I can still remember sitting in the birthing pool sure that I could not go any further. As I lay back in Eric's arms I finally understood why so many of my mum-friends were surprised when I told them that I was not planning on using any pain-killers. (While I am glad that I was able to have a drug-free birth I feel strongly this is a personal decision which has to be made by the mother.)

Sitting there in the pool, wondering how I could possibly go on, my next contraction started and it was the strongest one by far. Suddenly, Zoë shot right out of me like a little rocket. She skipped crowning, went right past right 'Go', and all of a sudden she was deep in the water. It happened so fast we couldn't find her with only the candle light. Eric reached down, found the umbilical cord and followed it to find her swimming along in the pool. He lifted her out of the water and I saw her for the first time. My first reaction was amazement. I must admit I had been in denial that there was a living, breathing baby inside of me.

Eric put her in my arms and I gazed in complete wonderment into her eyes knowing my life would never be the same again. She looked back at me, deep into my eyes and soul; it was a moment I will treasure forever.

One of the beautiful things about a homebirth is that I wasn't rushed out of a hospital bed. I simply stepped out of the pool, dried off and then crawled straight into my own bed with my now slightly larger family.

I had read that smelling the baby's head, and letting the baby smell you, is important in the bonding process and the production of oxytocin. It was so special; we laid in bed with Zoë breathing softly between us. She was so peaceful and relaxed wrapped up in a bubble of calm, safety, and love. I remember thinking what a gorgeous first few minutes of life she must be having.

I didn't sleep much that night. I was so excited and amazed. I kept waking up to check on my perfect angel with her cute little fingers and sweet little toes. Everytime I looked at her my heart swelled with intense waves of love unlike anything I had felt before.

This was just the start of our journey together, a journey of the highest highs and, well, some pretty low lows. Some of those lows, ironically, came from doing too much research and, frankly, taking too much of it on board. For instance, as I read about "Attachment Parenting" and spoke to one not-entirely-sane mum, I somehow got the idea that I had to do everything myself. After all, I made her myself, so why shouldn't I take care of her myself? It wasn't long before I realized looking after my baby was much easier when she was inside my belly.

The more mothers I spoke to, the more I realized I was not the only one having this strange idea that I had to do it all alone. For some reason, I let guilt prevent me from asking for or receiving help. And when I did, I would feel terrible about it, like I was some kind of failure as a mother. After all, what good had I been to Mable and Oscar?

One day, perhaps a bit frustrated with my stubborn approach, Eric reminded me of something really important. During our visits with the Hadza people of East Africa, it was difficult to match the children to the mothers. They are raised by the village! The tribe shares the responsibility of raising their children, including food preparation, safety, and even breast-feeding. *I realized that in my attempt to be Supermum, I was hurting myself and leaving myself depleted. Ironically, my attempt to do it all was making it difficult for me to do anything well. The 'put your own oxygen mask on first' cliche should be the first rule of motherhood.*

When I think about what went into creating my birth experience, some of the key points were:

I had the right environment. In my research, I had found that stress can slow down the labor process. In nature, if a laboring mammal is threatened or disturbed, the stress hormone catecholamine shuts down or slows down the process to allow the mother to get to safety before resuming giving birth.

With this in mind, my husband and I created a quiet, softly lit, and safe birthing den in our apartment.

I had all the time I needed. The birth process can often involve a long list of unnecessary pressures on the mother. The more anxiety the mother feels, the slower the birthing process can be. Sadly, one source of this comes from hospital staff and administrators; they often want births to happen on a schedule that doesn't hurt their shifts, working hours regulations, or tee times. If this sounds a little extreme or like a conspiracy theory, *I can tell you that a director at my local hospital noticed a spike in births on Friday afternoons and almost none on weekends. She investigated and found the hospital staff actively worked to induce labor and ordered caesareans in order to avoid working late on Fridays or on the weekends.*

Due to pressures such as these, women are often given Pitocin (a synthetic version of oxytocin) to try to induce labor. The induced labor (strong and early contractions) often causes extreme pain, requires more pain medication, and can cause stress to the fetus which might in turn make a previously unnecessary caesarean necessary.

Learning about this, I studied everything I could about the birth process and decided that I wanted a carefully supervised and relaxed home birth within walking distance of a reputable hospital. This might not be for everyone, but many hospitals now offer 'home birthing suites' in the hospital as they improve their knowledge of the birthing process.

I had the right people. I had my doula, my midwife, my husband. And nobody else. It was perfect.

I had the right attitude. I felt prepared. I was fairly relaxed and, most of all, excited to meet my little angel. Also, I now had a sense that I was a bit more prepared for the motherhood that would follow.

I had the right posture. I learned that during the birthing process, having the woman on her back and legs up high was a man's idea! My mother-in-law, who came from a medical family, explained that it was all about saving doctors' lower backs. Surprisingly, the concept was apparently popularized by King Louis XIV because he enjoyed watching many of his 20 plus children being born.

Having done my research, set things up as I wanted them, and asked for help, I really stacked the deck in my favour. I increased the chances of having an easy, safe, and magical birthing experience. It benefited us all and gave us a foundation for healthy parenting.

In terms of parenting, *I admit, I am still working on this.* One thing that guides me is that, as well as being a good mum for Zoë, I want to be a great example to her. To live a life full of joy, fun, love and passion. I know she is always watching me and it is '*my walk, not my talk*', which will shape who she becomes and what kind of life she creates for herself. With this in mind, it is important to me that I take good care of myself, my husband, and her, with presence, love, care and respect. Ghandi says, "be the change you wish to see in the world," I believe this is the greatest gift that you can give your children.

IGNITE ACTION STEPS

*Accept the past; it helped you become the person you are today.

*Do your research. Create a birth plan that inspires you. Remember that as important as the birth plan is, pregnancy and birth is a 9-month project and parenthood is *forever.*

*Get the help you need so that you can sleep, eat well, and take really good care of yourself; that is the only way to take the best care of your child.

*Your child is always watching you. They learn from the example you set; so do your best to show them how to be loving, happy, fun and respectful.

Elise Edmeades - United Kingdom

ELYSSE GREEN

"There is no greater time than the present to break the cycle.
Together we can leave a positive footprint,
for generations to come."

It is my deepest hope that through sharing my story, you will be inspired to open your heart and mind to parent consciously. To guide your children wholeheartedly with love, respect, compassion, empathy, and understanding. I hope to spark an awareness within you to nurture the unmet needs of your inner child, so future generations are spared the wounds of their ancestors.

BREAKING THE CYCLE

Deep within me I always knew I would guide and parent my children differently from how I was brought up. I feel proud that I parent consciously, being present, patient, gentle, loving, nurturing, responsive, and respectful to my gorgeous son and the little one currently growing inside me. I have broken the cycle! It was time it happened. I never want another child to endure the pain, fear, sadness, guilt, and feelings of lack I did, which my mother and father also endured, and the generations before them.

I grew up in a broken home. My middle sister and I were taken from my mother by authorities when I was three years old and placed in foster care. The police came due to a disturbance complaint. They found us screaming from inside a locked cupboard; my mother was drunk, topless, and mentally unsound. Mum told Child Protection we didn't have a father so he wasn't immediately aware we were in the social services system. Two weeks later, Dad located us and became a single father of three girls ages three, five and thirteen. My oldest sister already lived with him because she refused to live with our mother, even though it meant she was separated from us. Being older, she understood about Mum's mental health condition and endured more of the unfortunate torment that went along with her mental illness.

People described my father as wild, strong, and hard; one who loved his beer, a smoke, and someone who wouldn't take anything from anyone, which frequently resulted in bloody pub brawls. Witnessing many beatings, I knew how powerful he was and what he was capable of. He seemed to attract unstable women who enjoyed drama and fighting. Each mother showed her children favoritism and spoiling. Some allowed their older kids to scare or torture me, causing more suffering.

I once witnessed one of my father's girlfriends intentionally run him over in front of me. I was age four, scared for my father's life, terrified watching what was unfolding a matter of meters away. I ran to him screaming and crying, the first there to care for and comfort him. She drove off into the night, yelling profanities, not looking back. You would think after being run over and severely injured, the relationship would have ended, but sadly they were back together the following day. These crazy events weren't uncommon. They seemed to thrive on drama and wild, erratic behavior.

I was too young to comprehend my world around me; I felt that way my entire childhood. I didn't understand why I wasn't allowed to see my mother and my half-brother when he came into the picture. At the time, I thought it was my father's doing. I didn't know my mother was unwell. Kept in the dark, I felt he was being horrible to keep us separated from our mother. I grew more and more resentful, thinking he was withholding our mother from seeing us, motivated by pride, spite, and hate.

I missed my mother every single day. Each night, I'd sneak outside, wave up to the glistening stars and whisper, "Goodnight Mum, I love you," hoping someone out there would hear my softly-spoken words and deliver my message to my mother for her to be solaced, also. I longed to hear her voice and be embraced in the warmth of her arms. I did this for years, right before I would cry and rock myself to sleep. Every. Single. Night. Noone else knew, except my middle sister who would occasionally hear my nightly sobs from our adjoining rooms. I wasn't allowed to express the sadness of missing my mother to anyone in my family. I would get in trouble for this. In fact, I recall times of being threatened if I did.

Threats and fear were always present when I was a child. I vividly recall being six years old playing in the school yard when I was abruptly grabbed by a teacher and frantically escorted to a classroom. She attempted to push me under a table where my sisters were already huddled. Scared and confused, I had no idea what was going on. I asked my sisters but they growled at me to be quiet. I turned, and directly outside the window I saw my mother with her hair half shaved, colored bright purple, wearing thigh high boots, with my little half-brother walking hand in hand along the corridor. Excitement and happiness raced through my body. Nothing else mattered. I tried to run and yell out to my mother, but my oldest sister grabbed my arm, yanked me backwards, pressed her hand firmly over my mouth, and dragged me further under the table, "Be quiet. Mum's here to try to steal us." I was so angry with her. In my head I thought how can my own mother steal me? I wanted to escape, to hug my mother and brother, tell them how much I loved and missed them. Every fibre of my being ached to be with them. Restrained by my sisters, I stayed hunched over in fear, confusion, and immense sadness. Tears welled up in my eyes, knowing I wasn't going to be able to cuddle them. Undisclosed to me, again, the school had been warned that my mother was unstable and she was not permitted to enter school grounds due to the abduction fears. Additionally, my oldest sister had a restraining order against Mum due to other events.

We three girls were often dragged in and out of court cases and literally stood between our parents amidst their fights. This was not ideal for feeling safe as a child. My oldest sister was repeatedly pulled into the courtroom while my middle sister and I were put in a separate room with a woman recording things we said. I would get in trouble with my father after this happened. Now as an adult, I know that he was worried we would be taken away. As crazy as he was at times, he kept us all together. Being a little girl who grew up in fear, feeling lack, sadness, lost, and alone, I am grateful for all he did that kept me with my sisters.

Growing up I remember always wanting to be seen and be heard, and sought validation from my father. My two sisters were always favoured and I was compared to them, particularly my oldest sister. I never wanted to put a wrong foot forward and be in the firing line. No matter what I did, it seemed unavoidable at times. I was often left at home alone to care for myself, which developed into a major fear and attributed even more to my feelings of abandonment.

As I grew older I was allowed to visit my mother. Every second weekend whenever she was well enough, or at times only short visits with a social worker. When my mother was 'well', she was beautiful, gentle, kind, and loving. I enjoyed our time together and the things she taught me on the occasions when I was allowed to see her. I started to witness more of my mother's other side, the one which I didn't comprehend when I was little. I began to experience firsthand her abuse, like the rest of my family had endured, which unfortunately continues to this day. My mother, who I longed to be with all those years, said and did unspeakable things to me and my sisters. I grew to believe she didn't love me, at times even hated me, when I hadn't done anything to provoke such behaviour. I always tried to overlook the anguish she inflicted in a desire to have a relationship with her. I desperately wanted to be with my mother so I put my own feelings of hurt and suffering aside as I wanted to enjoy the time with her when she was well, never knowing how long it would be for.

I have been the family peacemaker for as long as I can remember. On several occasions, I became the mediator to heal and attempt to bring relationships back together with my mother and my siblings; much of the time they wanted to give up. I aided in reuniting her with another younger half-sibling, who was devastatingly put up for adoption. I still remember holding that little baby girl in the hospital, loving her before she was taken away. It took 18 years before we found her and met once again.

Despite various attempts, unfortunately my estranged mother had once again been absent from my life for several years before I became pregnant with my first child at 29 years old. In the midst of my excitement of finding out I was pregnant, I had a dark shadow of sadness hanging over me at the thought of not being able to share my wonderful news and parenting journey with my own mother. It was at this time I realised that I didn't have anyone around to guide me to be the best mother I possibly could be. I didn't have a childhood that I could look back on for direction. Knowing this brought up many suppressed feelings and emotions which made me consciously reopen the doors of my childhood. Although I couldn't see this clearly at the time, I am now thankful for the challenges I faced as it allowed me to tune in and gain an awareness of my 'inner child'. I now follow my own true innate path, to parent in my instinctual way, consciously, without the noise and pressures that family could impose.

My son has awakened me. I laid on the table in the examination room with the ultrasound transducer pressed firmly against the cold, wet, sticky gel on my stomach. My fiancé was firmly grasping my hand, praying all was well with our little Being. With a nervous grin and mixed feelings of joy and fear flooding me, I heard my baby's tiny heart thudding for the first time. The reality hit. I had the biggest job now. I had to learn how to parent! Knowing I was bringing another sovereign being into this world turned on many lights. Deep within I was Ignited. This was a profound and life-changing moment. Hearing his heart beating catapulted me into my journey of discovery: one of healing, personal development, spirituality, and awakening. I developed a great sense of awareness, one I didn't previously have or could have even entertained the thought of, precipitating a massive shift. I had a calling to be incomparable to how I was raised.

In discovering my inner child I gained an understanding of how to nurture those unmet needs so I wouldn't pass the wounds of my past onto my son. His imminent arrival set me on the path of my purpose and opened the doors of what my soul was destined to do: to parent consciously, be of service to others, raise the vibration, and shine a light of awareness for parents to connect with their own children.

I am constantly growing and evolving in my parenting journey and do so with an open heart. My son is a caring, charismatic, strong willed wild-flower, and I love him that way. He has taught me patience, courage, strength, resilience and a love greater than I thought possible. I make mistakes and that's ok. I reflect and ensure that I learn through my mistakes and strive to do better.

Continuing my inner child work deepens my understanding of how damaged each of my parents were and how they recreated that in their lives. I appreciate that I live in an age of awareness where healing is sought by many. It is not a privilege my parents had. Abandoned by their parents, raised by grandparents, leaving home to get away from abuse, verbal assaults and shaming were things they managed with drugs, drinking, and repeating what felt familiar. My parents created a lot of havoc with each other and new partners, and we kids were exposed to it all. I came to realise I could not leave my wounded psyche unattended anymore. I needed to ensure I would never repeat the same patterns and behaviours. We either parent the way we were parented or we parent the polar opposite. It is a choice that requires looking at how we were influenced by our environment, events and people around us. Our inner child has stored memories which continue to impact us, particularly those memories from our first seven years of life when our brain predominantly operated in Theta, a very receptive state.

Many of our limiting beliefs, fears and blockages are developed in these critical years, passed down from our parents, which we too can pass on to our children. The way we react and respond to situations are all connected to this. Depending on past experiences, it may require in-depth inner work to heal our inner child in order to break the cycle, unlock our blockages and be fully present. It is only then we can cultivate whole beings through parenting consciously and wholeheartedly as they deserve with love, respect, compassion, empathy and understanding.

I invite you to open your mind and your heart. Be willing to explore and uncover your inner child's unmet needs and take the necessary steps to begin healing these wounds. Be diligent in allowing your children to grow into the unique sovereign Beings they have come here to be. We parents are here to gently guide them, whilst honouring their spirit, empowering their decisions, and encouraging them to just be Who They Are!

Through my life's difficulties, I have learned many lessons and aspire to help others like me. I remain grateful and have learned to forgive. I know now that I faced these challenges so I can be the person and parent that I am today, so I can make changes, inspire and awaken others to do the same.

IGNITE ACTION STEPS

Although it may seem different and at times isolating to parent consciously with respect, our children need this now more than ever. I hope some of these easy, yet powerful, self-nurturing tools help you begin healing your wounded inner child, so you can show up and parent consciously. I encourage you to practice these daily as I did.

*Firstly, I invite you to reconnect with your inner child and develop a relationship of love, kindness, value and support. Self-love and forgiveness is fundamental to healing. It may not be easy at the start, but be open to it.

*If possible, get a picture from when you were a young child, 6 or 7 years of age or younger. Put your picture somewhere you will see it; on the bathroom mirror, next to your bed, on the fridge, have it with you at your meditation practice... look at it daily. Get the image of your younger self crystal clear in your mind.

*Communicate with that child. Look at the picture or imagine your younger self and repeat loving affirmations daily, such as: "I love you, I hear you, this is not your fault, you don't deserve this, I'm sorry, I forgive you, thank-you..."

It's normal to do this through tears, you may not even be able to get the words out in your first attempt. It's ok. Please be gentle and kind to yourself. It's all part of your healing. You can add any other loving phrases that may apply to you and your wounds that you feel will positively affect you personally and in your parenting journey. For example: "I am capable. I am beautiful. I am confident. I am safe. I am abundance. I am patient. I am present. I am grateful. I am enough…" The beauty of this practice is that you can do it anywhere, at anytime, whenever you like – while driving, cleaning, washing, hanging out clothes, putting your little one to bed…

*Visualization is another great way to connect with your inner child. Find a comfortable place where you will be free of distraction. Relax, close your eyes and take a few deep breaths. Imagine yourself walking down a staircase; really feel and imagine it in detail - are the stairs wooden, tile, straight, spiral, what does the handrail feel like? At the bottom of the stairs is your safe place. This may be a peaceful garden, a beach, a field of flowers, or inside a warm cosy room. See your younger self entering the space. Greet and embrace your younger self in a loving warm hug. Make him/her feel safe and at home. When you are ready, you can ask your inner child a question, such as "When was the first time I felt scared? sad? alone? hurt? abandoned?" Ask your question in terminology that you would use with a child. Wait for their response.

It may take some time and may not be revealed in your first inner visualisation practice. That's ok. Make sure you let your inner child know you accept this. Regardless of being answered or not, thank them, let them know you appreciate their presence, how much they mean to you. Embrace them in a hug before saying goodbye and leaving your safe place.

When pressed for time, I use a shortened daily visualization which takes less than a minute and allows me to connect with my inner child at any moment. Simply close your eyes wherever you are and take a few deep breaths. Imagine yourself greeting your younger self and embrace them in loving arms. Tell them they are loved, heard, safe, secure… whatever feels right to you in that moment.

Ask yourself: "How do I want to show up in the world? Not only for myself, but for my children and their children and their children to come?"

We each have the power within us to make change and impact future generations. How do we use that power wisely? There is no greater time than the present to break the cycle. Together we can leave a positive footprint, for generations to come.

Elysse Green - Australia
Founder of Awake Parenting, Conscious & Passionate Parent
www.awakeparenting.com.au

GINA INGRAM

"Each of us is a diverse mosaic of cultures, wisdom and stories.
What we put in, we become. "

The greatest legacy we can give our children is experiencing the world and being raised by all the people they meet along the way. They take a piece of each person's love and wisdom into their hearts, helping them become true global citizens ready to change the world. Whether you do it globally or locally, my hope is that you expose your children to the diverse and rich cultures of our beautiful world.

MY KIDS WERE RAISED BY THE WORLD

When people asked how could we raise three kids while traveling the world, my answer was, "I'm not raising my kids, the world is."

From before I can remember, my dream was to be an explorer. I wanted to stand in the shadows of the Pyramids of Giza in Egypt, gaze at the beauty of the Parthenon in Athens, or go on a dig to find an ancient lost city buried beneath the sands. Even though I was so young, I had this burning desire to go to places across the world. Throughout my childhood this dream was the only thing that kept me going.

I was born with a very rare bone disease, which led to me in and out of hospitals for many years of my childhood, as I endured numerous surgeries—a total of over 35 surgeries to date. All I wanted was to be like other kids who could go out to run and play. I let my imagination take me to the far-off places I would one day visit, dreaming of them so vividly, I felt like I was already there.

The older I got the more this dream grew. I knew I wanted to share all those future adventures in life with someone special. That dream came true when I met Todd, in our senior year of college. Our connection was immediate, bonding over our shared love for travel and escaping the bubble in which we were living. We knew deep down we didn't fit into the normal, predictable lifestyle all our friends craved – corporate jobs, owning a home, fancy cars and living for the weekend. We wanted total freedom to explore wherever we desired whenever we chose to – we were yearning to break free.

We saved, schemed, planned and dreamed for years until our chance to escape the ordinary finally came. Immediately after our wedding, we embarked on a one-way journey to explore Europe.

We knew our money was limited so we scraped by on as little as $20 per day so we could stay abroad for as long as possible. We had the most incredible year-long adventure until the money finally ran out and we had to return to our home country and reality. Soon we realized ordinary life was even more painful than we remembered. We had changed. Completely changed. We knew we could never go back to the way we used to live— suburban life, 9-5 jobs, Tupperware parties, reality TV and fast food.

We did whatever we could to get back to Europe and the traveling life we craved. We both worked feverishly to save money at jobs we disliked and spent all of our free time teaching ourselves new technology which would help us get a job with an international company. After a year, all the hard work paid off when we were moved to Amsterdam to work for an IT firm.

Our daughter Kaitlin was born in Amsterdam, where we loved living for two years. We felt guilty, however, for having the only grandchild in both our families so far away. So, even though we had the most amazing life and jobs in Amsterdam, we moved back to Los Angeles to be with our families. Todd and I soon realized we were unhappy living the life everyone said we *had to have*. After languishing for nine months, we made our way back to Europe, doing whatever was necessary to return to the continent we loved, where we felt 'at home' and where we wanted to raise our kids. We spent the next magical year living in both Germany and France.

Still the pressures of society and family expectations overcame us once more. When I was seven months pregnant with our daughter Cassidy, we returned again to Los Angeles to try to 'settle down' this time. We bought the deluxe minivan and a house full of new furniture. We invested in landscaping and private schools – you name it. This time we would make it work, or so we thought. But again, we soon knew deep in our souls this lifestyle was not right for us.

Many people thought we were being irresponsible for moving our kids around so much, not giving them the stability everyone thought they needed. There were days and times when we gave into their pressure, but in our hearts, we felt we had to break away from the rules—we had to find our own paths no matter what the voices around us were saying.

We made it almost two years this time, but when my husband got a job offer in Rome, Italy, a place I had always dreamed of living, we immediately packed up our stuff and put it all in storage. Within three weeks we arrived in the Eternal City—two exhausted, yet ecstatic parents, two jet-lagged, yet extremely energetic toddlers and eight overstuffed suitcases—ready for the next big adventure!

We spent four magical years living *la dolce vita* in Rome, yet life in the city was often chaotic, so we decided we'd try a more normal suburban life for the sake of the kids (now seven and five), who were starting school. We found a beautiful home on the outskirts of Paris, but within six months the pressures of French school and Todd's job became unbearable. Italy was beckoning us to return!

This time we traded gladiators for gondolas—moving into a medieval palazzo on a canal in the heart of Venice. For seven years we lived as Venetians, the kids taking a boat down the Grand Canal to go to school and all of us finally learning Italian. During the second year, our son Trevor was born. We were experiencing the beauty of immersing ourselves into the Italian culture, getting our citizenship and watching the kids be raised as half-Italians.

When Trevor was only one and I was 40, I got the news my doctor warned me about as a child, but I had hoped would never come – I had bone cancer. In the process of removing the cancer, I lost my entire left shoulder and part of my collar bone, so I was completely unable to use my left arm. With the newly attached area so delicate, I wasn't able to lift anything heavy with my right arm either! No more lifting or carrying my one-year-old son, doing everyday chores or normal beauty maintenance (like putting my hair into a ponytail), carrying heavy bags on my adventures, or a hundred other things we all take for granted!

I was completely devastated, and overwhelmed with grief. *"Why me? What did I do to deserve this? Haven't I had enough setbacks in my life?"* I knew one way or another I had to push through for my family; I had to find a way to cope with my new reality.

As I look back on this event, I realized this was that crucial moment where my whole life took a turn for the better. More than ever, I knew deep within I had to take control of my life and lead it in the direction I had always dreamed of going. I had been awakened to the fragility of life and I would not let any more precious time pass, because I knew for certain that every moment is precious, and each new day is not guaranteed.

I saw the true meaning of my own mortality and I was determined to enjoy every moment with my kids to the fullest! There was no more time to waste or listen to all the cynics, I was ready to live my life full out while I still had the chance! Living in Italy was fantastic, but what about all the other countries and people I had yet to see and meet? I became restless and ready to embark on another epic adventure. I couldn't wait any longer, I had to experience the rest of the world!

As a family, we packed up all of our belongings and sent them to join the lonely home items in our storage unit. Many of these items we had not seen since our wedding; some were never opened. Leaving behind the life we knew in Italy, we embarked with one-way tickets to explore the world. Ready to push past ordinary into the bold, we took our kids out of school, to step into the 'classroom' of the entire world!

In the past six years we have, as a family, visited over 90 countries on six continents—traveling by plane, boat, train, bus, tuk tuk, sampan, camel and more! Instead of learning in only one classroom, our lessons happened in each and every moment through first-hand experiences and cultural immersion. We were surrounded by endless stories and knowledge of life, teaching Kaitlin, Cassidy and Trevor lessons that are only absorbed through true connection. Visiting over 450 cities in 72 months, stepping outside their comfort zones became the 'new normal.'

Our new style of education was about soaking in the vast richness of cultures of the world and challenging stereotypes by witnessing and experiencing places, people, history and current events, rather than just learning from the news or a textbook or studying for a test. Through our adventures, our children learned true life skills specific to new locations and global perspectives. They discovered their true talents and passions by being exposed to new ideas. There was stimulation from contrast to develop executive function, critical thinking, self-expression and creativity.

As we continued along in the flow of our curiosity around the globe, we encountered our greatest adventure and growing experience as a family – volunteering with Syrian refugees escaping war and seeking a new place to call home. When we first started working in a refugee camp in Athens, Greece, the self-doubt and voice in my head started to ask, "Is this the right thing for the kids? Should you really be doing this?" Yet that same feeling came back deep down in my gut, "This is right." Volunteering gave us the greatest joy and rewards we had ever experienced as a family. Kaitlin and Cassidy, who were 17 and 15, realized quickly, they were not too young to make a huge impact on the lives of others. They spent ten hours each day running a make-shift school and playing with hundreds of kids.

Although they had lost everything, these refugees were the kindest people we have ever met. Our perception of them completely transformed, teaching all of us the greatest lessons; never judge and always accept others. This experience of volunteering was a turning point for our family, a wake-up call that life is truly about how much you give to others and the joy you bring into their lives. During our months there, we connected with the families and children. I would come in to the camp day after day with my kids, dedicating our time to sharing the love we had in our hearts and give what we knew they deserved.

Each day working in the refugee camp was magical in its own way. Even with all the hardships we faced, there was always a beautiful lesson to be gained. There was a specific moment that changed my entire mindset, a moment that gave me the true understanding of why travel can transform who we are. As much as I felt this was impacting my children, the moment came when I realized how much it was impacting me! The sun was setting over the camp as I watched kids running through the tents coming to say 'hello', one by one coming up with a big smile on their face and a twinkle in their eyes, giving me the biggest of hugs. There were kids all around me, some older, some younger and all yelling one thing - *"Mama Gina! Mama Gina!"* It was my name to hundreds of people, adults and children alike.

I was there for them when they needed me most. When they needed to talk, or cry, or just wanted someone to listen or show they cared. Sometimes all they needed was a hug to make them smile. When their parents were not present or unaware because of the trauma they had experienced from the war, I was there for them. I looked into those children's eyes seeing the hope and joy on their faces, knowing I was helping them grow into the people they were meant to be. I was stepping in as their second mother. I was a loving figure not just for my three kids, but for hundreds more.

In that moment, I thought of all the people we had met around the world and realized they too, had raised my kids. They had been mother and father or aunt and uncle for a short moment, giving my children the knowledge and wisdom from their own experiences. These people offered valuable insights, making a positive impact in my children's lives; the global community had become their teachers, guides and supporters. It was the bread lady in Egypt who offered the warmest of smiles, the boat lady in Vietnam who, despite her old age, never gave up on the job she did to sustain her family. There was the old man in Chile who, despite not having much money, shared the true meaning of happiness. It was all the families in Jordan who welcomed us into their shops and homes, or the Palestinians who gave us tea and told us stories of their lives. It was the words and actions of the thousands of faces we have seen along the way creating who my children are today.

I finally understood that my passion for travel gave my kids the best gift they could have ever received – the gift of being raised by the world. As I was helping raise these refugee children, sharing with them the wisdom gained from my life experiences, so too were all of these wise teachers giving my children their stories and lessons.

We are all the fabric of diversity, a colorful tapestry of every culture in the world, all woven together and intertwined to create the people we are today – passionate and hospitable like the Egyptians, kind and gentle like the Burmese, connected to nature like the Maori and Aborigines, and warm and fun like the Peruvians.

Every person we met along our journey was my children's teacher and guide, giving them a glimpse into their stories, perspectives and wisdom. Every human has their own path and knowledge to gain. I exposed my children to all of these paths, interwoven into one soul. The gift of travel is not just about the experiences, it is about the profound change which happens within ourselves we can only truly discover over time.

In the same way so many people taught my children, I was a parent and a voice of wisdom for hundreds of children from other cultures, creating a beautiful cycle of many people raising children together to help them flourish. I finally discovered the true power of the phrase '*it takes a village to raise a child'*.

Embracing the wonders and diversity of the globe through love, knowledge and giving back is the greatest legacy I could ever leave for Kaitlin, Cassidy and Trevor. This is the gift that will carry on in their DNA for generations to come, raising them to be children of the whole world and becoming people who will carry on this wisdom.

The ancient Athenian statesman, Pericles, said it best: "What you leave behind is not what is engraved into stone monuments, but what is woven into the lives of others." In your parenting journey, I wish for you to find your village and seek the wisdom it has to share. Let many hands guide your children to live the magic life has to offer.

IGNITE ACTION STEPS

*Explore as a family - Whether you can only travel for a two-week vacation or months at a time, go and discover a new location and immerse your children into another culture.

*Connect with local people - Our most memorable experiences have been meeting people from other cultures and hearing their stories. In each, there is a beautiful lesson we can grow from, if we take the time to connect with others and learn to listen.

*Ignite Their Curiosity - Traveling as a family gives kids the chance to open their minds and discover something new by taking them to sights that are interesting and fascinating. Challenge their perception of the world by taking them to museums or on a tour. Let them ask questions about everything they are experiencing.

*Be Present - The most beautiful experiences come at the most unexpected times; when we allow ourselves to truly be in the here and now. As you travel, embrace every moment as an opportunity to learn something new. Show your kids how to enjoy the present; help them understand each moment is precious and worth living to the fullest.

*Storytelling - Sharing stories is the foundation of how we learn, so as you travel always remember to learn the stories of the place you are in. Ask questions of the locals, learn about the history and most importantly. Let your kids discover the vast diversity of the stories of the people and culture they are in.

*Volunteer - Let your kids experience the joy and beauty of giving back to others by having them volunteer in your community or as you travel. They will be forever changed by sharing their beautiful light with the world.

Gina Ingram with Kaitlin Murray - Greece
Mom, Traveler, Activist
soulexpedition.world

HELLE SIMONSEN

"The most important job we have as parents is to ignite the light in our children's eyes so they can discover the beauty of life from within themselves."

My deepest wish for any parent reading my words is that they shed the illusionary parenting role. That they free themselves from being the formers and shapers of the little human beings in their care. That they trust, that if they catch and then stop themselves, that is when their children will truly start living.

THE ILLUSION OF LOVE

I grew up in Denmark, in a sort of castle, not literally speaking, but I had everything one could wish for. My parents were wealthy, so my brother, sister and I were never short of new things or holidays. On top of that, I had been placed on this earth with a pretty face and many talents. I was one of those children that was good at everything.

From a young age, I was an achiever, constantly striving for success, wanting to be the best at everything. Approval from others became my number one mission. I honestly thought this was what life was about. I could see my path laid out ahead. Looking back though, I was never happy but I never thought to question my life. I didn't know any different. Slowly, I was losing the authentic little girl inside of me. She was taken over and disappeared in my pursuit of success.

I started feeling the pressure of expectations; rules and restrictions that were mainly self imposed. I only felt good enough when I performed well. Being the best became an obsession. The pressure I put on myself became more and more intense in my teens, to the point where I stopped feeling anything. Nothing. My soul was screaming but locked so far away that no one could hear it. I blamed myself for not being happy. I seemed to be living a dream-life and guilt became another factor in fueling the fire.

No one from the outside saw it coming; I didn't even see it coming. But one particular morning, 17 years ago, I had a row with my mum before college. I was mean, as in cruel and horrible. I took a real go at her. I don't even remember 'why', but I do remember making her cry. And my mum NEVER cried.

I rushed off to classes too confused and proud to make amends. I felt awful. My parents gave me everything and yet I'd said terrible things. Today I realize it was my soul screaming for help, but that day I felt I was the meanest and worst human on the planet.

When I got home later that day, mum wasn't there. I still felt dreadful but couldn't bring myself to pick up the phone and call her. The guilt and the feelings inside of me were agonising. I wanted to escape. Without even thinking, I went to the bathroom, took out two containers of pills and took them to my room. I emptied them onto the floor, sitting crossed legged staring at them. I swallowed them slowly in sets of two. I never thought the word 'suicide' – I just wanted to get away – to free my mind from the expectations and the feelings of 'not being good enough'. Except...

I played soccer in the highest league and had practise almost every afternoon and this day was no exception. Ironically enough, the thought of staying home from soccer practise never crossed my mind. Afterall, I was expected to be there. People counted on me. So, I got in the car, drove to practise and back home again afterwards. My body and mind felt numb now. I felt empty and *empty* was a relief.

I remember walking into the living room. Mum sat looking so small and sad on the couch. She looked at me, "Have you also had a bad day sweetheart?" I literally felt the last bit of willpower and strength leaving my body. Finally, I broke down. I cried, confessed what I'd done and apologized a thousand times. All I remember is being rushed to the hospital. They pumped the drugs out. I really don't remember much, only that I felt awful and extremely guilty for what I'd done to my parents.

After two days in hospital, I insisted my parents take me directly to my last exam for my college education. I passed with an A+, the shield was back up. I withdrew back into myself and into depression. My parents tried to understand me but I shut them out. For the two years that followed, I travelled to escape my life, the guilt and the expectations. I felt better when I was alone and far away from my life and the people who cared about me in Denmark. I was free, no one knew me or expected anything from me. Ultimately, I settled in Spain and this became the start of my healing.

Here I met Benjamin, an Englishman. I was in another world, another reality. We fell in love and five years later, when I was 25, we had our son, Charlie. Shortly after his birth the economic crisis hit Spain hard and we decided to move back to Denmark. Excited, we packed the car and set off to start our new life.

It was almost instant as we crossed the border to my home country. My body reacted viscerally as the expectations of myself came flooding back. Expectations and pressure to succeed in building up a new life from scratch for our family. It became my only goal.

Our relationship didn't survive the move, and we separated two years later.

One afternoon, as I knew our relationship had come to an end, I was crying in the bathroom because of shattered dreams. Little Charlie, who was two and a half at the time, suddenly stood in front of me. I had not heard him enter, not even noticed the door open and close after him. He looked at me with a look, that I will never forget. He dried my eyes with tissue paper in his little chubby hands, and just looked at me with an absurd look of wisdom. This was the exact moment I made it my goal, that Charlie and I could and would do everything on our own. A two-man army. Mother and child.

I became obsessed with the goal that Charlie should not suffer the agony I had in my childhood, nor be scarred from his parent's break-up. This led me to yet again constantly focus on proving myself—as a mum, employee, friend, daughter and sister. This was so deeply engraved in me. So I did what I knew best. I created an illusion of control to build up a new life for me and Charlie. Little Charlie was the perfect victim for me to maintain that illusion. Totally innocent, he was wrapped up right in the middle. He was the fuel that made me get up in the morning and make the plans I executed in the very best power-parent-manner. For three years, my only motivation was Charlie. During my obsession, I was providing, striving and chasing the means to create our perfect life together. I was blinded throughout this period and could only see the end goals I had set up for myself. Once a desire was met, I set a new one, not even taking the time to breathe or enjoy it.

Early one morning, I dropped Charlie off at kindergarten. As usual, I had already achieved 100 things beforehand, including: studying from 5 AM (I was obtaining a degree while still working in my job), working out in front of the tele, showering, ironing and making myself look my best. This was all done before waking up Charlie and then I turned into the calm, attentive super-mum with tons of energy. These were our typical mornings, planned neatly. Timed to the minute. But this morning, minutes were evaporating without my permission. I snapped and blamed Charlie for being too slow, and the feelings of guilt were intense as I waved him goodbye at the kindergarten and set off in a rush to catch my train for work....

I missed my train.

I couldn't really blame Charlie. It was me who had not executed well enough that morning. I had a meeting to run at work and there was no time to waste. Cortisol took over my body; I started running to another station, a different train. It was boiling hot, yet there I was running like a maniac in my neatly-ironed pinstriped shirt. It never occurred to me, to just let people at work know that I'd be late, that I'd missed the train. It seems so simple to write it here. It just wasn't an option then. Like it wasn't an option to miss my soccer practise.

I made the train. Jumping on just as the doors closed. Pulse racing, sweat breaking out all over my body, soaking my shirt. I stood, panting in the overcrowded compartment, certain everyone was staring at me, seeing through me, some judging me, others feeling sorry for me. I don't know if it was a panic attack or a moment of awakening, but, my whole body demanded, "Get off this train!" I don't recall which station, only that I could hardly see and that my body moved mechanically. I sank onto a bench, silent tears pouring down my cheeks. Sitting there I realized, no matter how much I fought for the perfect life somewhere ahead of me, I would never arrive.

I started walking back to the kindergarten, feeling a little lighter with every step, probably from the release of all the tears that I so controllingly had been holding back for years. Shutting down feelings in my frantic mission to create the perfect castle for me and Charlie. I'd been creating the same castle I grew up in, where I had every material gift and talent one could wish for, but the little girl missed her parents. Missed being kissed, hugged, listened to and looked at with love and compassion. I was now doing the same to Charlie. I loved him the way I learned to love myself— with control and precision. I was not only ruining myself, but slowly and surely Charlie too. I had no choice but to change.

I called in sick at work and picked up Charlie early from kindergarten. We had a day of just strolling around, no plans, just doing what came to our minds. I listened that day, really listened. My little boy had so many brilliant ideas, suggestions and love in him. I cried several times that day. Tears of gratitude and relief. This small angel in my life just accepted those tears, just as he'd done in the bathroom three years earlier. Through them, I saw Charlie again *and I felt him and myself.* It seemed as if Charlie had just been waiting for this day to come. So that he could show me his brilliance. That day became my true awakening, with help from my soul and the unconditional love of my five-year-old son.

A few weeks later, Charlie and I went on a spontaneous backpacking trip to Thailand and the connection we built was amazing. I felt and loved more authentically than I had ever known in my life. Charlie set the example every moment with his curiosity, questions and presence in the now, seeing all the things that I had not seen earlier being so busy in my mission for perfection. But this was perfect. My soul thanked me, thanked Charlie. These were the moments I wanted with my son. Just watching him, listening to him, seeing him unfold and be free without my constant disconnection, advice and plans. I was worried that the clarity and newfound connection would fade when we got back to Denmark. I quit my job.

I granted myself one year off to discover 'me' and to keep building the amazing relationship that had grown between me and Charlie. He had shown me all the amazing things and experiences we could have, simply by his curiosity leading and me following. I was amazed by this five-year old's view of life. How he met the day, waking up in the morning. I wanted to learn from him. So, I set up three values for myself to live by, inspired by Charlie.

Curiosity. I wanted to follow my curiosity. I had always set my mind on one thing and then strived for perfection. I was sick of that. I decided to try things I'd never done before and to be okay with not being the best, and even failing. Children just do without thinking of the outcome.

Honesty. A thing I admire so much in children. They speak their truth without reframing their words. This means they speak straight from their soul and heart. I wanted to be able to do that, instead of always over-thinking and spending so much energy worrying about what others thought.

Live Easily. I was so fascinated by the ease Charlie showed for life. He would always be 100% present in the now. He never spoke of tomorrow or next week. I wanted that. To stop my head from constantly making plans and organizing the future.

As I'm writing these lines, this all happened five years ago. Charlie is ten now, and our lives have changed radically ever since. Me, being gratefully aware of it, and Charlie just living his natural state that only a child knows how to. I thank Charlie for my awakening. I've learned so much about life and myself with him as my teacher.

These days, I stay aware to spare Charlie of my childhood experiences that are so deeply engraved in me. I work really hard on not having expectations of him or the outcome of the things he puts his energy into. If I do so, I'm back to mistakenly loving him with an illusionary and controlling version of love. I believe love with expectations serves neither child nor parent. How can we, as parents, *know* our expectations are right for our children? Each is a totally different human being, with a different soul, heart and purpose than ours.

I do my best to never judge Charlie's decisions or decide things on his behalf, even if I believe it is for his best. Only he knows. If it shows that the outcome of his decision is not what he hoped for, then it was still a decision he made as an individual and he'll truly learn from it. If I overrule him, because I can, as the parent authority, his authenticity crumbles as he starts to sense he must fit in to an ideal or live up to my standards of praise and approval. This is dangerous. This is when the head starts overruling the heart and the child has to think of their actions and not just follow their natural state.

The facades and masks small children put on to make their surroundings happy, are admirable yet devastating. Just like I did in my teenage years. Loving our children through our own illusions is lethal. We must shed these ideals and instead see the human beings in our care with their own dreams. It has been hard work, because I sometimes *think* I know best and probably often do. What I choose instead, is ask questions, that might or might not help Charlie identify his own learnings from within. Then listen to his answers and accept them. My job as Charlie's parent, is not to make his decisions or live his life. My job is to provide unconditional love without judgement. To create the space and experiences with which Charlie can grow. To go from being a boss, to being his guardian angel.

I have never doubted, that my brother, sister and I were the centre of my parent's universe. They would die for us. But they suffered their own emotional tragedies growing up, blocking their emotional involvement. Books about the Love Languages between parents and children had not yet been written. As a natural achiever, I was the one who drove myself to burn-out, whilst mastering the masquerade to perfection. What parents of their generation would recognize the danger signs of that? Today our relationship has completely shifted to being deep and connected. This has come with life-experience, wisdom and my awakening after becoming a parent myself. I treasure and burst with pride at what our family has built up.

It's never too late to find a deep authentic connection with your child, once we, as parents, strip away any illusions of being able to control another life. Our own existence becomes simpler and easier, and our children will discover the beauty of life and who they truly are.

Mum, Dad and Charlie – I love you.

IGNITE ACTION STEPS

*Realize** that your child is not a mini version of you. You don't know every aspect of your child's core essence. This is to unfold within a secure environment, set by you, free from your expectations and judgement. Letting go of the control may be hard, but it's worth it.

*Listen.** Let your child speak. It seems simple, but try to pay attention to this. As parents we interrupt and finish our children's sentences much more than we think. Don't. Be attentive, turn to your child and look into his/her eyes. And then truly listen. This will make them feel seen, acknowledged and accepted.

*Expectations** – notice everyday situations where you put expectations onto your child. An expectation is either met or it's not. Success or failure. This is judgement. Instead learn to accept any outcome. Acceptance comes from the heart.

*Take a day out.** Just sometimes. Never mind that your child misses school and you skip work. No school on the planet can teach what you both will benefit. Let your child lead the day, with you securing the environment. Just be.

*Surrender.** Release the illusionary view you have on how parenting 'ought' to be. Instead surrender to your heart. Back off, relax. Trust the journey and your child's spirit will thrive. Have faith, it will be the best thing you will ever do. I promise.

Helle Simonsen - Denmark
Children's author and Founder of CuriousMinds ApS
www.hellesimonsen.com

SUNAINA VOHRA

"As a mother, YOU are the center of the household.
If you are happy, everyone around you is happy."

My hope is that in reading my story you will realize that YOU need to take deep, long breaths. Looking after yourself is not selfish; is a selfless act. There will be more of you for those whom you serve. You need to fill your lungs with pure oxygen, have pulsating love in every cell of your being, acceptance in your heart, and calmness in your essence. You are the heartbeat of your family and everything in you echoes in their souls.

SELFISH PARENTING TO REDISCOVERING SELF

The flickering candlelight danced off my friend's sequined shirt as we clinked our wine glasses, toasting to years of camaraderie. All ten of us were celebrating our decade long friendship and reminiscing about the struggles endured and the good times had. We had shared memories of new jobs, humble homes bought, first pregnancies, and some lost ones, amidst tears and tantrums of little ones. We had picked a restaurant that was special to all of us, one we frequented as a group. I felt surrounded by the warmth and love of true friends.

The men were having a great time until they drew our attention to a little game they were playing around the table amongst themselves. I heard one ask, "So which country do you think has the most beautiful women?" I heard a friend shout out "Italy!" another, "Venezuela" and another, "Russia".

When it came to the last man on the table, he looked straight into my eyes and spoke from his heart, "The one at home." The men guffawed at his statement and ridiculed him saying he was just trying to earn brownie points – I knew better. The warmth and love in his eyes revealed his truth.

When our eyes met, my husband smiled warmly at me from across the table and instead of returning his smile in that magical moment, I felt a prick in my heart and in my eyes tears welled up. I pretended to cough while quickly wiping away a stray tear. I had no clue why my heart had suddenly given way and before I could pause, words tumbled out of my mouth to my girlfriend sitting next to me.

"I feel like I am the worst mother in the world. I should never have had kids. I don't deserve to be a mother."

My friend turned to me startled, "Are you okay, Sunaina? Is everything alright? What happened?" With tears gushing uncontrollably, I got up and pushed my chair away to make a beeline for the ladies' room. I had no clue why I was saying that, let alone what I was feeling. I literally collapsed on the plush bench within the room with sobs shaking my entire body. Two of my girlfriends followed me and thankfully allowed me the space to let out my flood of tears without any questions.

After fifteen minutes, I felt I could find my voice from below the dam that had just burst forth. Assessing the damage caused – mascara lines looked like meandering rivers across a pink rouge landscape, I looked up and saw two loving friends' faces covered with concern and questions.

I did not see this coming, not entirely. Yes, I admit I had these moments of doubt and guilt creep in once in a while, but this complete breakdown in the middle of a celebratory moment left me shaking. I felt a warm hand on mine and my friend whispered, "Sunaina it's okay. If you want to take some more time, we are here for you."

I allowed the wave of self-disappointment and deprecation pass over me. Taking a deep breath, I wiped away my tears and the slivers of wet mascara, touched up my lipstick, plastered a smile on my face and looked at my friends proclaiming, "Oh, I really don't know what that was all about! Must be pms-ing, sorry about that gals." Returning to the table, I slipped with *fake* ease back to the dining party, not meeting the worried gaze of my husband, because he would know.

I did not know, or more accurately did not want to know, what about my life left me feeling amiss. I could sense an emptiness had been gnawing inside me for a couple of weeks despite being surrounded by my lovely family: an adorable daughter, a toddler son and the most doting husband. I would wake up as the dutiful mother and wife, seeing my daughter off to school, toddler to nursery and husband to work with sweet hugs, and little kisses. But as they left the house, in entered dark clouds swirling around my very Being.

I kept busy with my household chores but I could hear these voices inside of me calling me a hypocrite and an undeserving soul. I battled with thoughts like I did not deserve this beautiful family. I was ungrateful. I needed to do more. I needed to clean the house so it was spotless. I needed to cook meals not only to nourish my family but also meals that would be the talk of social parties. I needed to exercise, be in shape, and to have my hair and nails done. I needed to say the right things. I needed to have the right friends and be seen and heard at the right events. If I continued to score high at all of this, then the Being inside would be okay. She would feel she had worked hard enough to deserve this family. So I kept going and going and going. The hamster on the wheel was me.

When volunteering at my daughter's school, a particular incident that marred me was when I went to her kindergarten class and had to count dried cereal to teach the kids numbers. I felt I had let myself down. Seriously, is this what I had planned for myself? I returned home not feeling like an accomplished mother but rather like a defeated woman. Was I even allowed to feel this way? I wondered. Wasn't being a mother all about sacrificing and enjoying these volunteering activities in schools? For the record, I could not bring myself to volunteer again after that experience.

I was a high-achieving, marketing professional and motherhood was immensely gratifying, a miracle in every sense of the word. But I had allowed ME to dwindle. I had drowned my ambitions and my desires in a mountain of nappies and play-dates. Splashing in the pool with my kids brought joy into my life, so did combing the hair of my daughter's Barbies. However, there were many aspects of motherhood I wished I did not have to deal with: the battle of getting the food laden spoon into my child's mouth and the constant wailing of my toddler early in the morning while getting ready for school. Yes, yes, I needed to be grateful I had borne kids healthy in mind and body unlike many others. Yet I was ill-equipped to deal with their constant demands on my mind, body, emotions, and time. I repeat, I was that hamster on the treadmill – constantly performing for everyone with no destination in sight. I had so much to do but no time to feel. There had been goals and ambitions which had been covered in nappies, oh did I say that already? Brain fog had become a norm. I had begun to feel like I was getting sucked into an abysmal chasm. I was meant to rejoice in the miracle of motherhood; still, I seemed further away from joy than I had ever been. I had somehow resigned myself to being *lesser than.*

Yes, I had friends who seemed to be enjoying parenting. No one complained. Everyone was out near the swimming pool discussing gym trainers, diets, exhibitions, nannies, and the next extra-curricular activity they were planning to send their Einstein to so he could become the next Newton. Yet, here I was, resenting sitting at home away from my corporate job which I thoroughly enjoyed… oops, did I just say that?

I remember in the middle of changing my baby's nappy, I had allowed the same words regarding missing my corporate job to escape my lips in front of my grandmother. She had turned around and said, "Becoming a mother is a privilege and you need to learn to enjoy it. Spend your time cooking up your kids' favorite meals and you will experience fulfillment." At that precise moment, I remembered the debacle of the 'cereal' assignment and felt my heart drop, defeated.

Motherhood was meant to raise me, wasn't it? Yet, with each passing day, I was feeling more defeated, more like I had let ME down, more like there was 'no exit'. Don't get me wrong, this was not about my babies – this was about ME. I could not for the life of me fathom what was *happening.* My health began to deteriorate. It was nothing serious, just small, niggly things, until such time my mother-in-law decided to visit us in Singapore.

She SAW me. I think she saw me, mother to mother. Being a very accomplished woman herself, including teacher, Ikebana specialist, and potter, she knew something was amiss. She had three children whom she had raised while she pursued her career and hobbies. Even after they had flown the nest, she had continued to enrich her life by following her myriad of passions.

Once, while accompanying me to one of the many doctors helping me resolve my health issues, she looked at me puzzled, asking, "What is going on?" I pretended to not understand her question and shrugged it off saying, "Let's see what the doctor says." But she persisted. This time the floodgates opened and between sobs I confessed, "I am really unhappy and I am angry with myself because, despite everything God has given me, I am unable to appreciate and treasure my children and my husband. I keep craving for something more."

My mother-in-law, having witnessed my corporate success, queried, "Do you want to work?"

I countered saying, "How can I? My baby is still so young I could not possibly leave two young kids and chase a career."

She said, "Who is stopping you? Is it your husband?" When I shook my head, signalling no, her answer changed the trajectory of my life!

"Sunaina, you are the center of this home – when you are happy everyone around you, your kids and your husband will be happy. Do what makes YOU happy."

To reiterate this, it was my mother-in-law who asked me to put myself FIRST, before my children and husband. Never before had another woman asked me to be selfish. Selfish… wasn't there a secret mother-code that demanded mothers feed their kids before they feed themselves? Wasn't a mother supposed to be patient and perfect or perfectly patient with her offspring? Wasn't a mother supposed to sacrifice the world for her kids? SACRIFICE? Wasn't sacrifice a synonym for motherhood? I was truly horrified by my mother-in-law's suggestion. She had literally asked me to think about MYSELF before her grandkids and her own son, my husband.

She obviously read my puzzled expression and sat me down to explain, "Sunaina, unless I love myself, pamper myself and care deeply for myself as a woman, I would not be able to experience the joy that I AM. How could I then love, pamper and care for my children and loved ones? Can you pour from an empty jug and quench someone's thirst? Your jug needs to be full before you can share yourself with those you love."

As soon as I heard this, all my pent-up frustration and resentment poured out. I shared with her, the doubt, guilt, and hatred I had directed towards myself for craving more in my life. I did want to work. I did want to contribute outside my home. My need for significance, as explained by Tony Robbins, was one of my highest needs and I was doing nothing to fulfill that, making me feel depleted and diminished. I was literally stretching the proverbial rubber band to breaking point.

Slowly and steadily I began to rebuild the woman I wanted to be, whilst still being a mother. I realized the significance of why the flight attendants stressed, "FIRST you wear the mask and then you help your child."

I chanced upon a friend who was a practicing life coach. Upon further understanding this relatively nascent profession, I first embarked on being a client and then on learning the ropes of the profession itself. To start with, I had to first accept I was where I was meant to be. I was not too early nor too late in the journey of parenting and becoming an aware parent. I had to learn there is no perfect parent and more shockingly, no perfect mother. The family commercials which I grew up watching were not the entire life of a family, rather a 10-second glimpse of what the advertiser's 'perfect family' could be, again leading me to a dead end. I had to forgive and let go of my parenting mistakes, including the ones I wanted to take to my grave.

This was honestly the toughest part of the coaching journey, somewhere my sense of self had become so enmeshed with the self-flagellating mother in me, it was the only way I could live with myself. I had to heal by giving myself permission to FEEL all the emotions which were showing up on my canvas of life. It was only when I allowed myself to go through the emotions, rather than circumvent them by daily distractions, I became aware of the emotional lesions the self-flagellation had caused.

Tears washed away years of negative self-beliefs of who I should be as a mother and how miserably I had failed myself. I began to see clearly how my overwhelm and emotional turbulence was impacting the way I was parenting my children. As I uncovered layer after layer, I felt a sense of lightness pervade my Being. The more I got in touch with my inner essence, the easier it became to be present for my children. I thought caring for ME was selfish. On the contrary, the more I began to fall in love with myself, the more love flowed out of me for my family. My eyes opened with wonderment as I began to unravel the wisdom in what Kahlil Gibran says so poignantly:

Your children are not your children.
They are the sons and daughters of Life's longing for itself.
They come through you but not from you,
And though they are with you yet they belong not to you.
You may give them your love but not your thoughts,
For they have their own thoughts.
You may house their bodies but not their souls,
For their souls dwell in the house of tomorrow,
which you cannot visit, not even in your dreams.
You may strive to be like them,
but seek not to make them like you.
For life goes not backward nor tarries with yesterday.

As self-awareness and self-love became my religion, I naturally gravitated towards building a coaching practice focusing on children and parents. I was drawn to helping others, especially mothers just like me who were burnt out and had lost touch with their essence. These parents were overwhelmed and exhausted, causing them to struggle with raising their children. I shared my personal experience to reinforce the fact that we, as parents, were responsible for creating a family environment conducive to the academic and personal development of our child.

Today, I help parents just like you to let go of the guilt and blame they put themselves through. I help them understand the impact their emotional baggage has on their kids. I inspire parents to truly 'raise themselves' by becoming more self-aware and to understand the role of self-love in emotionally resilient, mentally strong, and spiritually-evolved children. I believe through awareness and conscious parenting we play a key role in elevating the collective consciousness of the planet. I truly feel we can bring peace, love, and harmony to the planet – one family unit at a time.

IGNITE ACTION STEPS

I found the one thing which helped me through my personal parenting journey and that parents I now coach find the most beneficial: journaling. It is an opportunity for you to meet yourself in the privacy of the blank pages of your journal where neither the pen judges you for what you write nor the page for what you express.

*Start by pouring (journaling) out all the "stuff" you constantly admonish yourself for as a parent.

*Allow yourself to feel the depth of the emotions which flood your being. Avoid distractions and just sit with the emotions.

*You can create a simple ritual of forgiving and letting go of the above "stuff" because this gunk is exactly what is coming between you and your child.

*You can light a bonfire and tear the pages of your journal that carry your emotional baggage and feel the negativity dissolve.

*See the flames incinerate the stuff that has kept you chained to your past, recalibrating how you feel in the now and anchoring it to your present

Sunaina Vohra - United Arab Emirates
Youth & Parent Coach
www.athenalifecoaching.com

HILARY COLE

"Great sleep makes everything else possible."

What I want for parents reading this story is to believe that parenting doesn't mean sacrificing your sleep for months or years on end and helping kids become independent with sleep doesn't get in the way of them feeling secure and loved. In fact, the opposite is often true. Having children who sleep well is totally achievable and not at all selfish! Kids need parents who have the energy and patience to be fully present for them. And each of us—young and old—needs to sleep through the night to be at our best.

FINDING SANITY IN SLEEP

This was not what having a beautiful new baby was supposed to be like.

First, there was the excruciatingly painful first six weeks of breastfeeding when no medical or lactation expert could figure out how to get this baby to latch properly. I used to joke that my child got a dose of cortisol with every feeding as I gripped the armrests of the chair and stomped my feet in agony from the pain, determined that breastfeeding was best, and we would get through it.

We eventually did get through our breastfeeding challenges and my body began to heal. But our struggles in those early weeks definitely left their mark—by the time feeding got on track, we had created every habit in the book which prevented our baby from developing any kind of ability to fall asleep on her own.

Six months into this motherhood gig and totally sleep deprived, I hit the proverbial wall, walking laps around my condo building's underground parking garage in the middle of the night with my child strapped to my chest; the baby carrier was the only place my husband and I could consistently get her to sleep.

Trudging around in my winter boots and my husband's oversized coat covering us both, humming, shushing and bouncing as I walked – *at 2:00 in the morning* – I knew something had to change; this was not sustainable. Or normal. We needed help.

We were new parents with a (thankfully) healthy, delightful, sweet baby we adored. But from day one, she never slept like we expected her to. I was prepared for a sleep-deprived beginning, waking to feed my newborn every few hours but all the new moms around me seemed to be moving beyond that stage at three months, four months and five months for sure.

Even though I came late to motherhood (I had both my kids in my 40's) and had seen most of my friends go through this stage of their lives already, I actually knew nothing about infant sleep going in. *I actually thought the more tired a baby was, the faster they'd fall asleep.* Of course, nothing could be further from the truth.

I didn't mind those initial night wakings – they were precious time alone with my newborn. But when every three hours turned into every two hours and stayed that way for months on end, I realized our situation was not going to get better on its own.

I picked up my first sleep book, *The No Cry Sleep Solution,* when my baby was three months old and thought I had found the holy grail. I still think this book has one of the greatest titles in parenting books ever. I devoured it in two days, desperate to help my little baby learn to fall asleep without all the wailing, screaming and hours of rocking that seemed to be required. And without letting her cry it out. I got to the end of the book and thought, "Where's the *solution* part?!" I had already been bed-sharing and demand-feeding. We had a bedtime routine. I tried the gentle-extraction method outlined in the book when feeding her to sleep, ad nauseum. I was still up every two hours.

Then I read a book about timing naps with a baby's natural body rhythm. That helped a bit – at least I had some kind of schedule to go by. But the battle to fall asleep was still on, day and night.

Sleep became an obsession in our household and the only thing my husband and I talked about. It was definitely the only thing we fought about. Before having babies, my husband and I literally never fought. We disagreed like other couples (of course) but never snapped at one another or raised our voices.

But at 3:00 AM when we'd both been up for half the night and were operating on a six month sleep deficit, we snapped. We got angry. Every cell in our bodies was demanding rest but we didn't have it and it affected our emotional control, our mental capacity and the sharpness of our tongues with each other.

We were starting to fall apart.

The strange thing was there were lots of days when I would feel relatively okay. A friend whose baby was born the same day as mine and was sleeping seven-eight hours at a time, asked me how I could possibly function or even get out of bed on such little sleep. I remember telling her I was fine and that I managed to piece together about seven hours of broken sleep every night to keep me going.

What I've since learned from reading sleep research is that a key component of sleep deprivation is that the sleep-deprived person will "underestimate their impairments and overestimate their abilities." In other words, they think they're fine. In fact, they probably aren't even safe to drive. Getting less than six hours of sleep a night for just two weeks leaves a person with the cognitive function of someone with a blood-alcohol level over the legal limit. (And those are six *straight* hours.) When talking about the sleep deprivation caused by waking up with a baby repeatedly throughout the night, it's actually been called 'drunk parenting'.

I remember a lot of days that felt like hangover parenting.

Thankfully, my husband and I agreed we needed help and that everything we had tried so far wasn't working. The prenatal dream of sharing a bed with our child was blown out of the water. Not this child, not this Mama. What I thought would be the best sleeping arrangement for our new family actually meant none of us were actually sleeping enough. And for our baby, falling asleep was a constant struggle. I could see that she was as tired as I was.

So, we called a sleep consultant. Not in a million years did I imagine I would need to do this, mainly because I had never heard of a sleep consultant until my late-night google searches made me realize this wasn't just my problem, this was a common issue for many new parents. And there were trained experts out there who knew how to solve it!

We first met with our sleep coach on Facetime, which, let's be honest, doesn't always display the most flattering image of oneself. I don't think I'll ever forget looking into the iPad that day. Seeing the contrast in appearance between myself and our fresh-faced, perfectly coherent and highly functioning baby sleep coach was almost laughable. Except I was too tired to laugh. I looked *awful*: I had serious dark circles under my eyes, my hair was a mess and my face had deep lines I was sure weren't there six months before.

Thankfully, it didn't take long for the miracle to happen. Within three nights of using the plan that our sleep consultant had walked us through, our little peanut was sleeping through the night! She was in her own crib beside our bed and sleeping soundly for almost 11 hours! Every morning, my husband and I woke up to her happily babbling away beside us. And while there were tears involved, this was no shut-the-door, cry-it-out, see-you-in-the-morning ordeal. We got to stay right beside her as she figured out this new life skill: how to fall asleep and stay asleep.

It was like the heavens opened and the angels sang. It felt like the dream of having a blissfully sweet life with a baby was actually coming true. The first time she fell asleep on her own (not at midnight because we had bounced, rocked and serial-fed her until she crashed, but at 7:30 pm) my husband and I were so astonished, we didn't know what to do with ourselves. "Neither of us has a child strapped to us!" we realized. "What do we do now?!"

We high-fived each other every night at 7:30 for about a year. No kidding. We continued to work with our sleep coach to iron out our baby's napping needs and help her stay as consistent as possible so the miracle of sleep became real and lasting.

We later learned there was a huge bonus to our baby sleeping well: we would always know when something was *actually* wrong. She wasn't overtired anymore and she knew how to fall asleep and stay asleep all night. On the odd occasion when she did wake up crying during the night, there was a really good reason – a new tooth was erupting, or she was feeling sick.

Suddenly there was no more guessing, we could tend to our child how she needed. I finally realized what 'nighttime parenting' was supposed to look like. It wasn't about waking up all night, every night. It was about responding to my child with comfort and support when something out-of-the-ordinary happened. On those rare nights, there was never any resentment about being woken up; this is what I signed up for. This is what being a parent was about.

Five years after those chilly laps around my underground parking garage, another Little Bean added to our family, and we all sleep through the night, virtually every night. Our kids both feel safe and secure in their places of sleep and confidently say "G'night Mom!" and snuggle in at 7:30 for 11 or 12 hours of much needed rest.

When I read now about how broken sleep or too little sleep affects a child's behavior, learning and mood and how an inability to sleep on their own can lead older kids to have anxiety around sleep, I am grateful we made the leap and did the work when we did. Children have enough challenges to deal with and anxiety provoking stimulation to manage; we need to at least give them the foundation of enough sleep to get them through those struggles.

As for us big people, well, we need time to ourselves and time for our partners. I know how important it is for couples to have those precious evening hours to themselves after the kids are quietly tucked in. I am now a firm believer that sleep is the biggest part of the whole concept of taking care of yourself first so you can take care of someone else. 'Cause you can't pour from an empty cup.

As much as I need my nightly break during those much welcomed evening hours, I sometimes miss my little ones when they're asleep. I believe that's a good thing; I'm excited to see them when they wake up, which means my children (who can read me like no one else) wake up to someone greeting them with authentic smiles and enthusiastic hugs and kisses. That's something no words can replace.

Now, when I do have a snuggle with one of them in our bed because they're sick or scared from a dream, it is sweet, cozy and special. I don't feel resentful for having a foot in my face or an elbow in my ribs all night. I want my children to feel fully loved and acknowledged and that can only happen when I have the energy to honestly show them.

I am a Mom of two young children, and I am not sleep deprived. I'm just normal-tired. :)

Having sleep come back into my life (and stay there) seemed like such a magical transformation, when the opportunity came to learn how to pass this on to other families, I jumped on it. I became a certified sleep consultant and am now (at the time of writing this) about 200 super-sleeping kids into a gig which I totally love.

My constant wish is to help bring that same foundation of sleep to as many families as I can. I now teach parents that making healthy sleep a household priority allows space for love, joy and fun without that heel-dragging feeling so many of us have walked around with, babies and toddlers in tow.

My continued learning is leading me down the path of also helping older children who suffer anxiety around sleeping alone. In these cases, I work with both the kids and their parents to help them get past this painful stage and become confident, relaxed and independent with sleep so they not only get the rest they need but can join their friends at sleepovers and summer camp.

I will admit, I am grateful for having had to learn all of this the hard way. I would never have said this at the time but my little girl's tough time with sleep for the first six months of her life has been a gift and an experience which set me on a path to be a better parent. It has been my single greatest proof that there are no fixed characteristics in any of us, including our kids. My child was not born a 'bad sleeper'. It just would have been easier in the moment to chalk it all up to that and do nothing and I am so glad we didn't.

When my daughter stepped into the quintessential 'terrible twos' we decided to jump on the learning train again and see what kind of strategies we could find to get us through that next stage. We read books, went to a few seminars and saw a super parenting counsellor. It turned out, understanding the developing brain of a toddler went a long way to dealing with or even preventing those tantrums. It also made being mindful in the moment, instead of reactive, way easier.

When you understand what your child is experiencing, it's a lot less crazy-making. I've seen dozens of little ones' apparent hyperactivity and problem behaviors melt away once their parents have a few brain-centered behavioral tools up their sleeves. I share these tools with every parent I work with who has a child over two along with a clear plan to help everyone get the sleep they need. By coaching families through sleep-training programs, I've learned that so many aspects of parenting are, without a doubt, about creating clear boundaries around the things that are really important and helping kids learn how to stay within those boundaries.

I often say to parents that helping children sleep well is like a metaphor for everything else we do: we support them enough to help them learn something new but get out of the way enough for them to truly thrive and become the best little versions of themselves.

IGNITE ACTION STEPS

*Take a moment to remember how much sleep was your "ideal" night's sleep before having children. Then remind yourself that your body still has that same need (if not more because your downtime is now a lot less or even non-existent!).

*Before you go to sleep, take two minutes to sit on the side of your bed and check in with yourself: are you going to bed because it's time, or are you completely crashing from exhaustion? Are your shoulders tense with that walking-on-eggshells feeling of not knowing when your sleep is going to be disturbed by the next cry-out or little visitor to your bedroom?

*Decide, right then and there, what kind of parent you want to be: heel-dragging, patience-losing and resentful, or peaceful, present and energetic? Then decide how much sleep you likely need to make the latter option even possible.

*Ask yourself if there is anything holding you back. Write down all the reasons you want to make a change and then all the reasons you haven't yet. Then you'll be able to see, on paper, which list carries more weight for you.

*Start tonight with a bedtime routine. Begin about 30 or 40 minutes before your child usually falls asleep and do a consistent set of activities leading up to bedtime such as: having a bath, putting on pyjamas, having some milk or a quick snack, brushing teeth, reading one or two stories, then singing a quiet little song before laying down for lights out. Repeat it *exactly the same* way for at least five nights in a row and see if the battle to fall asleep gets any easier.

*If your child is falling asleep later than you'd like, move bedtime back by 10 minutes every second night. In just a week or two, your child will be falling asleep about an hour earlier every night (more sleep for them, more time for you!)

Hilary Cole - Canada
Certified Sleep Consultant
hilarysleep.com

BIPPAN DHILLON

*"Failure IS the gateway to success when it is met
with forgiveness."*

**When I became a parent, I never imagined the growth I would discover
in myself. My desire for those reading my story is to have you unlock the
opportunity that lies in every challenge you overcome. Just like seeing
your child grow, you will be amazed by what you witness within yourself.**

THE GATEWAY TO SUCCESS

Jaya, my daughter, said one day with a big smile on her face, "Mom, I'm
going to be just like you when I grow up." I smiled back, mostly in reaction
to how excited she was to share this with me. Internally I was having a
different experience. A moment of concern. I remember thinking, "Wait,
wouldn't all parents want to hear that their child wants to be like them?" Not
if they didn't believe in themselves.

For me, it was an internal dialogue that had me ultimately hoping she
would be a better version of me. My mind randomly did an examination of
all the ways I didn't measure up, the ways in which I fell short. At no time
during this experience did any worthy accomplishment cross my mind, nor
any acknowledgment of my contribution to my family. It was just an endless
list of evidence that had me believe I had not *done* or *been* enough. Why
didn't I see that I must be doing something right to have her say that? Why

did I fail to recognize the compliment in her statement?

The answer to these questions and more would reveal themselves to me. Although I am tempted to start with my excuses and my reasons to avoid accountability, I will refrain from that, as one of the discoveries I made is the habit of seeking forgiveness from others. The need for validation.

At the time the four of us, Paul, my husband, Ashaan, my oldest son, Jaya and I were living in this rather large home – big and beautiful but a lot to clean. Because there was ample room we had allowed our little eight-year-old Jaya to have her very own science lab. Sounds fancy – it kind of was. It was a small closet that when opened would give way to a cocktail bar. It included some cabinetry with a small bar sink and a couple of rows of shelving to display liquor and cocktail glasses which sat in front of a mirrored wall. A quintessential '80s entertainment space. There she proudly kept her gelatinous, playful *'slime'* collection she had made from watching YouTube tutorials, along with the ingredients and an array of Tupperware containers holding the various versions in the many colors and consistencies she had created. It was every eight-year-old's dream room. As you can imagine, it had the makings of also being a bit of a disaster.

One particular Saturday, I couldn't stand it any longer and told Jaya she had to go and clean that room. It was in its messy state, bombed with food coloring, and empty containers of contact lens solution and various other ingredients were all around, along with bits and pieces of slime residue on almost every surface area. We were in the kitchen when I made the request, "Jaya I need you to clean your lab today."

It was immediately met with, "I don't want to." I asked her again, "I really need you to go and spend five minutes down there and do your best to clean it."

This was followed by, "But Mom, we don't have any paper towels."

I came back with, "Okay, there are things you can throw away. Just start with that." Looking back, I was oblivious to her reasons for stalling. However, rather than being curious and going down to her slime lab to see what was holding her up, I took the drill sergeant approach and persisted with my request, "It doesn't matter that you don't have paper towels. Just go do something."

Before long my effort to take a firm stance led to screaming, "Mom! I told you I don't have paper towels. You're not listening!"

In the midst of all our disagreeing, she ended up pushing me. In our house, we have a consequence for hitting. It is 'together time', spending 30 minutes with the person you hit and writing a five-sentence love-letter to them. However, in the midst of this argument, I defaulted back to an old consequence, one we all had determined did not fit the devoted promise of being respectful. Despite knowing better, there I was saying, "Well, you just lost your computer screen time for the day."

Of course, this only led to more frustration for both of us. She continued to push and I continued to get more and more angry. My inner thoughts were, "There she goes again, not listening to me." With what was happening in my inner and outer worlds at the time, I was not able to gain perspective. She kept pushing. I kept threatening. "Well now, you lose your electronics for a week... a month." I knew it wasn't working but I didn't know what else to do. In an effort to give myself space, I thought I needed to get away from this situation and let her be. Of course, she continued to follow me, pushing and tugging at me. Echoing through my head, as I repeatedly asked her to stop, was "I don't know what to do." To find a distraction, I decided I would throw out the bathroom garbage. Paul had already tied the bag up. I just needed to grab it and throw it out. As I made my way to the door, Jaya was clinging to my legs, wanting my attention and rebelling against me. I was struggling to figure out how to control my frustration and holding back tears from the feeling that I was failing as a Mom – I pleaded, "Jaya, please give me some space. Please leave me alone." Finally pulling myself away, in complete exasperation, I turned around and swung the bag – right at Jaya. I heard the impact and then saw her tears. Shocked by what I had just done and not knowing what to do next, I walked outside to the garbage bin – now in full on tears trying to get some clarity.

I felt the bag and realized it had something other than normal bathroom tissue and hairbrush hairs. There was something more solid in the bag. Jaya would later tell me it was a plastic cup she had snuck into the garbage. There was a moment where an old version of me surfaced, wanting to blame someone, anyone, for not recycling but I had enough awareness to know I needed to take responsibility. There I stood trying to figure out what happened and what to do next. I went back into the house and knew there was no justification for ever doing that. I went to her room where she was crying. I was immediately aware of the consequence of having lost my temper with her. I cried. I was experiencing one of my worst fears that maybe I had a temper like my parents. I broke down looking at her, thinking, how does a mother do this? I knew I needed to say 'sorry'.

Trying to look into her tear-filled eyes I said, "Jaya, Mommy made a mistake. I am sorry, I was so angry and I didn't know what to do." It took a few minutes but we were able to talk further and she accepted my apology.

We decided that we would go look at the slime lab together and figure out how to start. She simply did not know how to clean up if she didn't have any paper towels. However, inside of my cloud-covered story of, 'I am not being heard and I am failing as a Mom,' I could not see what was missing.

The day continued with the kids staying at my in-laws that night. On Sunday, we arrived to pick them up. I went to greet Jaya with a hug. Underneath her eye was a slight puffiness with a bit of bruised discoloration starting to appear. I had to hold back my tears. Looking at her cute cheeks and dimples, I whispered, "I am so sorry, baby girl," hoping she would know how much I love her. Shyly, she asked, "Mom, is it that bad?" I didn't know how to answer. I wanted to say, "It's terrible – I'm terrible." Instead, I found the strength to say, "It's not that bad. It will go away in a few days."

I had plans to drive to Seattle, WA from Canada that day. I was working on a project to document my father's story of the 1947 Partition when India and Pakistan divided. I was going to go alone but given what had transpired I decided to ask Jaya to come along. She agreed that it would fulfill the proper consequence of "together time." After our argument, I felt compelled to spend time with her and be in her presence. I thought I needed to show her how much I love her; as I was dealing with overwhelming guilt. We got on the road to Seattle, her in the back seat, equipped with some snacks and electronics. We drove and along the way I had time to reflect. I was reminded of how parenting really takes conscious effort. So often I find it is like looking into a mirror that is reflecting back all of your own past hurts; showing you what needs to heal.

A few minutes into the trip, I allowed myself to cry. I had been holding it in since Paul's parents' house. As I wept, I realized not only was I grieving for the woman who clearly had a parenting failure but I was also mourning for my eight-year-old self. I was reminded of all the times there was arguing and yelling. All the years where we would be crying from our parents fighting. All those moments when my siblings and I were afraid, terrified of saying anything to anyone. Worried that we would be split up. Even though they acted in that way, I knew they loved us. All I ever wanted was for them to get help.

As my daughter and I approached the drive through border-crossing from the United States to Canada, I found myself paralyzed with fear. What if border patrol asks about her eye? What if she is taken away? The more I considered these thoughts, the more I cried. Jaya asked, "Mom, why are you crying?" I shared with her that not only did I feel sad about hitting her but I also felt emotional because I was having a hard time forgiving myself for something that really seemed unforgivable. I thought of the situation I had put her in. I asked her, "What did you tell your grandparents about what happened?"

She said, "Mom, I told them it was an accident." Her response transported me back to a time when I had to lie and pretend things were an *'accident'* in our home. My heart was heavy with my own childhood memories, yet I managed to keep it together as we crossed the border and as fate would have it, the Border Agent had no concerns. There I was driving down the highway, grappling with how to find a way to forgive myself. I had never hit either of the kids before. There had been plenty of times when the children tested the limits and had me feeling frustrated but this was the first time I had ever reacted with more than yelling.

The last time I had felt this way was back when Jaya was almost two and Ashaan was five. I was stressed. I was managing my business, raising two kids and dealing with the impact of having lost a significant amount of our financial equity. The stress was also taking a toll on my relationship with Paul. In the midst of everything, I lost my temper with Ashaan one day. Paul had bought one of those fancy face-creams for shaving. Something in the price point of $35 for a tiny bottle. I had left Ashaan in the tub, playing with his bath toys and making bubbles underwater like he often did. I returned after what seemed like just a few minutes. Ashaan had gotten his hands on the expensive cream and spilled out most of the bottle. It was one of those straw-that-broke-the-camel's-back moments. I lost it. I found myself yelling and screaming at him. He was of course scared and apologetic. I blamed myself for that moment and countless others where I had not been the 'perfect mom'.

Shortly after the 'shaving-creme' incident, I was introduced to a parenting method called 'The Nurtured Heart Approach'. It is based on rewarding and energizing your child for what they are doing well, rather than what they fail to do right. While I applied this to my interactions with the kids, I recognized I never applied it to myself. They say in life you are bound to make the same mistakes until you get the lesson. Back then, I knew reacting with frustration and anger was a mistake I had been repeating. What I didn't see was the impact of *beating-myself-up* over having reacted that way. I hadn't acknowledged that I had taken steps to change this behavior. Instead, I had been looking for others to validate the change. I was not seeing how forgiveness needed to come from within.

As Jaya and I were driving through Bellingham, the city where I grew up, my head was a flurry of thoughts. Somehow, amidst what felt like a tyranny of self-blame and self-judgment, I was grappling with how to forgive myself. I knew I wasn't the worst mom ever. I found myself shuffling back and forth between what had happened and the similarity to how I was raised; aware of the helpless feelings of my own childhood. My parents would often over react. The littlest thing would set them off. I would find myself walking on eggshells, trying to be 'perfect' to make them happy. It wasn't safe to make a mistake. Meanwhile, I had needed them. We had just moved from England and I was having trouble fitting in, making friends and keeping up with the adjustment. Instead, our house was chaotic and absolutely crazy at times. While my Dad yelled, my Mom made threats to her life. "I should just die," was a regular statement she screamed in the midst of an argument. Both had no sense of responsibility. Everything was always someone else's fault. It was one victim talking to another victim and with neither accepting responsibility there was no end in sight. Though I knew I didn't want to be this way, I had never experienced anything different.

As divine timing would have it, I was on the road that day to complete the project I had started. The 1947 Partition was a devastating time in India and had left a fundamental impact on my father. The interview process had made me deeply aware of his fear and skepticism from having seen so much horror. It brought out the worst in people, enough to take another person's life to protect one's own. Then there was my Mom. Her family was also deeply affected by the same event. My grandmother, unable to shake her anxiety and depression from all the terror, took her own life when my mom was only five. These brutal events undoubtedly shaped my parents' experiences of life, family and parenting. It has only been in recent years that we have started to talk about Post Traumatic Stress Disorder, something that may have affected them. As an adult, I recognize the impact that it had on them and on my childhood. Despite how I was raised, I asked myself, did I forgive them? Was I able to look past their faults? Could I get over their mistakes? Yes – it took time but I finally made peace and forgave them.

For as long as I can remember I have been the kind of person that didn't accept failure. I had had a successful career. It wasn't until parenting hit, coinciding with starting a new business that I discovered I did not accept failure. I did not know how to deal with and share failure. I had been raised in a household where I learned to fear failure, to keep it to myself – in an effort to avoid painful criticism and anger. Not seeing failure as a normal part of the growing process touched every aspect of my life. It kept me from sharing the challenges I faced and seeking help. It compounded the fear of judgment. It amplified the impact of the failure itself. I did not understand growth came from failure. It is only when you can forgive failure that the lesson and gifts emerge. You can leave behind judgment, have compassion, and stepping into responsibility. I recognized failure is the gateway to success when it is met with forgiveness.

When my kids were two and five, I had this epiphany. I remember thinking, "Wow, look at how much these guys have changed this year?" Jaya had learned to walk and Ashaan had learned to ride a bike. Both had extended their vocabulary. It was amazing to witness. I remember asking myself if my kids could grow this much in one year, why couldn't I do the same? So I made a declaration, I decided I was going to transform into a new person each year just like them. As well as watching my children grow, I have been witnessing my own growth. It has not been an easy journey. It has taken discovery, curiosity and wonder – qualities children embrace naturally. I have left no assumption unexamined. Where I had been previously blaming others, I have embraced responsibility. I have taken power back in all the ways I had unconsciously given it away. I have transformed my beliefs from being a victim to being at the source of any change I need and desire in my life. I forgave myself that day, for not getting parenting perfect every step of the way. I forgave myself for the habits I brought from childhood and I forgave my parents. Without forgiveness we lack compassion and without compassion we are left stuck with no way forward. Forgiveness clears the way.

IGNITE ACTION STEPS

*Parenting is a challenge. There will be times you will not know what to do. It is a road you will have never traveled.

*Be patient with yourself.

*Don't be afraid to fail. Do so and share your failures – and most importantly share them with your kids.

*Forgive yourself and you will forgive them.

*Children are here as teachers. They will trigger you. These triggers are our teaching moments. Be curious and ask yourself what has triggered you? What actually happened – separate what they said from what you made it mean and you will grow. Not only will you be celebrating their growth, you will be celebrating your own.

Bippan Dhillon - Canada
Entrepreneur, @b_growing

KARA ANN BLOCK

"Recognizing challenge as the ever-present gift for growth."

My hope is that by reading my story, you will feel the connection to your centered core and the desire to come from that place of health within, while supporting your child's place of wholeness and connection.

THE CULTIVATION OF LIFE IS THE PRACTICE

Birth..

My best is good enough...

What I first realized about becoming a woman, is the deep capacity that women have to not only nurture human beings, but to cultivate the entirety of growth and understanding. Birthing life into creation was the moment in my life I recognized the truest capacity of women. The amount of energy given to nurturing a human being is remarkable. The focus of energy necessary to cultivate healthy life is immeasurable. Herein lies the first new balance as a mother. How much is enough? How much do I give to the other? How much do I take care of self? Will my child be okay?

Before giving birth, a wise woman explained to me that contractions during childbirth was the inside of the uterus, twisting itself, like a small wet towel you twist, to remove all remnants of liquid. The purpose of the wring out is to pump all the nutrients from the baby's growing greenhouse, through the umbilical cord to the baby. Without this surge of life nutrients, the baby would be unable to make it through the birthing canal. From the moment the zygote arrives in the womb to the advent of a mini-human, the temporary baby-rental-space quadruples in its square footage.

By the time I moved to an organic farm, seven months pregnant, I was in search of the calmest, most 'back-to-the-land kind of transition to mothering' as possible. As I sat staring at the grassy hillside, I felt the direct Californian sunlight on my face. This was the first spring-day where no winter-chill was left in the air. My view from the bluff over the creek bed, was spectacular. There was a cow's skull hanging on the fence. This same view had, some years earlier, showed me a mountain lion gracefully walking along the far creekside. It has shown me many full moons, starry nights of wonder, planets aligned with slivered moons, hawks and one Christmas morning, a momma cow crying over her dead calf. The land gave me the deep connection I was always looking for, just in time to have the most monumental experience of conceiving, growing and birthing my first and only child.

Contraction–Expansion; Inhale–Exhale; Life force–Pranic breath; Expand–Contract…

Once having a baby and embarking upon the journey as a parent, it was clear that every human was once so new, so vulnerable and needing to be cared for and loved. Becoming a mother humanized me in a way I could not have imagined; building compassion for all beings as an intricate part of the greater community.

Your best is good enough.

I grew up running to the beach as much as possible, escaping the Southern California suburban life. I remember yearning for the kinetic energy of the ocean, almost addicted to that recharge my system felt from nature's fullness. The beginning of my fascination with the natural world, only magnified after child-birthing. How could existence be so deep? What is this thing geologists call 'deep time'? How could we be caught up in the shallows? How is it all interconnected? The world of nature is wondrous, producing geometric patterns consistent throughout all of nature. I began seeing the interweaving of these natural implications in the growth of people, society and culture.

Fumbling through sleep deprivation and grieving the loss of familiar freedoms, I was playing constant catch-up on developmental stage changes. Learning how to raise my child embarked me on the journey of re-raising myself into wholeness, through the love and guidance of motherhood, with the best co-collaborator of my life, my son Benjamin.

He pees, I freak.

It wasn't until my son was almost two years old that I realized the depth of the issues underlying my anger, trauma, upset, hurt, failure, immaturities and shame.

I had casually tried to place my son aboard the potty-train. Sick of diapers, ready for my son to enter underwear-land, I began to discuss peeing on the potty. I heard from friends with older boys, that starting them too early could backfire. A few days later, diapers were back on and I had moved past it for the time being. Benjamin, however, had felt my desire for independence, my hunger for past freedoms, my abnormally strong drive for success, my avoidance of failure, and my push....

This slight push literally lasted less than three days. A week and a half later, I threw up my hands in complete surrender to a rushed illusion of recapturing any ounce of independence. My previous self had vanished, and I wanted it to return desperately. Like most first-time moms, the surrender of childrearing was challenging, the result however, is the capacity to be beautifully present while providing mind, body and soul guidance to another living being, the greatest gift of all; Transition into Motherhood.

The expectation and forceful energy backfired, and its shrapnel penetrated my chakras. It was so dependent and yet so independent; such quick development and growth. Then more independence and dependence. My goal for both of us was, and still is, how do we find the homeostasis of interdependency, knowing we are forever changing? And knowing that my job, as a mom, is to understand my son's developmental stage accurately so I can meet him there.

What I didn't know then, is that with each changing stage, a different expansion and contraction begins in mothering. In order for me to meet my son where he was, whatever age he may be, I first had to clear the hurt, the pain, the shame and the fear of my own experience at those ages. Next, I needed to clear the lineage before me—those who had not healed their traumas before raising children.

Motherhood...

At the time, I had no idea this was at the root of my upset. Loss of self, someone taking something from me, an imbalance between giving and an expectation of receiving. My son must have felt all the pressure I place on my own accomplishments and therefore, his peeing on the potty. A week of difficulty with night-sleeping, nap time rituals, eating and putting on shoes followed. The basics of our once functioning system were crumbling as my internal defense-systems of safety began to crash like a thick whiskey glass. A slight chip here and there before realizing I needed to, in full trust, drop it from the highest point I could reach on this earth, to its demise. It would take many more years to keep shattering that glass. It is still underway. I will keep you posted.

That day, the Groundhog Day of sucking-it-up, seven loads of laundry, struggling for gratitudes, dashing to be outside in nature, cooking, cleaning, was just another day. I finished the housework, preparation, laundry and all the fresh new bedding for my tempurpedic bed, my therapeutic topper mattress, my Restoration Hardware down-comforter. I love my bed. I also had just finished bathing my cutie-pie. The one who had been resisting me for days. I placed him naked on my bed. Through all my tidying up, I had forgotten to bring the after-bath diaper into my room. I said to him, "If you have to go potty, just scoot off the bed and go to the potty, I will be right back." I grabbed the diaper like jumping-jack-flash and when I returned, he had peed on my bed- through all my hard work and comfort. I got the most cross I had ever been with him. I banished him to his room and through gritted teeth explained that I was very angry.

The next day we fell apart, only to be put back together in a way I never could have imagined.

A brand new day, wiggle your toes. We woke with the sunrise, per farm-life usual. Dad went to work and the resistance against eating was stronger than ever. I was lucky enough to have a dear friend living close by on a ranch. I drove with my son, past California rolling hills and total beauty, to her house and resigned as mother for the day. I handed the job over to her and sat in all my emotions. Emotions too big to understand. Feeling so rich and full, I thought I may explode from the intersection of love and pain. The expanding and contracting I had felt through child-birthing felt like the physicality of the same expanding and contracting I was experiencing now, emotionally. Somehow, I know it was growing me, growing us, though it felt devastating. I watched, I breathed, I surrendered, my control fading. I witnessed my son be fine with no food. I allowed my resistance to our schedule to wash away. I had done my best and it was good enough. Not only could I not control outcomes, I didn't need to control anything, and I decided to be okay with all of that. The spiritual practice of accepting what is.

With my invisible energetic acceptance, he returned to the natural rhythms of being. My son finally ate when he was so hungry, being super picky was now a thing of the past. My son finally fell asleep, when he was tired enough. The time and space continuum started to synchronize and recalibrate.

Once asleep, I picked him up and put him in my arms, reclaiming my motherhoodship. We returned to the farm. He slept on my bed for the remainder of his nap. I continued integrating the contraction and expansion of the experience, knowing that this process, coupled with surrender was the only way back to presence and center. It is always the breath that leads to moments of grace.

Birthing is a metaphor for life. There were many moments throughout this memorable day, where my breath returned me to me. In all honesty, it was the only thing I had left. Within this cross-section of duality, the practice is the oneness. I drifted off into my practice and landed on a thought plane as my son continued to sleep. My birthing experience was the flight that my mind decided to ride on. It was, clearly, our beginning. I used to talk to him while he was inside me, sharing with him that we are a team and our learning to work together will dictate our experience of life with one another. Birthing was our first go-round. We did good. Because of my practice, I knew deep down that this broken potty-training train was another experience for us to find our togetherness, our team strategy for life. For the duration of my mental flight, I explored regions of cultivating a healthy life from far east Buddhist practices, to western freedoms of individuality. How do you achieve these states of being with the ever-flowing contradiction of human and soul, other and self? I had finally answered for myself.

Love...

Love is always the answer. But how do we love when we are fearful? How do we love when we react from hurt? How do we *not* evoke trauma when we have been traumatized? How do we parent through our children's resistance? How do we heal our own fear-triggered resistances? Being truly alive is the cultivation of life itself.

My meditative flight concluded as I noticed my son waking. We snuggled. He still is the coziest thing I ever did see. As the love-energy coursed through me, potent and visceral, I saw my suffering was not suffering at all. It was clear that my child's resistance had poked into all of my dark, unknown places. I lay there with my son in the grace of release. As he woke from his rest, I don't say anything. I showed my love through my presence and my physical closeness. He turned and looked deep in my eyes. I ask him, "Are you upset with Mommy because I got mad at you yesterday?"

His "Yes!" – is the beginning of resolution...

I build on his one-word answer, "I am really sorry."

He put his arm around me, "I'm sorry, too." He took off his diaper, looked right at me, walked himself to the bathroom and went potty, never to put another diaper on again.

In that moment, in taking responsibility for myself, I realized this experience was the first time where I had to stand still and not run from the resistance of looking deep into my own unknown. In that surrender, in healing, we healed.

A different and deeper gratitude for my son and for the process, were seeds planted that day. Expanding and contracting together, we managed to refine this developmental healthy place of homeostasis. A place where he felt heard, seen and respected because his resistance demanded it and so did mine. A place where I felt honored and where he met my feelings. By accepting, allowing and feeling, I was guided into the freedom of *Agape* (principled) love, which healed and allowed the release of past pain and trauma. In turn, we rejoined the natural place of human existence. A space of what is, of all being, of peace and of health. This grew our mutual respect, understanding and deep gratitude for our love and its power to transform. I intuitively knew that by continuing to show up in this way, to meet my pain and trauma head on, that once closed void from within, could burst open at the seams. That connection reinforced and assured me that by surrendering, you create what you need.

What I realized is that I had to choose to go inside. The funny thing is, every time I show up for myself, family and community, the resistance diminishes. By surrendering to what is, the next contraction always appears until the life cycle of the trauma is complete. The choice of actually going there creates the expansion, the surrender, the awareness and the growth within, essentially the rebirthing of self. This parental love integrating with self-awareness is conscious parenting.

Birthing holds on to this accepting like a big hug, not wanting to let go, until all the life force and nutrients pump again through the umbilical cord to sustain and create another life. I believe the same is true for growing children and ourselves. There is not one without the other. This becomes the life-cycle journey...

Ignite Action Steps

My gift is a visualization for You to experience:

There was once a girl. She twirled in the sunlight and danced under the stars. She found herself so thankful for the sky and sun. This was the beginning of her presence, her peace with life. She thanked the stars for their appearance. Like musicians on a stage, the stars entertained her and inspired her. She found awe in the vastness of her surroundings. She knew when she was thankful, she was part of the whole, that her peace was the peace of the galaxies, of existence itself. That connection was her connection to self, to all.

She went walking through the stream, feeling the cold water on her feet and the unknowingness of the stream bed under her toes. She had a moment of fear, uncertainty about the unknown. She trusted. She let go of the "un." Certain, she felt known. She grew. She moved past a thought. A thought can take us on one path or another. Her gratitude for the Earth and her awe of the ethers, allowed her to let her fearful thought float away down the river like a fallen twig from a tree. In this, she was alive.

The girl came to a cliff edge overlooking the valley. A sunflower that had already lived through its prime had scattered its seeds around the fallen stem. She was tired from her day and the hot sun. By taking the time and planting the seeds she was the cultivator. In this she realized her own strength in showing up to participate. She swirled and twirled and ran about, ecstatic about growing her surroundings, until she was out of breath. It took some time, but she found her breath again. In breathing, she felt her lungs fill, air moved through her and calmed her body.

Again and again she stayed focused on her breath, until she wasn't thinking of stars or sunlight, flowers or the growth to come, the space or the view. She was just breathing, not even realizing that without this breath she would have no existence at all. And so, she continued to breathe. In this, she found total freedom.

In that gratitude, she cultivated herself. In that trust, she freed herself. In letting go of fearful thinking, she awoke herself. In that aliveness, she found herself.

Kara Ann Block - USA
Lead Creative & Process Designer Dakine Creatives,
Co-Founder Land of Dreams.
Karablock.com, Dakinecreatives.com

JODI ANNE LAW

"Heal yourself, play to your strengths, walk the walk,
talk the talk and your children will follow."

It is my hope that every parent finds and establishes a way to be in their flow. And then from that flow realize children are on their own journey. Your role as a parent is merely to guide and encourage your children to play to their strengths so they too will be in their flow.

TALK THEIR TALK, WALK THEIR WALK

From the start, my husband and I formed a habit in our marriage to *his* liking. I paid no heed to the more than obvious warning signs. Friends and family dropped away whilst we moved thirteen times in our 20 year marriage. Cut off from family support with too little time to develop friendships and community, I was alone. I was never clear on what I wanted and hadn't even thought about being a mum and having a family. The habit of disappearing inside myself and the pattern of spiralling into depression, started at age fourteen at boarding school. There I became an expert at internalizing things. Both at school and as I became aware in my marriage, I felt trapped, suffocated, like a caged animal; I never felt good enough or that I belonged and certainly never felt loved. Alone and abandoned was the norm. To cope at school, I just stopped eating. Everyone commented on how good I looked as my chubbiness vanished. I stuck my head in books, did well at school and I was praised for that too. But I was dying inside.

With those beliefs I went to university, earning my nursing degree. After graduation I decided to travel. But whatever I did, I couldn't get away from that same mindset.

Returning from my travels and totally disillusioned with life, I met a man 13 years my senior. Thinking he would be the answer to my sad, sorry life, I married him. There must have been something between us at the beginning but over time it grew to be a distant memory. We did everything together. Everything. I felt suffocated.

Twelve years after the vows, along came a baby girl. Having no community connection, my guide during pregnancy and childbirth was a book. Morning sickness and having milk-engorged breasts are the most vivid memories of that time. Day three in the hospital, getting over the blood loss and breastfeeding complications, I lay next to my little girl, marvelling at her perfectly manicured nails and long eyelashes, seeing the perfection, charm and beauty in this little creature I was to have in my life. I gazed at her in awe. I didn't want to go home because he controlled the house and controlled me.

Two years later, along came a little boy and it became more obvious the focus was no longer on me. I was cast aside. I was living in a household with a husband and two beautiful children, having no input into their lives – still feeling trapped and isolated. My designated role was to make money and walk the dog. He worked from home with an intermittent income and took on the role as 'Mr. Mum'. The children would eat their meals together early; we never ate as a family. Often I'd leave for work before they woke and by the time I got home they were in bed. When I did spend time with them and asked about their day, I was told, "Don't talk to them like that, don't ask 20 questions. They'll tell you when they are ready."

I wasn't allowed to play with them because they would expect that from him when I wasn't there. When we did play we would all squeal with delight, wrestling and laughing together. He would tell us off. We were three children and he was a sensible adult. With his office in the living room, there was no escaping the toxic energy. I didn't want to come home from work.

Next came our differences over the sleeping arrangements. Our initial intention as new parents was for my daughter to sleep in her own room in a cot, progressing to a bed when my son came along. Only my little girl had other plans. She would only sleep when she was in bed with us. To make life easier, we allowed it. Somewhere along the line, my son decided he didn't want to miss out, so there were four of us. Realizing this was not sustainable, something had to give. With no discussion, I was ousted to the back guest room with the dog.

Every day I walked Toffee, our mongrel terrier dog. Rescued from a rubbish bin at birth as our first 'child', he and I had a strong bond. One afternoon, he set off with his usual strut, tail held high, wagging back and forth but this time pulling on his leash. He led me to a house where he promptly sat himself down, refusing to move and started to whine. The owner of the house came out with his two dogs, one of which was a bitch in heat. This began many intimate walks between us through the botanic gardens, discussing the universe and me realizing my dreams with a man who made me feel alive. The impact of being seen Ignited something inside me, giving me the power to question my miserable existence and take action.

After a life-time of feeling trapped and 20 years of having no control over my family life or babies, I took a suitcase and two canvases and with complete heaviness, I walked down the front steps one at a time towards the end of my marriage. With tears running down my face, I waited for my one friend with a broken heart, feeling as though it had been pierced with a knife, then twisted. I felt violated, vulnerable and completely exhausted. I had nothing left to fight with. I hadn't told my children I was leaving, I didn't know what to say. I left because I needed to work on me. I was of no use to anyone as I was, let alone my children. I needed to show up as the best version of me, to be there for them. To say I had a plan would be lying. I just knew that for the first time in my life there was a speck of light at the end of a very long, dark tunnel. I felt Hope.

When I left, I hadn't been alone with my children for almost three years. He was that controlling. I was told he would have to chaperone me when I did see the kids. My first outing with them was to the botanic gardens, where he dropped us off and picked us up. I spent two whole hours with my children on my own and revelled in it, letting them lead. We played chase, watched ducks in the lily ponds, observed the turtles and interacted with other people as opposed to utter control. It was magic. It was freedom.

Not long after the separation, he decided to move to the city. I had post-graduate studies to finish that would keep me stationary for a few months but that did not deter him from leaving immediately. My reuniting with them three months later meant I had missed my son's sixth birthday. During my visits to see the children, everyone was on guard, their father would loom over us, not even allowing them to talk freely using their own words. They were always glancing at him for approval in case they spoke out of turn. Three months is a long time in the life of children aged six and eight. My son was very wary of me. He was nice and polite but he didn't trust me. I'd sit and watch him make lego models and ask him what he was doing at school, trying desperately to make a connection. I wanted to just hold both of them in my arms, let them know how much I loved them and never let them go.

The bond my son had with his father was very strong. Emphasis was placed on how brilliant he was with the private tuition his father paid for in math, English, Chinese, piano and guitar. Then the cricket, football and tennis lessons helped to reinforce this. Once they moved to Melbourne, then came the expensive clothes – his father dressing him up in jackets and ties that he was wearing for their 'café breakfast' time. I felt so small and humiliated whenever I visited and with each encounter I felt a piece of my heart being cut out, a brick wall getting thicker and thicker. I visited like this for a couple of hours at a time for two months before I could coax my son to come and visit me.

Doing what society suggested, I took a casual nursing job in a large teaching hospital. It was the job that got me out of bed each morning. Each day on remote control, I walked 45 minutes to work. Long hours in another toxic environment and a $200 dollar a week drop in pay meant I felt some satisfaction seven months later when I handed in my notice. I took a full time nursing job in a large, private hospital in the cardiac area which would require inhouse training.

Things were looking up, so I rented a two bedroom apartment close to my children which cost me a third of my pay. In the nursing trade you can get by but you certainly have no luxuries. I was working full-time, emergency on call for a cardiac catheter lab and totally exhausted. When I did see my children, I felt so inadequate I couldn't do the parenting thing properly. When on call, they couldn't stay with me because if I was called in, there was no one to look after them. I was stressed 24/7.

Not leaving any stone unturned and recognizing the ongoing stress as a danger to myself, I took out a mental health plan and saw a psychologist. At the end of twelve months I was still in my same *sorry* story. I still wanted every area of my life to change. I went on antidepressants. All they did was numb everything, solving nothing. It was time to take the bull by the horns and listen to me.

I moved to the country believing I would have more time to work on me. Also, because of schooling complications, I took advantage of an opportunity for my daughter to come and live with me. We grabbed the chance. She moved up for the beginning of the school year. Ahead of us lay the task of learning to live together. The scenario wasn't ideal, with me waking her as I walked out the door to work. She had to get herself to school and back. There was quite a challenge in her lack of input into household duties which caught me unaware and created conflict. There was a lot to alter if it was going to work for us. At the end of our first term together, she spent the second week of the holidays with her father. The day before she was to return I rang to find out the train she would be on. His casual conversation defied the intensity of anger and rage I felt as he calmly told me she wasn't coming back. He had pulled the rug from under me again. My way of coping was to go to bed for several days, heavily depressed.

Fortunately, I had just started a yoga and meditation teacher-training course which ran one weekend a month, 13 hours each day, for 12 months. On the first weekend, I was the angry opinionated one, full of venom and rage about life and everything in it. Yet, right from the start these weekends became my sanctuary. I didn't want to leave and go back to my 'real world'. There I was, surrounded by amazing, gentle people, full of love and in search of their truth. I opened up to every piece of the love they offered.

I also started a Diploma in Energy Psychology, which meant I began earnestly working on me. The door had been opened into a new world and my life began to change.

My kids began coming up every second weekend, so for the first time I started to get to know my children on my terms. We went for bike rides and picnics, played at the lake or hung out with friends. They enjoyed simple, fun things they had never done before. I got a job in an area of my choosing and surrounded myself with a fantastic group of friends.

Life ran relatively smoothly for 18 months but one thing you can be sure about in life is change. Unbeknownst to me, decisions were being made about my son's education. He had been accepted into Sydney Boys Grammar school and his father was making plans to move there. I was informed of this in the shopping center car park. The four of us were standing there when I just screamed and swore at the injustice of what I was hearing. Later that week, when I was more composed, I rang the school to find out how the process could get this far without my knowledge. They were very apologetic, assuming I knew as the correspondence had been going to both parents.

Six months later their father, originally from Britain, took both children on holiday to the UK. An exam at a Grammar school there had been arranged for my son without my knowledge. He was accepted. I refused permission for him to go. How could I agree to them living on the other side of the world? The following year the exams were repeated in the UK, again he was accepted. My son came back saying, 'Mum, can I give this a go?' I was worn down by refusing him and feeling bullied by his dad, yet I realized this might stabilize their lives. It might also allow us all to ground in one solid place and establish consistency for myself and them. So I agreed to let them both go. They packed up and left for the UK in May.

My intention was to go for a holiday at the start of their new school year, return to Australia and apply for the unusual 'Access Rights To Child' visa for Britain. I went through experts to ensure a smooth twelve week process. Fifteen weeks later, I still hadn't heard but had the confidence to pack up my rental property knowing I had to leave quickly to meet the visa's activation deadline. In week seventeen I received a phone call and made the two hour train journey to Melbourne to arrive at the stipulated 3 pm appointment where I was supposed to receive my visa. I organized for my belongings to be collected and bought a plane ticket to Manchester. With a feeling of excitement, I opened my parcel from the visa office. Frantically wanting to see the visa, I ripped the envelope open...only to see... no visa inside. My heart sank, anger rose and a deep feeling of defeat engulfed me. I felt betrayed and insignificant.

Dealing with a visa expert brought the devastating, bureaucratic reason to light. With tears running down my face and overdosing on yoga and energy healing, I still felt full of rage. I resigned from my job and bought a ticket to a month long conference with a group of people who live their life through infinite possibility through inner connection, in Tallinn, Estonia. My daughter flew and joined me there. I didn't feel confident with my parenting situation but was surrounded by a community who held my values. If the Universe couldn't get me to them on my own, then I would use this new community to assist me in connecting with them. I needed that comfort and so did my daughter. It was as though, for the whole time I had been working on me... it was for this very moment, a whole month of uninterrupted time together. Two weeks in Greece followed, with my son joining us for fun and laughter.

I returned to Australia alone. I had to wait another six months to apply for a British visa, then three months for it to be processed. Whilst waiting, the kids and I corresponded via Viber and Skype. The frequency depended on the seasons which determined the time differences. It was better for me to ring at night but if they weren't in a talkative mood the call ended on a low note. I kept myself very busy. I returned to work at the hospital. However, things were deteriorating as management was being restructured. Micromanaging dominated the environment and I didn't stay around. I had bigger fish to fry.

Living out of a suitcase since moving out of the rental property, I spent five months in a livable shed at the back of a friend's house. Surprisingly, I felt safe. I had my own space and company if needed. Finally, fifteen weeks later, I received the visa! I was ecstatic, despite the grueling process and time it took. None of that mattered now, despite my inner fears. I was on my way to being with them.

I'm now living in the UK. I hadn't realized how much of an impact not being with my kids had had on me. My heart feels full. I see my role as being there for my children, offering an alternative view of the world by simply being my authentic self. Being around them, I offer them guidance and they teach me. They are on their own journey and I accept that. They chose me as their mother to learn whatever their soul needs. I honor that.

At fourteen, I had begun a path that didn't serve me because of beliefs I'd taken on. It wasn't until 30 years later, because of my children, I started steering myself back on course. All the pain I went through to get back on track has been part of my journey. Now I show up in life fully and present for my children so they too can have the opportunity to talk their talk and walk their walk in their power. I invite you to do the same.

IGNITE ACTION STEPS

Transform by healing yourself first - Start to learn about yourself. At any moment ask: What am I feeling emotionally? What am I feeling physically? What am I feeling energetically? What am I thinking? Just notice. Journal if it helps with your flow.

What stories are you telling yourself? Are they serving you? If not, change them.

Strengthen - do one thing intentionally, for yourself, every day, no matter how small eg. take a bath, do a yoga class, walk on the beach or amongst the trees. Fill your cup first, so you can give to others.

Connect with the 'Real You' by being creative, being grateful and meditating.

Jodi Anne Law - Australia
Life Energy Coach, Author, Speaker
https://jodiannelaw.com/

MADALINA PETRESCU

"Parenting offers the greatest gift of all: the mirror
to see our true self within."

My intention is that through my story you can discover that connection is the portal to a deep, loving relationship with your child. This connection becomes possible when we as parents remain grounded in our higher selves, so we can attune to our childrens' emotional needs with awareness and compassion. By seeing and accepting them for their authentic selves, they grow into their loving, empowered, and resilient selves.

RETURN TO CONNECTION

There are beautiful moments which are so stirring and life-changing, that we can never forget---experiences which carry lifetimes of joy, such as the day our children are born. I still remember the birth of my daughters, Sofia and Elise, like it was yesterday. I recall the blissful moments cradling them in my arms for the first time, inhaling the smell, and feeling the sensation of initial skin to skin contact between mother and child. There is perfection in this gift of connection, marking the beginning of a precious bond.

Connection is one of my greatest life values. It is as important as oxygen. Why? It's because I know well what it was like to feel the opposite, separation at such a deep level it motivated me to desire it like air. I was nine when an experience forever changed the trajectory of my life. I grew up in Romania under Ceausescu's communist regime. Freedom was scarce under his tyranny. I remember my parents having late night hushed conversations which frightened me. They were planning to escape but told no one...until my father's job as a surgeon provided him the opportunity to work in Libya. My mom was able to visit him, and soon after our family received the life-changing phone call. The only thing I grasped from my mother was that they were not coming back. I became speechless with fear.

My grandmother explained the devastating news to us. Her voice quivered and her eyes flooded with tears as she relayed the shocking news: my parents had declared their escape. My younger brother and I were forbidden by the government to join them, which shocked my parents. We did not know when we would see them again. My ears heard the truth, but my young heart didn't. I felt the floor dissolve underneath me, leaving me lost. A heaviness rolled across my body paralyzing me. I felt I would die at the reality of being separated from my own parents. There was nothing anyone could do. Now being a mom, I can't imagine the trauma my parents must have felt to be torn from us.

Two long years later, thanks to Grandma's persistent effort and bribes to the secret police, we were granted approval to join our parents who had immigrated to the USA. Our parents were waiting as we got off the plane. Once our eyes met, the four of us started wildly running towards each other. Tears of joy were profuse in our reunion embrace.

Our happy reunion, however, was quickly tempered due to the harsh reality that my parents had lost all their financial valuables in the escape process. They had no choice but to work multiple jobs to put food on the table, therefore, we barely saw them. As they were off working, I faced the culture shock on my own. Kids rejected and made fun of me for being different, and barely able to speak English. I felt alone and disconnected from this new world.

From that moment in childhood, connection became vitally important. Years later I deliberately married a wonderful husband to whom I felt deeply connected. Prior to having our children, we would dream endlessly of having the most meaningful deep bond with our babies.

I had the right intention, but life happened. I became a mother while I was building my career in medicine. Cardiology is intense, often dealing with complex life and death situations. I was the director of Echo Lab and head of Structural Imaging. I served on the Board and Workforce Committee.

As a faculty member I was asked to deliver presentations at conferences. Often I did not see my girls in the mornings or take them to school. Late night work hours also meant missing precious moments over dinners to share school stories. Prepping for medical talks on the weekends and being on call stole opportunities for cherished time with my family. I had no clue how to balance work with family. Distracted by my desire to succeed in my job, I became a workaholic. I lost perspective and family took a backseat. I was living in a state of survival, arriving home exhausted from the workday. Even during family time, I would be on the phone responding to texts and emails, earnest to be there for my colleagues and patients.

There were multiple "cries for help" from my girls, but I failed to recognize them. Over time, my older daughter Sofia began speaking less and less, her face looked sadder and sadder. She started 'vanishing acts' in which she would hide in some corner of the house. We would have to look endlessly to find her. Elise was the opposite. She became louder, more demanding. She was having impulsive screaming fits at the smallest thing that didn't go her way. Dealing with their disruptive behaviors was more than hard. I relied on traditional parenting methods to discipline and correct their misbehaving, but nothing worked. I felt exasperated! Until one distinct evening, when an ignite moment pushed the edge of what needed to be seen and changed within me!

It was a typical situation. I had arrived home late from work in my usual rushed, anxious state, just in time for dinner. Sitting down at the table, I started probing the girls with questions, feeling my own desperate need to connect with them. I glanced at Sofia, who was seven at the time, and saw her sad, long face. Concerned, I asked her to tell me what was wrong. All she said was, "Nothing." Meanwhile, Elise, age 5, began tugging on my shirt to listen to her drawn-out story from school while jumping up and down, spilling peas all over the floor. "Elise you're making a mess!" I exclaimed, raising my voice. My husband nudged me, pointing at the empty chair in which Sofia had been sitting. Ahh! Again! Feeling that familiar pang of deep worry, I got up to search for her. I eventually found her in the bedroom closet. Her tearful face was covered by her hands. I reached to touch her, pleading with her to talk. She retreated, shaking her head. It was like she didn't trust me. "Are you sad because I have to leave for the medical conference tomorrow?" No response. "Mama feels hurt when you don't talk to me." I did not realize I was making it about me, using emotional coercion to get her to open up.

Meanwhile, a commotion was developing upstairs. I could hear Elise screaming, making note of her perfect timing, exactly when I was focused on Sofia. I ran upstairs to find Elise stomping and hollering wildly. My husband had taken away her electronics. Despite my ongoing efforts to correct her behavior with discipline, all was in vain. Time outs only seemed to make her more frustrated. Punishments such as taking her toys away only provoked her resentment towards me. I was also concerned her behaviors were suspicious of attention hyperactivity deficit disorder (ADHD), considering her overactivity, impulsive outbursts, distractibility, and difficulty controlling her emotions.

Frustrated by her misconduct, I run out of patience. I begin to scold her "bad" behavior. Defiantly, she looked at me directly in the eye and angrily shouted, "Go away, Mama, I don't trust you!" Her assertive voice sent shudders down to my bones. I opened my mouth but could not speak. Her words threw me into quicksand, with nothing to hold on to. That moment my aggravation turned into sadness and powerlessness. I realized how utterly distant I felt from the girls. The one thing I desired so much, felt so unattainable.

I could no longer look her in the face. I backed away and headed to my bedroom to escape the anguish I was feeling. In the doorway I saw a note in Sofia's scribbled handwriting. This was not the first time she had left me tiny notes to communicate. This one was asking: *What's more important to you? Choose: (a) work or (b) family.* Her innocent question created abysmal guilt within, realizing her plea was for me to choose. I went into the bathroom, crashed on the floor, and did the only thing I could: cry and cry more. How did I get here? How did I fail so miserably as a mother was all I could feel.

I had previously contemplated the possible detrimental impact of my unhealthy work/life balance. This time all I felt it in my heart was a deep gnawing ache. Focused on my career, I stopped being emotionally present with the girls. The disciplinary parent skills were not working. On the contrary, the more I tried to change them the worse their behavior became. My attempt to control them fueled their resentment toward me, causing them to push me away, widening our separation. After crying out all my tears, I pulled myself up and looked in the mirror. Who am I kidding? This is not working.

I saw my own reflection staring back, my eyes challenging me to look deeper to see through the discomfort and discover the truth. It dawned on me. What if I had it backwards? What if the path to my connection to the girls was not about making them the focus of change but rather me? Instead of trying to fix *them* what if I focused on the way *I* showed up as a mother?

I felt brave enough to ask more: What if their behavior is not the problem to punish, but rather an expression of their unmet emotional needs? What if the external behavior is the messenger of the internal cause which we as parents are meant to decipher? Instead of questioning how to get Sofia to stop disappearing or how to curb Elise's impulsive acts, I ask why is Sofia feeling the need to disappear? Why is Elise acting out? I dared further. What kind of an energetic and emotional environment was I creating that might be contributing to my girls' behaviors? Asking those questions felt right.

The pain of emotional separation from my girls reflected how I felt as a young child when I was separated from my parents. History repeating itself, evoked a burning desire to do whatever it took to become the best mother possible. I allowed myself to see the truth I had been running away from. Before I could genuinely connect to my girls, I had to connect to myself. Only then would I have the capacity to have an authentic relationship with them.

Inspired by Socrates' words "know thyself," I plunged into the greatest journey of all: the one within. To discover and connect with my true self, I read books by the masters of spirituality and experts on emotional healing and conscious parenting. I read Eckhart Tolle, Wayne Dyer, Dr. Shefali, Don Miguel Ruiz, Esther Hicks, Lau Tzu, and more. I attended spiritual retreats which helped me to process unhealed emotional experiences and connect to my spirit. I went through a conscious parenting program and earned my coaching certificate. I engaged in a morning ritual that involved meditation to enter a state of presence and elevated consciousness. I also cared for my emotional well-being by journaling to process my feelings. I spent time outdoors in silent self-reflection.

I felt the answers flow through me as I tapped into my inner wisdom. The girls became my greatest life teachers. Their behaviors mirrored my unconscious patterns which needed my awareness to process, heal, and transcend. Only from this space of inner presence and grounded in my higher self, would I have the capacity to see beneath the girls' external behavior, to recognize their real emotional needs.

Sofia's pattern of disappearing was an external expression of the pain she felt internally. She felt so insignificant she could vanish. Seeing me making my career #1 priority, she did not feel she mattered. Hence, she did not feel important to me and consequently in life. Her soul wanted to be found, seen, and loved by me.

Sofia became my teacher to help me get my act together, to create a healthy work/life balance. I had to authentically make her feel loved and seen, not just through words, but through my actions and choices. I committed from that point on, the family will always be more important than my job. I made radical changes at work by creating boundaries in my schedule to ensure I either drove the girls to school or picked them up, which made them extremely happy. I developed a rule of no electronics during family activities, after work hours, or on weekends. I started being more selective about work projects by holding off on saying 'yes' only after consideration of how that would impact family time.

It was not easy for Sophia to open up but I persevered. I experimented with different ways to connect. When talking did not work, I expressed my love through artwork and writing letters, asking her how I could help. The letters worked magic; we started exchanging notes like two schoolgirls. I also slipped love-cards in her lunch box. Our closeness strengthened. We began having daily intimate talks, giving her my undivided attention. I'd snuggle with her and give her massages. Now I am happy we have such a deep, trusting relationship. Her vanishing acts have ceased, and have been replaced by her vibrant laughter, lots of hugs and one-on-one, soulful conversations.

As for Elise, I discerned her tantrums were her way of protesting my parenting approach, in which I was trying to change her true nature. Her animated, determined, energized self wanted to unfold but I was rejecting her natural inclinations by putting her in the box of my expectation. Wow, her fierce spirit was a close resemblance to the younger me! She wanted to be as she was, not as I wanted her to be. As for her ADHD-ish behavior, the issue was not a deficit of attention but rather of authentic connection to me, and hence to herself. This lack had led to her inner agitation, which physically manifested as hyperactivity and emotional outbursts.

My path back to Elise was initially met with resistance, yet I was patient. The answer was through play and games. I surrendered to her guiding the fun and adventures no matter how silly. I allowed myself to match her spontaneous, energetic nature wholeheartedly. We would do dance-offs, jump up and down on the couch, make funny faces, and tickle each other until we laughed so hard it hurt. I let her choose her outfits and her hairstyle no matter how eccentric. As our connection through play deepened, her impulsive act-outs dissolved and she started to feel free and safe to be herself.

Over time, our family life has evolved toward beautiful unity. My journey within deepened my own connection, which has cleared the path to see and bond with the girls. I continue to look within for my opportunities to embody the calm, conscious energy which allows me to meet my girls' needs. We prioritize our quality time above anything else. Every weekend we plan a family-only activity to strengthen our bonds and enjoy being together. We love to be adventurous, play outdoors, go camping, paint, build Legos, chase each other around the house laughing hysterically, and read books for hours. We also created one-on-one quality time with each girl to deepen their connection with each parent.

As parents, we have an amazing opportunity to discover our unresolved inner work, reflected through our relationship with our children. Our role and impact is not a minimal one;the way our kids relate to us determines their relationship with Life and themselves. I invite you to have the courage to look within and embark on an inner journey of personal growth and awareness with your kids. This magical key of connection will unlock boundless possibilities for a healthy, harmonious, close family bond!

IGNITE ACTION STEPS

*Lean in with curiosity when your child displays an unfavorable behavior. Rather than Focus on the desired change by asking, "What is the unmet emotional need beneath this behavior? What is my child saying to me? How am I contributing to their behavior?"

*The capacity to decipher their emotional needs is only possible when we respond from a state of open-heart. It is natural to be triggered by our kids when they are acting out. Resist the urge to react to their behavior, which only intensifies it. Take a deep breath to ground yourself in your higher conscious self and respond by asking "What is going on within the child that I need to tune into?" Rather than giving them a time out, it is healthier for you to take a time out. Remove yourself if possible and safe to do so. Reflect on what is coming up for you *emotionally*, which is being triggered; direct your attention within.

*Create a daily ritual to connect within and expand your consciousness creating an open, loving, energetic container for your kids. Establish emotional well being through free journaling your feelings and awaken spirit with meditation. Become attuned to your kids' needs when you are grounded in a state of presence and awareness.

*Play! Drop to your kids' playful childlike level and let them guide you to whatever game they desire. Be silly and let go!

Madalina Petrescu Agafi - USA
Cardiologist at Swedish Medical Center, Seattle
www.heartq.com

MICHAELA DE SAPIO-YAZAR

"Open your mind to the world of a child. Ask, guide, awaken...
take their hand and follow them into their universe."

My story is about learning how to make decisions for the benefit of my children, not based on what I believe, but on their hopes and goals. Hearing and acknowledging children on the path to adulthood, we as parents can offer guidance versus control. I believe this allows them to grow at their pace and in the direction they seek. It is my wish you open your heart and mind to walk beside your children on their path, enjoying the adventure of exploring life alongside them.

HEARING THE CHILDREN

My journey began when I first realized my children had similar traits to me. I have Dyslexia and they showed signs of those with Dyslexia.

What I observed when my three children were young: one was artistic, loved to draw and create things from whatever he found around him; the second built structures beyond his age with his LEGO sets; the third loved to draw and paint. All three children, had an immense curiosity for learning and hated going to school. As preschoolers, they experienced moments when they loved school and moments when they didn't. Their personalities, and needs continuously challenged my perspective of what parenting meant and caused me to reinvent myself.

When my children were born, I was a University student. My goal has always been to keep a balance between caring for and connecting with them while finishing university, later building my own path in life. As our family grew and the children went from one developmental stage to another, I would search for answers, looking for the best path for our family. Bookstores became our hangout. Parks were our places to release energy. Libraries turned into our research center.

The first important parenting decision I made was to breast-feed on demand. My mother had shared her experience, "When you were born, we were told to bottle feed on a rigid three-hour schedule. I'd get upset when I saw you were hungry before the next feeding. I wish I would have breast fed," my mother confessed. When I had children, I never questioned the idea. I started breastfeeding on the first day... From there, each decision I made be a child-centered decision.

As my children went through toddlerhood, I quickly realized normal time-outs or setting limits without an explanation, stressed all of us. What caused the meltdowns was often hard to gauge. I discovered any imbalance, too much or too little of anything, not the right food, too little food, too much food, too little sleep, too much sun, not enough outside time could trigger negative behavior. Punishing them wasn't a natural consequence. I found it better to hold them on my lap and connect, so my time-outs were about emotionally supporting and understanding. I gave up on making rules and chores mandatory or assigning unrealistic jobs to keep things in order. I focused more on creating responsibility towards oneself and one's own things. That was facilitated by setting solid daily routines. Everyone thrived.

My oldest often had difficulty falling asleep and still does. Our habit when he was young, was to read bedtime stories. He has continued reading and/or using audiobooks to this day. Reading books at bedtime has turned out to be very helpful and better than just requiring our son fall asleep.

The type of food they ate changed as they grew. I ensured they received a widely varied diet with breastfeeding until they were weaned. Trying ethnic foods from many cultures and avoiding traditional baby foods was important to me. To my dismay, my middle child, who ate all types of food until he was two, became a picky eater, suddenly interested in a few very specific things. My oldest would show off that he could eat anything, and the baby did not mind either way, until later when she also became picky. My solution was to cook one meal for all of us, with a variety of dishes where everyone found something they would eat. To keep their pallet broad,

I introduced the 'eat-one-bite' idea, "If you do not like it you don't have to eat it, but at least try one bite" This worked well to reintroduce foods and try new ones.

When disagreements arose between the children, our approach was to find the common ground, or if necessary, agree to disagree and move on. This applied to games, toys, activities, (kept in the living room as communal property) and all other objects which could create a dispute. My kids were good at communicating their thoughts and feelings; they also respected having healthy disagreements. This helped me from a parenting perspective because it gave me insight into the situation and more to work with when I needed to step in as a referee or arbitrator of the discussion. My parenting style meant stepping back and trying to guide the solution. The younger years were about distracting them from situations that may cause conflict and as they grew older, it was more about finding ways to solve disagreements. Finally, they took the reins in their own hands and I became more of a sounding-board.

I loved being a mother and had fun. I felt like our family was doing well as we traveled and grew together. I was a young mom and busy, both working and still completing my university program. It wasn't until my son wrote his name for the first time perfectly mirrored did I realize he may have dyslexia. I was flabbergasted by the vision of his chalked name written on the driveway. Looking at the writing, I remembered my mother telling me, "The first time you wrote your name it was perfect, except that to see it correctly you had to look in the mirror." I couldn't believe it, here was this very articulate child, who played for hours, building things with his siblings, being a journalist in nursery school, praised for his articulate conversations with strangers; yet he wrote his name backwards. This was the beginning of life with a child with learning differences.

As my son grew, his learning style and personality came to light. When he started school, he had trouble getting to class before it started, despite being dropped off on time. After seven tardy-slips in the first month, I asked, "How is this possible, when I drop him off early?" It turned out he would be playing in the sandbox with others, so preoccupied, he wouldn't hear the bell. That was a trait of hyper-focusing and being more interested in three-dimensional activities over flat books and papers--another layer of his learning style.

As he and his siblings grew older, we noticed similarities in acquiring reading and writing skills. All three demonstrated signs of dyslexia, while simultaneously showing abilities in creative tasks, thinking outside the box, strong memory of historical stories and abundant curiosity. I concluded that I needed to learn more about raising neurologically diverse children. I read parenting books, education practices and homeschooling magazines, which had innovative ideas. These books helped me find ways to work with and create an environment that would be successful for them.

At school, homework was a nightmare, teachers would report lower than expected abilities and the nursery school for my daughter was not the right fit. *"We spent the first five years in curiosity-driven learning... now my children can't stand school... Yikes!"* This was my major ignite moment, recognizing that no matter how hard I worked at finding a "good" school and creating a positive environment, my kids were becoming stressed and so was I. I asked myself, "How did we go from using a computer at one and a half, physics questions at four, reading the Odyssey (kids version) at five, to watching too much TV (only allowed after sunset) or playing games which caused arguments and disliking anything that had to do with school?" *My motto, I need to fix this!*

By this point, my two oldest children were referred by teachers, for IEPs (Individual Education Plans) I had no idea what this was. I knew the meeting was called because they were below grade level in reading and writing. When I had time before work, I would hang out with other moms. One, whose child had Dyslexia, kindly shared the information I needed about IEPs. She also told me about a local office that offered assessments and services, to help Dyslexia and ADHD children.

My quest was to figure out why, what and how I could help my children succeed, academically and emotionally. To find out my options. To discover if it is viable to teach my kids. If so, how am I going to get there? I needed answers for now and long term. To begin, we took a break from school, testing out homeschooling by going on field trips. I said to myself. "I can teach my own kids!". When I spoke to my husband he did not agree. He could not understand why I was so adamant about homeschooling.

When the school set up two IEP meetings for our two older children, I attended but my husband did not. He decided to attend the final meeting. After all the professionals gave their reports, including one teacher who said our son did not belong in the school! Finally, my husband spoke up, "We're taking him out of this school!" **"What, he agrees?"** was the thought that crossed my mind. Ok, I was shocked and relieved.

With a new decision, I started rebuilding my childrens' curiosity, allowing them to choose their path. To circumvent their dyslexia, I used lessons that targeted interests to stimulate reading. Finding other people who did the same, the kids became more of a team than they already were in a more positive way. Yes, I allowed a ten-year-old, a seven-year-old and a four-year-old to quit school. They joked they were elementary school dropouts. What lay ahead was a lifetime of adventures.

With homeschooling, the children could succeed using their strengths and take extra time on their weaknesses. The biggest question asked was, "What about socialization?" Socializing became our primary activity. My "little" school grew with the kids' friends and their friends. We took field trips out on the town, to park days, co-op groups and Mr. Mac's science classes. The "students" were respectful despite the lack of written rules. They created projects of their choice, played games and did "homework" in the mornings. During all of this, pranks were a way of life but boundaries were respected. Each kid picked the books they liked to read and each kid created a curriculum that fit their interests. For example, for my daughter, who did not like history, I brought home women's history books which she found more interesting. The days were so full of activity, it became a whirl-wind, yet everyone's stress level went down. Anxiety and their dyslexia lessened. Writing was the last academic difference we finally overcame. To this day every once in a while one of my kids complain that writing is difficult.

Another stress-free gain was I did not have to get them up and ready at the same time every day. Some days we started at a normal school time and others we did not. The kids were more relaxed and we were relieved of the difficulties with executive function. Other examples include a not having to remember homework and lunch boxes for school. We learned by doing, and using different tools, such as video games, books on tape, internet or library documentaries and going on field trips. We avoided rote memorization. As time passed, aspects of parenting changed. Homeschooling gave us more time to talk about our ideas, our likes and dislikes. When a majority showed interest in a topic, we read about it or discussed it. Also, we spent more time together and learned to deal with each other on an interpersonal basis.

In a small homeschool, my job was working with all the personalities that had to fit together, as the children who came and went became a big part of our life. I decided our best bet would be to have a democratic system, after all I was outnumbered and I had no admin to help me. It was on me to be disciplined enough so I could sense when things became intense. Some guest students, just coming out of the public system, had to transition from structured to unstructured learning. With these children, I had to decipher how much freedom I could allocate, depending on their personality. I set up a system (a set time to study and designated books to finish before going off to play) until they became used to being able to make their own choices, exhibit self-control and become more self-driven.

The school ended up resembling a large family, where the kids would work things out, point out dangers or outright report an argument if one broke out in our yard. Arguments were dealt with as a discussion. Only one time I had to ask a teen student to go home. He got too hot-headed and I was not sure how far he would go. Naturally, he was welcome back the next day. He never again let his temper rise to the same level in my home. He understood that he was accepted for who he was in our group and continued to return and visit through college.

In building my parenting style, I developed a balance of guiding the child while being child-guided. I later read and identified with the concept of "Authoritative Parenting" (versus authoritarian, permissive or uninvolved). The kids can make choices but the parents set limits, while still considering their children's feelings and needs. I also integrated Montessori methods of creating an environment where children could design and deep-dive into a project, taking charge of each part, respecting the community at large, benefiting from whole-brain learning experiences as they worked.

To reach these goals I read many books that were all about allowing children to lead while parents guide the child and help make decisions without dictating. There were times that required me to make an adult decision that didn't necessarily make sense to the kids. At those rare times, we would declare a dictatorship, i.e., when traveling on a schedule.

With all these kids coming in and out of our home I did not give any specific chores to the children. Instead what the kids learned, was when you finished eating WE all bring our dishes and glasses to the kitchen sink. (Ok, so, if I would do it again, I would include, we also rinse our own dish and pan we used.) We made our own beds, most of the time. We put away our own things, most of the time and we did a spring cleaning every season (minimum). If there was a fort in the living room it could stay until the game was over, then we all put it away together.

Then came the yard. (Absolutely a dictatorship!) Every Sunday the garbage bins went out so every Sunday the yard needed raking and the piles of leaves (so many leaves) needed to be put in the bin.

Finally, at 11 my eldest while playing Pokemon, said to me, "I want to learn how to make these games." And that started a whole new adventure...

I have learned when raising children, to truly hear what the child is saying. Be focused--- show interest in what they say. If your kids are struggling and say they are not being heard or someone is bullying them, Listen. Ask questions, find out the cause. Each child is specific and needs different things. Get to know yours. Then, take action.

IGNITE ACTION STEPS

If you choose to become child-centered, do it because you believe it is best for the children, not because it is cool or the latest thing for parents to do. Practice care, engage in family games and work together.

*Believe in your kids. They have insight into what they need, what interests them.

*Don't make assumptions. Find out WHY, your child gets pouty, angry, aggressive, manipulative, happy, silly, funny. Many times their internal talk affects mood or external pressures increase anxiety. Focus on their good-heartedness, while looking for the trigger that caused the situation or outburst. Staying calm is key to keeping the path clear for growing healthy, capable and caring people.

* Create a map of success to help your child see their accomplishments. My favorite line by a parent was, "I know this doesn't look like you." This spelled out how I felt every time my kids ran into a situation they did not deal with in a positive way. Accentuate the good, even as you acknowledge the not-so-good, in order to brainstorm solutions.

*Acknowledge your own shortfalls: admit when you react inappropriately or make a mistake. It goes a long way to helping your child accept themselves as imperfect.

*Practice mindfulness. Parenting takes a lot of energy and emotional stamina. Taking time to have a practice of self-care, reenergizing yourself helps you stay positive.

*Read books on positive child-raising: I enjoyed the following: *You can't say you can't play*. written Vivian Gussin Paley; *Positive Discipline* by Nelsen Ed.D.; *Raising Your Spirited Child* by Mary Sheedy Kurcinka (see my complete list in the Resource Section of this book).

Michaela Angela De Sapio-Yazar - USA
Educational Therapist

OLIVIA M. DAM

"Meet darkness with a magical light."

My main driver in life is to be my version of the best mother and parent to my children. Only you have the power to move your life forward in the direction you want it to go. I want you to read this story and to know that if you dream it, anything is possible. I wanted to be a better parent, believed it and made it so. You can, too.

TO BE A GOOD MOTHER

My mornings started early if I wanted to get any work done. My natural state was to wake up at 2 or 3 AM with my mind racing and my mental list of 'to do's nagging insistently to get done. What a relief and rush when I was able to take items off my overflowing plate! These were the days when friends, staff and colleagues would wake to numerous emails from me ranging from planning for dim sum to managing patient care details.

This early morning period was my only productive peaceful time, free of distraction to accomplish any organizational and focused tasks. Within a couple of hours, the house would be bustling with little feet and cries of "Mommy." Followed by the morning rush of breakfast, packing school bags which should have been prepped the night before, running all over the house in search of keys, wallets and phones, and finally, out the door.

On days when I had to perform surgery, out of the house sometimes meant 7:15 AM with a drop off at the grandparents. Then I returned home after the children were in bed at the end of the day. Certainly, not every day was so grueling and, certainly, it was not everyday I felt absent from the kids but this was more often than I care to remember.

That same absent feeling nagged at me when I got off the plane in beautiful Mykonos, Greece. This was the first time I had traveled on my own for almost a decade and I felt a strange combination of emotions: fear, excitement and bravery. I reminded myself that in my early twenties I had set out for Zimbabwe, Malawi and South Africa on my own. I traveled like a local; on foot, in beaten up taxis, on local buses even when warned that it was not safe. I was young and lived the naivety that went with youth. I believed I was surrounded by angels who watched over me during that trip. Now, almost two decades later, in my early forties, it seemed somewhat ridiculous to be fearful of traveling to a safe and sought-after tourist destination.

My week in Greece was a time of emotional growth. My walls crumbled, walls I did not know existed – I cried and cried and cried. There was no time or space for me to be this person at home. There was too much of my world to hold up, to keep together: loving and mothering my 2-year-old son and 5-year-old daughter; being a caring daughter, constantly grateful for the wise teachings of my amazing parents; supportive wife to an incessantly aspiring husband; being a meticulous surgeon who looked forward to seeing her patients; administering the clinic. The list of responsibilities and duties was long. Now, having traveled literally a world away, I could let it all out – an ugly blubbering cry. I bawled and snorted as I caught my breath. How many of us need this space to cry?

At that moment, with the help of those around me, I knew my life was going to change. It *had* to change. I was not going to stay in a place of *not knowing* my children. I was not the loving focused parent I wanted to be. It was not the fulfilling life I wanted to live. I was not afraid to do the work of change, set new priorities! My goal: make time for my children – quality, dedicated time free of distractions, however small.

Not an easy goal for a dedicated eye surgeon. For ten years, my clinic was manageable, employing three staff members. I was in full control, able to manage all the pieces. Six years after my clinic opened, I became a mother. Balancing bottles, breastfeeding and diapers with work demands, necessitated finding a second physician to help at the clinic.

I was lucky enough to find a newly graduated eye surgeon who possessed the flexibility to cover for me when parenting demands arose and also had the same approach to patients. He made balancing work and motherhood easy for me. We were so in sync in our care for our patients we continue to work together today.

I am not going to lie. When my first child was born, I felt like I had been hit by a Mac Truck. I reasoned, "Teenagers have babies. I'm 36, a successful professional, with many years of schooling and life experience under my belt... if a 16-year-old can do this, I can, too." I really thought I was mentally prepared, but I had no idea what I was walking into. My daughter was born weighing six pounds, dropping down to five pounds at one point; not gaining as she should. My life consisted of feeding her, pumping what I had left, every hour for what seemed like forever. This was a non-stop, never-ending cycle. I did not leave the house for six weeks, it was a real shock to me.

All the while, my practice was okay. I was able to get family support with my new baby and I went back to work when she was two months old, focusing on surgery. I went to work one week on, one week off for almost two years and spend what I believed was good, dedicated time with her. At first, afternoons belonged to my daughter, a ritual of feeding, playing, reading, and going for walks. But there were days I left the house before she woke up and I counted the hours I was away from her. We were also both grumpier in the afternoons, more apt to be short with one another, as only a 3-month-old could be.

For me, thoughts from my morning at the office persisted so we traded afternoons for mornings. Mornings were heavenly. She was giggly. I was silly, feeling so lucky to have this time. Our ritual was the same but the timing was a better fit. After a morning with her, my heart was at peace; I'd go to work not missing her. During my working weeks, I was only working afternoons so I could spend bonding time with her. Life was good and it all worked smoothly. With this arrangement, I had minimal mommy guilt, that feeling you get when you think you haven't done enough for your child.

When my daughter was two and a half, my son was born. Just prior to the pregnancy, the decision was made by my family and myself to expand the clinic. Serendipitously we found a perfect space. For the next year, while pregnant, my life was consumed by the many details necessary to build this new surgery center. I'd gone from managing a space where there were 4 of us to upwards of 29 staff. With no formal managerial experience, it took everything I had to get the practice up and running.

All the while, I was a brand new mother. He was an easier baby, which only made it "easier" to put all of my energy into the building. He was easy to be with, easy to play with, but, before long, I was missing all of it. *The clinic had become my new child.*

My life was go, go, go, decisions to be made, go, go, go, work to be done, go, go, go and there was no option to stop.

I had to get on that plane to Mykonos.

I had to find a way to make the work demands stop.

I had to find a safe place to let go.

I had to allow this wall - this dam that was holding back the tears and flood of emotions to break free – to allow me to break through and meet the other side.

This was not the mother I was meant to be.

When I thought about the first two years of my son's life, I couldn't recall much beyond what pictures remind me of and a tremendous feeling of absence in his life. Whether due to lack of sleep or simply not being there, I don't remember his 8-month cuddles; I don't remember his first steps; I don't remember much of anything. This was a devastating realization as I lay there weeping. How could I, his mother, not remember?

It's difficult to admit how absent I was from myself, my family, and worst of all, my children. Even when I was 'home', I wasn't present.

For too long, work was all-encompassing, requiring all my resources, all my waking hours. My four-year-old daughter, my sweet unicorn, and almost two-year-old son, my happy angel, needed me. He was born in the midst of setting up the new surgery center and almost two years later, it was so painful to realize, I didn't know my son. I couldn't tell you what he liked to eat or what made him laugh. I was so distracted and into my work. It was devastating to me that even when I was with him, I was not mentally there. I am grateful that my parents were there. Except... I, his mother, didn't know who he was. How was that even possible?

At that moment, and with the help of those around me at home, I knew my life was going to change. It had to change. I was not going to stay in the place of not knowing my child a second longer. It was not the mother I wanted to be. It was not the life I wanted to live.

I had to ask myself...Who do I want to be?

My number one job is to be a mother. There is a very small window in which we are our children's world. They look to us to be their everything; they depend on us to show them the world. When our children turn into young adults, they do not want to play with us anymore. They don't turn to us first for comfort. We are no longer their universe. We have the first 10 years. I had to wake up; I only had eight years left with my little one.

I had to find a way to be involved in my children's lives. I knew I had to partake in the things they loved to do and be with them as much as possible. Recognizing they also needed time without me was important. Parenting was the most significant job I would ever have. I could not let another day go by where I would be so distracted that I would be left with 'no memory'. We needed Balance. It was important for me to make sure my patients were well cared for. I did not want to trade one absence for another.

I had to do two things.

First, I had to reach out. Asking for help was now mandatory. I could not divide myself anymore. I was split into multiple parts: the home part, the mom part, the wife part, and the surgeon part. To integrate, I reached out to colleagues and friends asking if they knew of an excellent surgeon who would consider moving to my beautiful town and work with me. Another gifted colleague with everything I needed came my way. She was my lifeline. Trusting my practice could thrive, and knowing my patients would be in exceptional care, allowed me to release my grip and create the balance I sought. I went from working seven days a week, my mind consumed with daily minutiae of the office while I was at home, to working four days a week and allowing myself to leave work once I walked out the door. I made room for being a more present mother.

Second – I needed to envision the parent I wanted to be, then write out a plan as to how to achieve that. I had to set down some basic principles. Prior to my moment of clarity, parenting was something I fit into the cracks. Even when I was physically there, my mind was elsewhere. I began to schedule in time when my son needs one-on-one time with me, or my daughter has a school performance as a dedicated part of my schedule. These 'appointments' were as sacred as office and surgical time.

Previously, I did not see motherhood as a job that deserved the scheduled time, to be honored. Rather, it was done by default. I had to be conscious of my thoughts and be focused whenever I was with my kids. This was the mind shift. In every job you have responsibilities and you are accountable for achieving the goals. One of my inherent parameters was time. If you don't spend time with your children, you will never know them. It sounds simple enough! We dedicate eight or more hours a day to work, but how much time do we dedicate to our children? Often it is just what is left over. That was no longer good enough for me.

My goal was to make time for my son. To ensure that when we were together it was a quality, dedicated space free of distraction. The journey was not always easy but 3 years later, I no longer carry this burden. I found it is the small moments that are so easily lost and yet enjoyed the most: singing together on the drive to school, blowing kisses at drop-off, chasing my son at pick as he runs and plays, listening to him intently tell me about his Superhero books where there is no fighting... because he knows I don't like reading stories of violence.

I don't think my struggle is different from many working mothers and fathers with important priorities to balance. I have walked the journey of many parents with much more to come. I share my story because if there's a dream you hold and carry if there's an image of the parent you want to be, you can make it happen! You can get there!

Ignite Action Steps

*Meditation was absolutely critical for me to be the parent I wanted to become. It took me from being reactive to responsive when facing adverse situations. The ability to better manage my emotions changed my life. Meditating regularly has rewired my brain to be more effective, grounded and intuitive. I have improved clarity when making decisions in all parts of my life. On days I don't meditate, I feel the difference.

I meditate two times a day on most days. My routine is to meditate in bed for 20 minutes in the morning when I wake up and 20 minutes at night before I sleep. I find guided meditations work best for me. Sometimes I drift into a peaceful sleep during my evening meditation and that's a positive benefit since rest is so crucial for us to be at our best.

There are those that believe that they cannot meditate. I believe everyone can and that meditation is helpful for everyone. Meditation can come in many different forms and through trying different methods, you will find what works for you. It can be for one minute, five minutes, 20 minutes or more. It can be while sitting, showering or walking. It's simply allowing your thoughts to focus on one thing. The important steps are to begin to meditate and do not to be hard on yourself when you do.

*Make time to evaluate your current life – It is crucial to create time in your life to think and work on making your life better. Whether that can be accomplished where you live or if you need to physically leave your home, establish that space.

Once I had the time and gained the conviction, I began by making lists of all the tasks I do or wanted to do in all the different areas of my life. I categorized them into tasks I had to perform or tasks that could be delegated to others. I separated them by whether I enjoyed doing them or not. You may have other methods of evaluating your life. In order to create space for my children, it is essential to determine what can be delegated away.

*Do the work to make your dream possible – I started with items I did not enjoy and could be delegated and let them go. I rank items according to importance in my life. The unimportant and unnecessary ones I release and let them go.

Delegation does not necessarily mean paying someone to do the work. The solution can be creative. It may mean a grocery delivery service that can save a couple of hours or trade with someone to clean your house. It may be a job share, a carpool for the kids or trading expertise. It may mean getting a few families together to cook meals for each other so each family doesn't need to cook dinner every night. The goal is to feel good about all the roles that you are fulfilling. Anything is possible.

Olivia M. Dam - Canada
VICTORIA EYE Medical Director and Eye Surgeon
SEE International Board of Director and Global Ophthalmology
sustainability lead
www.victoriaeye.com

PARTH NILWAR

"The IQ and EQ of a generation is directly proportional to the
PQ (Parenting Quotient) of the generation raising them.
All parents stepping into their roles with this consciousness
possess the power to change the course of humanity."

The power of procreation is different than the power of raising those creations. My intention is to create a global movement to empower parents to become conscious of this difference. I envision a world where all parents allow their children to flourish into the powerful beings they were born to be. In addition, I hope parents reignite their own wonderful lives.

POWER OF PQ

She was finally in my hands, our hands, maybe just three kilograms in body weight but maybe 300,000 tons in weight of her being. After giving us a few moments to feel her presence, she opened her eyes for the very first time. I cannot express what I felt to be in front of her gaze as she experienced the first ray of light from the outer world.

As gently as she opened her eyes, she closed them again, as if soaking in my feelings. I could almost hear her say, "Don't worry, I am here." She turned her head and opened her eyes again as if she knew she had missed something. This time she saw her mother, my wife, just recovering her breath after all the pushing. That was the beginning of our journey as parents. Usually I am excited about such moments, however, this time I felt calm. The little one definitely had a presence more powerful than we had expected.

My calmness, at that moment was potent with a lot of past experiences. Fifteen months prior, in the last trimester of an earlier pregnancy, we were in Dr. Hermann's clinic waiting for a 4D sonography scan. He was a renowned pre-natal diagnostic expert. We were based in Berlin, Germany and scheduled to fly the next day to visit our families in India to celebrate the occasion with traditional Indian rituals around pregnancy. Everyone was excited as both sides of the family waited for our baby. My parents in particular were brimming with enthusiasm, eagerly awaiting their first grandchild.

I had even more reasons for my very positive feelings. I had finally managed to break through my wife's resistance to attending a course on conscious parenting. I had known about the course for almost a decade and had it on my to-do list to undertake before becoming a father. But my wife Hricha (pronounced Ru-cha) was not convinced. Her biggest reason was that she felt parenting was intuitive and no course was going to help us become better parents. "Our parents did not take any courses and we turned out fine," she had said. We were living a good life but I was unable to explain to her that we were not living to our full potential and we didn't know what we didn't know. "This course will help us remove our blind spots," I tried to convince her. After a lot of discussions, she had agreed to give it a try.

Organizing the logistics was not easy because the course was being held in a traditional classroom and not available in our parents' towns. This would mean staying in another city for nine weeks, a duration not feasible so late in our pregnancy. So I invested considerable effort in organizing a trainer to travel to my hometown to conduct the course in a custom made, week-long workshop with our family and a few others attending. I was very happy that all had fallen into place a day before our flight to India. We were just awaiting the medical approval to start our journey. I was really looking forward to the conscious parenting workshop while the rest of the family were feeling excited about the traditional rituals.

But fate had something else planned for us. Dr. Hermann looked at us with a very grim face and broke the news in a straight-forward German manner. He explained to us, as sympathetically as he could, that the baby had a condition called Hydrocephalus which was so severe that most of the brain's space was filled with cerebrospinal fluid. He said it would be a tough life for everyone involved and recommended a few follow-up tests to be very sure of the diagnosis.

The ground beneath us shook. The news came completely out of the blue. None of the tests in the first six months had detected anything and the last one was just a week ago. We canceled the India trip. The following tests concluded that the condition was due to a genetic defect caused during the fertilization process, affecting only the brain. It could be detected only when the brain had grown big enough to be seen in the scans.

We were left with the decision to continue or not to continue with the pregnancy. Frantic research and intense discussions ensued as time was limited. The German system was on the whole, supportive but it was definitely not empathetic when handling delicate situations. The law required since it was so late in the pregnancy, that we would have to register the birth, which meant giving the baby a name and we had not yet finalized one.

At the hospital where we would go through the delivery procedure, we were informed that if the baby weighed more than 1000 gms, we would have to carry out the last rites, as is done for adults per our faith. As a young couple, and in a foreign country without the support of close family, we were in no way prepared for this and felt completely on our own. No one in our social circles in Berlin had ever had to carry out the last rites. We were to be admitted on the following Monday to start the termination procedure. Throughout the preceding weekend we had to research and finalize a name for a baby; one that we would not have.

We were haunted that weekend by a decision we had made after discovering we were pregnant right after getting married. We were about to move to Germany and felt we did not know each other well enough to be a parenting team. After a brief but intense discussion, we decided to have an abortion in the first month of the pregnancy. Little did we know then, that the decision would create a strong undercurrent defining our relationship over the next couple of years.

Hricha feared that her chances of being a mother were diminished and threatened by our choice to let go of our first conception. We were in agreement that the conception had not been a conscious decision and that we were not prepared for such a responsibility. That choice shook us more over that weekend than anything had in the first two years of our marriage. We were devastated. Now in the seventh month of this pregnancy, we were facing the medically-advised abortion of our second conception. We painstakingly researched for an appropriate name and ended up choosing *Aadhya*, which means '*first one*' in Sanskrit . This name gave us hope for the *next* ones, while still honoring the loss.

On Monday morning, I was heartbroken to see my wife staring at the thin November snow outside of the hospital window and waiting for the heart in her womb to stop beating. Until that point in our relationship, I felt I had grossly underestimated her feminine power and strength as a woman. I dearly wished that there was a less tragic way for me to experience her gentle yet indomitable will.

The procedure involved waiting 24 hours for the medicine to take effect and induce labor for a stillbirth. We were strongly advised by the doctors to accept, interact and say our goodbyes to our child, all the while knowing there would not be any response. Never had I imagined I would go through this in my lifetime. No past training, classes, workshops or graduate degrees had prepared us for dealing with such a situation.

Everyone at the hospital kept saying, if we wanted, we could be back for a healthy delivery within a year. Further tests confirmed there was nothing biologically wrong with us. This pregnancy was just an anomaly and usually nature takes care of such situations by initiating a miscarriage in the first three months. This is when I realized why we are advised to hold off from sharing news of an impending birth until the second trimester. We were learning all these things the hard way. Why doesn't our mainstream education system prepare us for something so many people go through?

In my childhood days, I would get home from school and ask my father, "Dad we learned *this* today. I was wondering how you have been using *this* in your life?" Irrespective of the subject, I rarely got convincing answers. This made me question the utility of the curriculum in real life. I started to think that we spend a lot of years studying stuff that we do not use. What we needed in life on a daily basis like basics of finances, authenticity in relationships or even managing our emotions are not part of any mainstream education system. As a child, I aspired to make this change in the world when I grew up. I had not yet realized that my dad had a master's degree in Chemistry which had nothing to do with his profession in a bank where he worked all his life. As I moved through the traditional education system, I don't remember when it was that I lost track of the aspiration I had as a boy. I graduated as an Electronics Engineer, yet I never worked in that field.

After two pregnancies and no child, I began to feel how inadequate the education system was in preparing me for necessary life skills. Parenting needs much more preparation than society offers. Reflect on how much we prepare for our professional roles with years of studying, and postgraduate degrees from top universities. It becomes apparent how little we prepare for our roles as parents. How many parents in this world could raise their hand and say they are prepared to support the intellectual, physical, emotional, social and spiritual development of another human being?

It was a no-brainer for both of us to opt for the parenting course when we conceived for the third time. My wife wanted to do everything possible for this new pregnancy. We found a great mentor in Dr. Atul Abhyankar. I had attended his orientation session making me aware then that *there were courses* we could take to prepare us for parenthood. He had evolved his parenting program before we reached out to him. He had evolved his parenting program and could offer it via remote video sessions which made it possible for us to do it as he was based in India and we were in Germany.

Friends who had completed similar courses strongly recommended we get our parents involved as they were typically our sources of all things parenting. My parents and in-laws joined this *'Genius Babies Joyous Parents'* program together with us. It helped us understand how all babies are born geniuses and even though we want the best for our children, we unknowingly 'degenius' them as they grow up because we don't understand the needs of the child in the early years.

I have learned that the largest amount of brain development happens in the first five to six years along with our belief systems and inner voice. I was convinced by the time children start formal education, it was too late to make any use of our biological development. The whole of our life is governed by our subconscious. What appears as rational, conscious decisions on the surface are actually deeply influenced by emotional factors programmed in the formative years. Apart from putting us in a very positive state of mind for this pregnancy, the program helped us immensely in becoming aware of and breaking through patterns we had picked up in the past. It gave us clarity on how we could experience the joy of parenting while raising a genius.

Our conscious parenting started during the pregnancy, with simple exercises that led to powerful results. I had already built a strong bond with the baby, even though my physical proximity as a father was not anything compared to my wife who was carrying our child in her womb. We had established such strong communication, it was evident in her eyes when she opened them for the first time, that she knew me. That, I feel, was the biggest reason for my calmness at the moment of her birth. I had a strong feeling of certainty in my role as a father which was profound, having heard of countless experiences of first-time parents for whom this is not the case.

We came to believe, through the program, it was going to be a great journey ahead. We would be learning and growing a lot, along with our little one. My wife found a very apt name for our daughter: Sarthi. It means 'Life coach'. It is another name for Lord Krishna, one of the ten Avatars in

Indian mythology. The entire Bhagavad Gita, the holy book of the Hindus, is a narration of the wisdom of life by Sarthi to Parth. Parth is another mythological character, after whom my mother had named me! Parth was the receiver of universal wisdom from Sarthi. My wife and I also broke a stereotype by naming our female child after a male character, one who holds a strong place in Indian mythology, religion and culture. We would not have built up the confidence to defy norms had we not developed the belief in our child even before her birth.

What transpired in the following months established how critical the program has been in setting the right framework for our role as parents. We started noticing things you would not expect from children of her age. At 18 months, she could show and tell 100+ countries on the globe, identify any car brand on the streets of Berlin and name scores of paintings and their artists. Because we were aware of the hunger a growing brain has in the early years, we started nourishing that appetite with simple exposures, similar to what we do for the nutritional needs of the physical body. She was already conversing in our mother tongue, Marathi, reading in English, singing Hindi Bollywood songs and picking up spoken German from her time at kindergarten – all before her 2nd birthday. The depth of her observations and creativity in her thought process has also been evident. The other day she pointed to the signage of a roundabout and exclaimed: "The arrows are playing ring-around-the-roses!" A few weeks after she turned two, she was her usual self, continuously chatting while on our way to the kindergarten. I was a bit lost in my own thoughts and probably not responding enough to the chatting. She turned around in her stroller, looked at me in the eye and said, "Dad, you are not listening. What happened?" She keeps surprising me in new ways at such an early age!

I strongly believe that each of us are born with this potential. All children need is exposure and for the people raising them to have the right mindset. Plenty of research and books on early childhood development have been published. Yet, the vast majority of the population is not aware that alternatives exist and as parents they have immense potential to enhance early learning years. My experiences with Sarthi reminded me of my childhood dreams and inspired me to found *WonderLives Organisation* with the goal to bring this message to parents around the world.

It has become my life's mission to spread awareness about conscious parenting. Little Sarthi did not take very long to stand true to her name – she awakened my own inner wisdom! My dream for *WonderLives Organisation* is for good quality content about parenting be made not just accessible to the masses but for it to be understandable and implementable as well. What drives me now is to inspire people to have mentoring for their role as parents, just like they do for any other professional roles.

My parenting journey, although not long in years, has already ignited in me an inspiring life goal of raising what I call – the PQ (Parenting Quotient) of humanity. Given my own experience, I strongly feel that every parent holds the potential to reignite the genius they were born with. The key is to step into our parenting roles sincerely with all the knowledge and tools which are available and travel together towards the wonderful lives we always dreamt of as children.

IGNITE ACTION STEPS

- **Start preparing even before conception** in terms of what this role entails. Prepare your body and mindset for the same.
- **If you already have children**, don't underestimate the reparation you can do at any stage of the parenting journey.
- **Read books that resonate with you.** I have listed some that really helped me in the resource section of this book.
- Sign up for newsletters and blogs that will lead you to info without you actively seeking for it.
- **Find a parenting mentor.** Seek advice from experts.
- **Keep a parenting journal.** Write about the beautiful moments you experience every day. You can share your entries with a messaging group, with your partner or just keep them to yourself. Record questions that come to mind for you as a parent. The more conscious you are about various questions, the more fluidly the universe will bring the answers to you through any of the earlier pathways listed.

Parth Nilawar - Germany
Co-founder of WonderLives Organisation, Motivational Speaker,
Conscious Parenting Evangelist
www.wonderlives.org

VIRGINIA L LEHAY

"We all have an innate knowledge and wisdom – tap into it."

It is my desire that all who become parents – know we have an innate 'parenting manual'. Tap into it and do a rewrite where necessary, to create a magical experience of gestation and parenting for ourselves and our children.

INNATE WISDOM

"I hate when babies cry." This, out of the mouth of my 15-year-old son...

My ears perked up with curiosity. I wanted to know what that statement meant in his inner world. I probed, "Why do you say that? That's how babies communicate." On hearing my qualifier, he added, "I hate when babies have a whine in their cry."

I carefully consider my next words, "If there's no whine in their cry, then what...?" His reply was immediate. "In church, I watch the mothers pick up their babies and take them to the Mother's Room, then bring them back. If the mother puts her baby down and the baby is happy, then her actions were for the baby's needs. If the mother brings the baby back and the baby isn't happy, that trip was for the mother."

I was astounded at the insight apparent in my son's observations. I responded with a story from his infancy. "When you were around six months old, I went to visit a friend. We sipped tea while catching up on each other's lives. You were awake and on my knee. I had forgotten to bring any toys, so I gave you my teaspoon to examine. Which you did for some minutes, eventually dropping it on the floor. While continuing to converse with my hostess, presuming it had slipped out of your fingers, I gave it back to you."

"However, when you dropped the spoon a second time, I observed it was not an accident. After retrieving it, I placed it back on the table. Within a moment, you began fidgeting on my knee and I gently edged you off to stand supported on the floor by my leg. You soon stretched out your arms to be picked up; I brought you back onto my lap.

"At that point, I began to divide my attention from the conversation I was having, to decipher what you were communicating. You were patient with me, as I was preoccupied. You quietly persisted until I tuned into the message you were sending. Once again you squirmed on my knee, an action you knew was pushing a boundary. I turned to my friend, informing her you were bored and asked if she had any toys you could play with? Her children were older and all baby toys were long gone. At my suggestion, we gathered plastic kitchen utensils and containers. I spread your blanket next to my chair and you sat there happily examining all your new stimulating 'toys'."

My teenage son leaned in to hear more about his young-self.

"During this interchange between us, you did not once make a sound, not a whine or cry, not so much as a peep. You *knew* I was comfortable in my skin and in my surroundings and you didn't need to take on my feelings or 'take care of me', by creating a distraction. I can see why it distresses you now when you hear babies cry, with or without a whine. At six months old, you knew you didn't need to cry to communicate with me."

My story made sense to his way of viewing things and he resonated with it. It also did the same for me. I was able to see that my earliest ways of being with him had a profound impact on the person he has become. To this day, he has an intuitive awareness and gentle warmth which draws friends and strangers to want to know him.

Back then, my hostess, after witnessing the interactions between my baby and me, marveled, "He's so good." This was not the first time I'd heard this comment. I had birthed five children, three sons and two daughters. From my firstborn onwards I heard this kind of awed admiration in the voices of observers. Even my mother was among those who said I was 'blessed' with good babies. Initially, I said "Thank you" with a sense of pride.

Upon hearing that phrase for the umpteenth time – 'you're so blessed' – which gave zero recognition of my skills as a mother, I blurted out, in frustration, "I have disciplined all my babies while still in the womb." After my hasty words, I wasn't able to satisfactorily explain what I meant, although my whole being knew what I said was true.

Finally curiosity displaced pride. Compassion replaced frustration at seeing babies needing something it seemed their parents didn't know how to give. I believed I had some parenting know-how that they lacked, but I could no more tell them *what I had* than they could tell me *what was missing for them*. Seeing such difficulties with child-raising stirred me into researcher-mode. I first absorbed baby-knowledge in the '50s and '60s when I was a child. I had mothers and babies all around me: aunts, cousins, as well as my elder sister with her firstborn. Then my mother had my baby sister when I was nine. Our house was often brimming with babies and toddlers. My mother was highly observant and an advocate for all children. She often spoke up on their behalf. If she held back, I'd hear her thoughts later, usually in a rant of vexation. She observed everything, was instinctive with babies and from her I learned so much, adapting it into my own parenting style.

When my mother was five, she had younger siblings while her older siblings were already having their own babies. At that early age, she was minding her nieces, nephews, and others. In winter, house-bound moms looked forward to the privilege of leaving young ones, even newborns with a wet-nurse and willing hands at my grandmother's house, an early version of a day-home, to sleigh into town for supplies without children in tow. My mother recalled placing sugar-rags, an early form of soother, into tiny mouths while rocking cradles. Hearing these experiences together with my own early observations made for a rich smorgasbord of information, which brought me to the conclusion – *how I was* and *what I did* had a great deal to do with how my babies and I got along. I had innate knowledge and awareness, a veritable internal parenting manual... I was blessed! – not with 'good' babies, but how to *be* 'good' with them.

By the time I birthed my last baby, I had long since ceased thinking my relationships with them was only due to being 'blessed' – as if I had gotten the luck of the draw every time – five times in a row. My response to my friend extended to, "He's also disciplined." As she raised a curious eyebrow, our conversation shifted.

I had always talked to my babes in the womb, in loving, accepting, welcoming and disciplinary tones, using a full range of motherese. I conversed with them about how I was feeling, what was going on for me and future plans with them. By the time my babies were born, they knew my voice. Familiar with tones that voiced love and soothing... humor and playfulness... empathy and connection... but also with tones indicating they were pushing limits and crossing boundaries. When my fetus put pressure on my bladder, I let them know that it was uncomfortable. I empathized with them, how crowded they were, as I have a short body, yet modeled honor for my own discomfort. When they kicked me in the ribs, I applied pressure back, sometimes with stern words and queries. "What are you doing in there?" With my first son, it became a game for him to push back. I could feel the imprint of his foot against my palm.

After my babes were outside my womb, if they fussed, I'd lift them up so we had eye contact with one another and we talked it out. Right from birth, I kept the conversation flowing. When they awoke from naps, I entered their space conversing brightly about what I had been busy doing while they slept. I'd keep talking, sharing how I was getting a fresh diaper, folding a blanket, etc. If they were making fussy noises or crying, I'd wait for cooing responses from them that matched the tone I was setting, before I picked them up. Only if I had missed their first wake-ups sounds and they were justifiably crying in hunger, did I pick them up prior to having an amicable conversation.

I observed many mothers speaking to their children in monotones. New humans are attuning to their environment at all times. They soak up information. A great deal of the incoming data comes from us, their parents. Motherese is key: for soothing, training, imparting love and care and also for those first deep conversations. Letting my emotions play across my face was a huge part of my communication with my babies. They could read my facial expressions, which were congruent with my words. I also devised many hand signals, slight pressure on their body, a 'shhh' with my finger, a 'stop-sign' with my palm. Teaching respect by modeling respect for myself and my energy was imperative. My body was not a climbing gym, my arms were not a jolly-jumper… to maximize on the energy available to me, I had boundaries with all my infants. If I was tired or over-stimulated, I wasn't as competent a mother as I was capable of being. Of course, I still gave recognition for developmental limitations, but I didn't stop being who I was.

Babies are very sturdy little creatures and extremely intelligent. They may not comprehend language, but they do understand tones. Adults don't enjoy boring conversations; neither do they. Having a full range of speaking tones makes for a rich dialogue with your infants. Varying your tone to match what you're speaking about, to convey a boundary and your own feelings, are foundational to later emotional intelligence and executive function. We are their earliest environment. To provide richness, breadth and depth to their world, we need to be fully human, fully ourselves.

As adults, we develop intellectual intelligence, but the very young have access to innate intelligence, which I believe surpasses any other kind. I retained a strong connection to my early, inner wisdom and treated my unborn and young babies as equals and asked the same in return. Inherent in being this way hinted at another aspect I didn't have the words to explain. I found them in reading the book, *The Secret Life of the Unborn Child.*

Dr. Thomas Verney spoke of the detriment of parental *ambivalence* and the benefits of what I call 'whole-hearted assurance'. I know I had little to no ambivalence when pregnant and raising my babies to toddlerhood. I view ambivalence as the opposite of both healthy parameters (boundaries) and whole-heartedness. Ambivalence being: the state of having mixed feelings or contradictory ideas about something or someone: *Synonyms*: uncertainty, unsureness, doubt, indecision, hesitation, vacillation, tentativeness; conflict, contradiction, confusion, dilemma, quandary.

The fertilized ovum of each of my unplanned children received a whole-hearted, whole-bodied welcome into my womb. From as young as nine or ten, I envisioned myself being a mother. No amount of outside turmoil, and I had my share, interfered with my vision. My womb was 'pink', warm and welcoming. I emanated the untainted assurance of that ten-year-old. My babies were housed in amniotic fluid permeated with unconditional love and acceptance. They were born into arms that held those same values. I was present with my unborn from even before conception, as both I and my womb knew I was in child-bearing years.

On my honeymoon, bent over tying my running shoes, I felt the 'twinge' of ovulation. I looked up at my husband and calmly announced, "We are pregnant." Our first child was on his way. I'd feel changes in my body upon each conception. I had no ultrasounds, but called each one by the pronoun 'he' or 'she' as I had a strong 'sense' with each one what their gender would be. People would ask if I wasn't afraid of being disappointed. I wasn't. After my fourth was born, I didn't intend to have any more. After all, my second husband and I already had five: yours-mine-ours. (he had one, I had three and now one together). When our daughter was nine months old, I sensed I was pregnant again… Breast-feeding had delayed my period, which I used to deny the familiar signs. I *knew* but refused to know. He's the only one I had to apologize to, for ignoring his presence for two months. Which I did eloquently out loud and at length; with my hands on my belly, he received a formal acknowledgment of my oversight. I promised him we would have a great time together and we did.

During those child-bearing years, my internal computer was running a welcome program in the background, no matter what was going on in the foreground of my life. The first time I ran that program was the Christmas I was nine. When I unwrapped my wishing-well piggy bank, Mom gave pennies to each of my three brothers and me. Then she told us to 'wish' for a baby sister. With my older sister married and gone, another sister was what I longed for. For the rest of my mother's pregnancy, my mind and heart were right there in her womb, alongside my developing baby sister.

My dad worked camp jobs, so my mom milked cows, hauled water, stoked the woodstove, baked bread, planted, harvested, cooked and canned plus a myriad of other farm chores. I had the opportunity to practice mini-parenting with my baby sister. Much of the wonderful privilege of her early care and nurturing fell to me. I was ecstatic. The loving connection I solidly established with my sister while she was in my mother's womb, blossomed outside. It is a bond that remains to this day.

My early experiences around pregnancies and babies, then wombing and parenting my own children, along with gleanings from observing parenting going on around me – shaped my own unique parenting manual. It brought what was innate in me into action and eventually into language. Over the years as a parent, grandmother, and now, great grandmother, I am still learning how to language and share what I 'learned' – accessing my own innate 'parenting manual'.

I feel immense gratitude for all my life experiences which taught me about myself as a person and later as a parent. There is no occupation more important than being a parent. That means accessing your own knowing – your true parenting manual. Know that creating a great relationship with your child means doing what feels right for you having an intimate knowledge of you are from your own beginnings.

Ignite Action Steps

*Prepare ahead of time – Create a visioning board you can put on the wall. As you assemble the pictures, operate from the consciousness of yourself at a chosen age in your childhood, youth or teens. Connect with the innocence of that age.

*Whole-heartedly welcome your child – as soon as you know you are pregnant, even before if possible. However, if like me, you never really planned your pregnancy, your 'welcome' is welcomed at any time.

*Commune with your Sesame Seed – They are sentient at the very earliest stages of development, from before they are the size of a sesame seed. Be available for their emotional growth. Be aware of their ability to emotionally connect. Send 'nutrients' for that growth. Their heart is beating by three weeks gestation.

*Communicate every moment of every day. Think of yourself as a computer with several programs open. No matter which program you are in, a CEO, home-making, volunteering, playing an instrument, raising an older child, wife, husband, lover... keep the window of communing with your unborn child open. S/he feels your presence, is aware you are there with them, busy at times doing other necessary tasks, but still always available – always present. This is attachment parenting at its best.

*Seek out a coach – If you feel blockage or resistance to the above suggestions, this does not mean that you aren't 'good' parenting material. It simply means you have residue from early-life events to clear. We can access the best of the early part of our lives and make over the rest to create clarity of intention for our parenting journey.

Each of us began with a womb experience and have had others along the way, which may not be conscious. Bring them into the light for examination and perform a do-over.

You can create a warm 'pink' space to receive the fertilized ovum of your child-to-be. Hang an energetic 'welcome' sign in that space to create a loving energy and aura.

I encourage all parents to clear as many of our issues as we can before raising children. With the level of consciousness available, the support of a world of people growing more evolved by the day, we can create an even more evolved generation, one womb, one baby at a time.

Virginia L Lehay - Canada
Coach – Author – Speaker
www.transformationaldialog.ca

SAYDEE SHORT

"Parenting is really about self-reflection."

Dig deep inside yourself and find compassion for others regardless of how you want to feel at that moment. Your children need to see you practicing forgiveness even in the hardest times. They are watching you. Be a role model for forgiveness and finding love in your heart.

SHAPING YOUR MIRROR

Parenting is the hardest experience I have had to date. But it isn't because of night feeds, grocery store tantrums or having to convince them to brush their teeth at bedtime. It's not because of having little mouths to feed or needing to find a babysitter to get some time alone. Not to say those things aren't hard, because they really are. They can break you a little at a time and you have to put yourself back together. But that still is not the hardest part.

It is because... I am shaping tiny human beings. Young boys who will turn into men one day, that could so easily slip into the world without a strong sense of the compassionate and loving values I am trying to teach them. I struggle daily, wanting to become more solid in my own morality and beliefs. I try to teach lessons on human and animal value, yet scream when I see a spider in the house and flush it down the toilet. I try to teach compassion for people who do bad things, but then I get mad when stuff is stolen out of our yard. I try to show kindness when others are rude, but I catch myself with a crappy attitude towards my husband when I'm mad at him. I want my boys to know there is always a way to sort things out, but

I get anxiety when the bank account is empty. I want to instill self-love in them because I *truly* believe they are amazing little souls, but I struggle with my own self-admiration.

Parenting is really about self-reflection. After everything is said and done, there are two little mirrors looking back at me. They think the world of what I do and how I do it. They see every move I make and internalize it. In the end, I want them to remember the love and compassion I have shown.

The summer my beautiful, curious, silly little boy became a toddler, my husband and I decided we were ready to add another child to the mix. A few days before Halloween, I woke up extra early to take a much-anticipated pregnancy test. A faint, but very real, second line showed up on the stick. It was a joyful morning, which went on to be a blissful Halloween with our son.

In the months following, my pregnancy was difficult with many ups and downs. Nausea and exhaustion meant not having the energy to play or do much with my son. Not long after the two test-lines showed up, the economy took a nosedive, and my thoughts of anticipation and excitement were replaced with the nagging question of how much my husband's subcontractor pay would be? We were fortunate to always make it through, but we also knew that my small business of childminding, which helped to supplement his income, would be coming to an end when my pregnancy neared its due date.

Under so much stress, my husband withdrew. I didn't understand at the time what was happening inside his mind and the tension made me uneasy. It made me question everything. Was it the new baby coming? Was he upset that I spent so much time laying on the couch, ordering take-out because I couldn't stand the smell of cooking? Or was it knowing that in only a few short months we would be the parents of a toddler and a demanding newborn? I took the time to read books on marriage and communication, in case I was the problem. It wasn't until one day at work after he suffered his first anxiety attack he finally opened up. The overwhelming stresses of providing for a family alone now, with debt and adding another mouth to feed, added to pressure he could almost feel physically; he sensed the weight of holding his family afloat.

Opening up to me helped ease the tension a little and our lives smoothed out. Together, we found small ways to cut back such as canceling subscriptions and lowering the grocery bill. The birth of our second son was beautiful and we threw ourselves into parenting our two happy, healthy boys. Enjoying family time helped to lessen the focus on financial stress and kept us from dwelling on the reality we were close to the edge of collapse. Facing any new hardships required a lot of self-reflection. I thought about choosing words carefully before I spoke to our son. My heart would squeeze a little when I would watch his brow furrow and his voice quiver when he inquired about our private conversations. He could feel our nervous energy and took it on. I was always hoping I could preserve my little one's innocence, but it felt that my attempts were falling short.

As our oldest son grew, so did his curiosity. His questions became more thoughtful and harder to answer. I was always on my toes with the things he might ask me, such as "Why does my body make poop?" "How fast is this?" waving his hand as fast as his little body could muster. "What is a vitamin? Why do I need them?" "What happens when you die? What makes you die?" That last one is still pondered and mulled over in many different ways. One question, in particular, shocked me at how difficult it was to answer. "Why do you have to go to work Dada?"

I often pondered my answers while my kids and I stood by the door in the mornings waving and yelling good-bye to their Daddy. He would slow down his old white Ford truck before driving away so we could see him waving back. We yelled above the sound of the ladder rack squeaking with each bump he drove over. Everyday weather permitting, our children would run to the sidewalk to watch as that same Ford rolled back into the parking lot. They were trained to wait till the rumbling engine shut down before they could sprint towards the truck where their tired Dad would meet them with mud-covered hugs and kisses. They would beg and plead to hop into the cab of the truck, pretending to turn the steering-wheel, messing with the radio settings, dreaming of the day they would be old enough to work alongside their father. We watched him go even on days he was tired or sick. They would again ponder the question of why he had to work, and I'd attempt to explain again it was necessary to put food on the table. I did not know if they grasped that his job was not just a game that he could choose to call quits on in favor of snuggles on the couch with cartoons like they could.

When I was growing up, my mother taught me an 'us vs them' mentality. We lived frugally with a sense of lack, but as a teen, I tried to trust that there was a reason for everything and people were genuinely good regardless of financial status. Once I grew up and had children of my own, I started to see that my once soft heart, full of compassion for every walk of life was clouded by anger. The adult world of money and finances had changed me and I reverted back to the feelings I had absorbed from my mother. This man-made construct was deeply intertwined into the structure of society. I felt it dictated how we lived our lives and the opportunities we could give our children. I couldn't tell my kids that hard work would always pay off with a big reward because it had proven to be untrue. After I'd been burned too many times, compassion for others became harder. I knew in my heart my mindset needed to stay strong and positive, but my emotions didn't always follow suit. When I found myself staring at unpaid bills, it was difficult not to blame the world, 'society' and everything that has crossed my path. Our children and I watched my husband go to work every day before the sun came up and stay till it went down. The truck that got him there safely and allowed him to get the job done was broken into over and over. Tires only used two winters sitting in our yard, were gone in the night. Suffering these thefts slowly broke down my resolve to have faith in humanity and a sense of security. I always felt a tug and pull between compassion and anger when I spoke to my children about the world's injustices.

In December, we prepared to cross the ocean, plane tickets gifted to us by a family member. Children squirmed in their beds each night, they were counting sleeps till they could see their relatives. We were counting dollars in the bank anxiously, "Could we really take time away from work?" The young innocent mind of my son only understood the joyful side of preparing for an airplane ride, seeing the cockpit, and soon sharing toys with his cousins. My husband worked lengthy hours every day for the entire month prior to our travel. Most days were a chilly -20 Celsius, Canadian winter. He worked thirty days straight, while I was deep in the trenches of wiping bums, kissing owies and trying my hardest not to raise my voice too much; I felt his absence from our parenting team. No break for him, so when our trip was over, we could still pay our mortgage. It was hard on his body; it was hard for us as a family to not see each other. Many midday phone calls from the kids asking, "Daddy will you tuck us in tonight?" So caught up in his own angst to put money in the bank, we lost sight of how our stresses were impacting our sons. As luck would have it, the truck heater stopped working. No more warm-up breaks on the days he worked alone. His dedication and determination to provide as a husband and father were almost palpable, but his patience for cranky children wore thin.

When we arrived at a family member's full house in England, we were all mentally, emotionally and physically exhausted. Our children's emotions shifted from excitement to overstimulation. My energy for motherly connection with them felt low while we tried to stuff every second of our visit with activities. The close quarters and sleep deprivation of sharing a room with our jet-lagged baby caught up with us, and what was supposed to be a break from our daily life was really just a new challenge to conquer. It felt strained to speak with loving, gentle words to my little ones when I just wanted a break from it all. I spent almost every waking moment of our visit on my feet, cooking huge batches of food for our large family, minding children, and trying to navigate their emotions while sorting through my own.

Three weeks later, it was time to hop on a flight back to Canada returning to reality and the daily grind. Not even recovered from jet lag, back to work my husband went. I felt so many emotions seeing him with bags under his eyes, barely any rest under his belt, heading back out to a cold truck, to a freezing day at a hard job. I felt such admiration for his dedication and sadness when I knew he had to go. A pang of guilt that I was unable to provide more than the household management I did. My job as a mother is hard, but at that moment, I wished I could take it all on, let him rest. I preach self-care to everyone who will listen, but I wasn't able to facilitate it for my husband at a time I knew he needed it.

When the dust had settled from our trip abroad and the parts arrived to fix the heater in the truck, our little family, children and all, celebrated that Daddy would finally have a small, but essential, comfort back. Our boys were excited to get into the old Ford truck and once again be allowed to mess with the radio and pretend to steer.

One January morning, we all woke up to the chit-chats of peckish children looking for wake-up snuggles. My husband gathered work clothes and tools with a tail of busy children munching on bananas. Snuggles, hugs and promises that he will call us from the job when we took a break to warm up. As I am standing in the kitchen preparing a simple breakfast for children and getting lunch ready for their dad, he goes out to start the truck to warm it up. Instead of it parked in his assigned spot, all he found were tire tracks, broken glass, and plastic door handle bits. He walked back into the house and just looked at me. "Truck's gone."

I still hadn't woken up fully. "What?" I was trying to comprehend what he said.

"Truck's gone! Stolen. Just... gone." I have never seen such a look in my husband's eyes. Utter defeat. But then, we remembered to look down at the two small sets of eyes looking back at us. Our boys, who idolize their Daddy and quiver with excitement when they get to go places with him in that magical truck, also dream of one day driving it themselves... those eyes were staring back with confusion and worry.

The rest of that day was a whirlwind of finding paperwork, multiple insurance calls, filing a police report and tallying up losses. Even worse was how we couldn't slow down for the many questions from a sweet innocent little person who just wanted to understand. His mind raced along with ours. "Why did they take it? Why don't we just get it back? What will the police do?" We felt blessed to have a child who feels things so deeply, but his need for connection with us as his parents, his human security blankets, was extra apparent. As our shoulders tensed and jaws squared, his demeanor changed from happy and carefree to anxious.

When my world felt like it had crashed down around me, with no light at the end of the tunnel, I looked in my children's eyes and questioned how I could still be the rock to hold them up. But the emotions I feel, or more accurately, what I do with those emotions, will be mirrored by them. After other thefts over the years, and now a much bigger loss, I struggled to find composure. I wanted to scream, cry, swear and hurt the person who did this. I admit, to deal with the amount of fury I had, I daydreamed of sleeping in my car with a shotgun for the next time someone tried to take what wasn't theirs. I had so much negative energy around it, that I didn't know what to do with myself but this daydream, that is so-not-me, made me feel less powerless. But every time I held my son and told him the details of the situation, I attempted to release the dark thoughts to focus on soothing the tension in his small body.

We filled our unhappy silences by talking to our children. Despite negative feelings, we tried to hold together the pretense of positivity on the outside. We told them that sometimes people do bad things because they think they have no other choice. Every word I said felt forced like I was trying to convince myself of the message at the same time as I was trying to teach it. I wanted to mean everything I said, but anger flooded my body. Until my thoughtful four year old, filled with innocence and worry, said a humbling sentence that tore at my heart and brought me back from the depths of my anger.

"Are they going to come back and steal our car?"

Tears came to my eyes and a pit in my stomach settled in. A realization washed over me that during the waves of emotions I was feeling, I had forgotten that my children were also getting swept up. Just because I used words of positivity did not mean they didn't know what I was feeling on the inside. I began to see that I needed to set aside my hardened heart, feel true compassion and forgiveness, regardless of the new financial hole we found ourselves in.

We immediately shifted to an obligation to help our children feel safe and secure. The truck was just an object, and money is just a construct, but our kids had a very real need for our comfort and stability. I didn't share a fear that our car would be stolen next, but I saw how my holding anger and hurt of losing Daddy's work truck could cause a young mind to create concern where it didn't need to be. We knew that making up for missed wages, buying a new truck and replacing all the lost tools would take time and money. But we also had to recognize our kids could not wait that long to see us gain confidence back.

I wanted to stay angry at the person who did this to our family, but I knew I had to let it go. I wanted to assume that a person who could do this was a horrible human being, but I had to find a softness. I had to dig deep to find my own understanding, they must already be hurt, to do something so awful. Instead, I looked at my sons and dug deeper to find forgiveness. I realized I didn't want to carry on my mother's bitterness. Instead, I choose to pass on a belief in the innate goodness of people. As a teen, it was something I had challenged myself to remember. An odd-looking man walking homeless in the streets – maybe he has a brain injury and lacked any support. An angry customer yelling at a cashier maybe just heard devastating news and had no appropriate outlet for their despair. Good people made poor choices because of the hand they have been dealt, not their character or spirit. I cannot teach my children to hold onto their loving, open and unfearful hearts, if I cannot keep my own heart open, loving and strong. Money does not divide us, people do. Our judgments do. Support and love bring us together, no matter what.

This experience made me look at our situation differently and let go. We have a responsibility to model what we want our children to observe. This was a clue to shift my thoughts and see things through their eyes. Kids are a mirror to what you put out into the world. Be conscious of your emotions and how your children might see them..feel them.. absorb them...Or take them on as their own.

IGNITE ACTION STEPS

*Stop and look at your situation from another point of view.

*When you are struggling, take time to remember children aren't just watching you, they are feeling your feelings.

*Be the mirror you want your child to see.

Saydee Short - Canada
Self-Care Coach
www.newleafwellbeing.com

SALLY DANIELS

"If you want to fly, you have to let go of the things
that weigh you down. "

**My journey has taken me from believing I knew what was best for my
children in regard to their schooling, to giving them the freedom to make
their own educational choices. I challenge you to examine your beliefs
around education. Are they working for or against your children?**

LETTING GO

My 15 year old son held up a mirror to my life, slapped me around the
face and woke me up to who I had become. His announcement was the slap
I needed. He was leaving to live with his dad in another country. I felt like
my heart was being ripped from my chest, but no one knew.

Oliver hated school. It was destroying him. I remember him, as a 6
year old at school in England, building Lego dinosaurs with his best friend
Freddie and then excitedly writing and telling stories about them. He made
an awesome papier-mache woodlouse which he still treasures to this day. He
learnt to play the recorder.

As a 16 year old, seven years of Croatian schooling had beaten all
creativity out of him. Studying and testing left him lifeless. He loved
gymnastics but had no energy to train. He enjoyed the piano but by the
time he had completed his daily homework, he had no time or inclination
to practise. He got on well with his classmates but never socialised outside

of school. Any free time was spent online gaming with friends in England.

I could see his spirit dwindling but did nothing. I kept telling him to get on with it---get good grades---join the dual-language class at grammar school--- it will get better---in two years you can change to the baccalaureate programme---smart kids go to grammar school. That's how it is I insisted. So he got good grades, kept me happy, and I kept pushing him. My stupid belief flew directly in the face of my own experience.

The first time I remember switching off from life was when I was 17. In England you take exams at 16 and then choose what to do next. Studying towards 'A' Levels for two years followed by university is the gold standard. Mid-way through my second year were mock exams. I sat with my history paper in front of me for two hours and only wrote my name. I was numb. Over the next few months I managed to re-engage enough to pass my final exams and I was offered a university place. Good news, or was it? Two of my friends were planning a gap year. I wanted to travel, but my parents said no. So I accepted the offer, still numb. I wasn't invested in my studies. I almost failed my first year and left with an average degree, a sense of failure and no idea as to what I wanted to do next. The system had done little to prepare me for life.

Fifteen years later, when my children were 6 and 8, I started looking at alternative paths for them. Graduate unemployment, increasing levels of student debt, rising mental health problems and suicide rates among teenagers terrified me. School should prepare you for life, not destroy your self worth and leave you feeling lost. I wanted my children to love learning and to be free to choose their future path. I wanted them to be happy.

Following this idea, we moved to a village in Croatia. We were "successful" in England. Good jobs, lots of friends, nice house in a good area with excellent schools and three fantastic children – Ella, Oliver and my-step daughter Laura (then aged 12). But life had taken its toll. My husband, Martin, was doing a long daily commute, leaving before the kids got up for school and arriving home after they went to bed. We'd also spent years in and out of court, fighting to spend our allocated time with Laura. By the time we left England to pursue a new life, due to custody issues we hadn't seen her for over a year. Her brother and sister asked when they would see her, my reply was, "I don't know."

Moving to Croatia was a means of escape. It was a huge decision, a leap of faith. We had no real plans. I had a romantic vision of my kids soaking up another language like sponges and us living an idyllic country life. We lived in a caravan and renovated a near derelict house. We created a beautiful home, grew vegetables, kept chickens, raised animals and became a part of the community. Our kids joined the local village school. From classes of thirty in crowded England to a class of seven. I thought it was perfect.

Ella took to her new school like a duck to water. She mastered the phonetic alphabet easily so could read Croatian like a pro, even if she didn't understand it. She was outgoing and gregarious and threw herself into the new situation. Oliver was naturally more cautious. Being two years older, he joined third grade where the work was more difficult. He began studying Croatian literature and learning German when he didn't yet know basic Croatian. With our support he aced the year, as did Ella. Except top marks, great students, endless studying, and pushing to achieve felt like I was being sucked back in. What was happening? I didn't realise it then but my beliefs that traditional education was mandatory were deeply embedded within me and would eventually come back to bite me.

We were constantly busy that first year spending more time together as a family than we have ever had. We ate meals together around our beautiful, wooden table--- wedding present that had travelled with us from England. It held many happy memories and we created more. Our table was an informal classroom where we talked about anything and everything. Ella pointing out of the window and shouting "duck sex!" prompted hilarious, but important, conversations about procreation and relationships. Together we calculated how much wood we needed to build a new chicken house. The kids saw first hand where their food came from. At night we gazed at the huge, star-filled sky, talked about the universe and watched for the International Space Station as it passed by. We were happy for a time.

It took awhile, but sadly, seven years later, the shine had worn off and things weren't so bright. Life hit rock bottom and the only way forward seemed to be for my husband and I to go our separate ways. Martin had been back working in England more often. I felt he wasn't engaged in our family life, he felt he was funding it. Amazingly, Laura was now back in our lives. At age 16 she had contacted us out of the blue. Unable to live with her mother any more she had moved in with her grandma. Visits soon followed. She slotted right back into our lives as if she had always been there. She arrived that summer just after we had made our decision to part. I picked her up from the airport. As she chatted away I sat silently, as I often did, knowing what was coming later that day.

That evening the five of us gathered around our table, the centre of our family life for the past seventeen years. I took a deep breath and, in a shaking voice, broke the news that we had decided to divorce. To this day the rest of the conversation is a blur for me. Emotions were so high I couldn't even stay and watch as my husband of seventeen years packed his life into a few cardboard boxes and left for England. No parting hug or kind words. I hated him, blamed him and was relieved he had gone.

Two months later Martin returned to visit the kids and Oliver dropped his bombshell. I found out he had been talking to his dad privately and had arranged to move to England with him. The pain this caused me was not because he was leaving, I knew that was likely to happen, but because I had been completely excluded from the discussion. My son couldn't talk to me. It was easier for him to speak to his father a thousand miles away than to me in the next room. That was when I realised I was like that numb 17-year-old again, totally disengaged from myself, life and now my kids.

My son was miserable. He was on the very path I had wanted him to avoid but had forced him into taking. That was the moment I knew I had to change. Initially I ran away scared, leaving my husband and kids alone. After a day of soul-searching I returned. My son had shown me how broken I was inside and I had to improve things. I had to seize that opportunity with both hands and make it count.

Walking back through our front door was one of the hardest and bravest things I have ever done. I was shaking. I had no idea what was going to happen, only that it was my last chance to have any sort of meaningful relationship with Martin and, potentially, my children. After the longest, most honest conversation we had had in years, (if ever), Martin and I cried, laughed, kissed and agreed to start again, although, not in Croatia. I was shocked when he suggested leaving. We had invested most of our money in a small business there. Surely we couldn't just walk away? I didn't think we could. But why not? What was more important; money or happiness? Everything is a choice, I decided.

A rented house in England gave us six months' breathing space. A time to reconnect as a couple and a family. As we contemplated our future Ella joined the local school and Oliver prepared for exams which would pave the way for him to start studying 'A' Levels the following autumn. The warning bells with the children soon began ringing. Ella was bored in school. Oliver initially enjoyed catching up with old friends but the novelty of life back in England soon wore off. It wasn't long before he was back, spending most of his time sitting in his room, gaming with friends who only lived around the corner. The only time he seemed truly happy was when he was outdoors playing rugby.

We were struggling to settle back into life in England and began contemplating taking the kids out of school to travel. But what about their education I kept asking myself? I already knew the traditional route hadn't worked well for me...why was I so attached to it? It certainly wasn't working for Oliver either. So I looked into home-schooling. From there I discovered world-schooling and the even more radical concept of unschooling. Allowing your kids to choose for themselves what, when, and how they want to learn.

Martin and I had been investing in our own education and personal development for some time via seminars, workshops, books, and online courses. We were choosing what to learn and enjoying it. Why couldn't our kids do the same I kept asking myself? We were already sharing what we were learning with them. Maybe we could take our teenagers now 14 and 16 out of traditional school to experience something different.

I considered what they were learning in school and then thought about all the things that people struggle with once they leave. Relationships, managing their money, simply being healthy and happy; all things which traditional education barely touches. They could stay in school or we could free them to experience the world. We could introduce them to new people, places and opportunities, allowing them to take control of their own education. Surely this would be better preparation for today's rapidly changing world. How exciting it would be to see them thinking in terms of how they want to contribute to the world rather than what they want to do to survive. My perspective shifted and I saw a world where leaving them in school would limit them more. My only worry was that having no formal qualifications would limit their future options.

We took a bold step and asked our kids if they wanted to leave school and travel the world. Ella was an immediate, "Hell, yes!" Oliver, more cautious, took his time to make his decision. Two weeks later he was in. When Ella told her friends, one girl commented, "You won't even be able to clean toilets without qualifications." Her reply, "I don't want to clean toilets!" Such confidence and belief---I felt so proud of Ella!.

We decided to sell everything to give us absolute freedom to go anywhere, for as long as we wanted, without having to return. This was a truly transformative process and is a whole other story. The hardest thing to part with was our trusty dining room table, our oldest friend. Yet, we still have the memories we formed around it. Oliver even sold his games console and bought a gaming laptop instead. We set off on our adventure with a 20kg bag each. Well, mine was 23kg and Oliver managed to scrape together 15kg including a pair of my shoes. He's got minimalism mastered.

Our first stop was Estonia. We spent a month at a new style university city campus mixing with people of all ages from all around the world, learning, socialising, and coming into contact with a myriad of new ideas. Oliver made the decision to play full out. He made friends, started journaling, meditating and reading. I watched him open up, connect with new friends emotionally, and he even found his first girlfriend.

From there we visited Finland before heading to Croatia. We saw our old home through new eyes. Oliver started meeting up with his old school friends, something he had never done when we lived there. His long distance relationship was a challenge. We hosted his girlfriend for a while as we travelled but her mother wasn't supportive. I watched as he opened up to her and tried to navigate this new emotional world only to be told that he wasn't good enough. It was heart-breaking to witness as his mother but also wonderful to be there when he shared with me. It demonstrated how much better our relationship had become. He was now able to talk to me about how he was feeling, conversations I never had with my parents.

From Europe we headed south for the winter. Bali, Malaysia and Australia. In Bali we attended a personal development event, the attendees were mainly adults, many were successful entrepreneurs. In a workshop on the first day my cautious first born opened his heart and cried. In a small group, he felt safe to let go of all the emotions he was carrying. He began to learn from his recent experience and to forgive. For the rest of the event Oliver set an intention to speak to five new people for twenty minutes every day. His opening line was, "I'm 17, what advice do you have for me?" This was the teenager who, four months earlier, was spending most of his time alone in his room.

We travelled slowly. Enjoying the time we had. Journaling, meditating, talking, eating well, exercising, having fun and laughing. We followed online courses as a family and worked on improving our daily habits. We allowed ourselves the luxury of time. After nine months of travelling, we realised we were all starting to yearn for a base, and a home. The kids were even keen to go back to school. We headed back to England and decided to settle there. Within the space of two and a half weeks we agreed on a town, found a college with courses the kids wanted to study, applied, went for interviews and secured places. Neither Oliver nor Ella had the required qualifications but both received unconditional offers. Now I could see just how ridiculous my old beliefs were.

I know some think we are crazy: in our late forties, no home, few possessions, dwindling savings, starting out on yet another new adventure. We could have been enjoying a safe and secure life, mortgage paid off, pensions accruing and kids collecting qualifications. But what we have is worth so much more than all of that.

We are the closest we have ever been. Our three kids are confident and excited about learning and life. The decision we made to follow our hearts has rubbed off on Laura, too. She feels free to follow her dreams and to set off on adventures of her own. We are all growing as individuals and sharing the new benefits of that with each other and the world around us. An initially reluctant Oliver said it is the best thing he has ever done and he wouldn't change it for the world. He's a changed person, looking forward to studying and making new friends. He is even planning to sell his gaming laptop!

IGNITE ACTION STEPS

Everything we do, or don't, in life is a choice. How often is that choice the result of conscious thought rather than acting on ingrained, often limiting, beliefs? Becoming aware of the beliefs behind your choices can help to open up a whole new world of possibilities.

*Make a list of things you would love to do, see or experience - from simple things to your wildest dreams!

*What is stopping you doing each of these? Write down your answers. Is the barrier real or simply a belief that you can challenge?

*What practical steps can you take to start ticking things off your list?

*Take the first step!

If you could make one or more of the things on your list happen, what else might change in your life? How would it feel to really be you?

I thought I had a fear of heights but, in a new place, I always head for the highest point to get the best view. So, earlier this year I did a tandem skydive from 15,000 feet. My kids don't quite know what to expect from me next.......

Sally Daniels - United Kingdom
www.reallybeingyou.com

SARA FELDMAN

"Lead with love."

It is my hope that through reading my story, you will begin to see the hidden opportunities in making your children and those around you feel loved, sometimes in the most unlikely places.

BUILDING A BUBBLE OF LOVE

As I sat on the small cement ledge at the base of the counseling hut, trying to shield myself from the unrelenting sun, I had a tired feeling in my body like nothing I had ever felt before. Sitting there in the middle of that refugee camp in Ethiopia, all I wanted to do was surrender to the exhaustion. It seemed like a cruel joke that we are told to keep our pregnancies to ourselves during that precarious first trimester when we tend to be tired in a way like no other. I gazed down at the dirt at my feet and contemplated laying down in it and taking a nap. I determined that doing so was probably not the most appropriate move for an "Expert Psychotherapist" to make in front of my staff of psychosocial counselors. Especially not as our clients were beginning to arrive for the group counseling session for survivors of torture, trafficking, and forced displacement that I was about to facilitate.

I had been sent to Ethiopia to launch and oversee a psychosocial program for survivors of severe trauma in the refugee camps in the north. Upon arrival in the country's capital of Addis Ababa, I met my son's father, a clever, funny, thoughtful, charming, and enthusiastic Ethiopian tour guide. I was based in another part of the country near the refugee camps, but somehow we managed a whirlwind long-distance romance that resulted in engagement, pregnancy, and marriage, in that order. Looking back, I can now see that the stress of work and life probably contributed to the self-deception that led me to make a wholehearted commitment to a relationship that was doomed to fail.

I flew home to Los Angeles for my annual one-month leave and saw my OB/GYN. Due to the malaria risk, she told me that I couldn't stay in the refugee camps during my pregnancy. I wouldn't be able to return back to the work that I was so committed to.

The reality was the baby growing inside of me might have been the only thing that could have made me leave that job. The job I was devoted to even as it was running me into the ground. I used to be one of those women, particularly those in the 'helping professions', who are all too willing to sacrifice their own health and happiness to serve others. The ability to walk away from a situation that was affecting my well-being is just one of the many gifts that my child would give me.

Towards the middle of my second trimester, I returned to Ethiopia in time to attend the events my staff had organized for the United Nations International Day of Support for Victims of Torture. I then had to announce to the team that I had assembled and trained that I would be leaving. It was a difficult goodbye.

I went to live with my partner in Addis Ababa and spent the last half of my pregnancy settling into a new foreign city and trying to build a foundation and home for our little family. It wasn't without challenges. My husband and I found ourselves trapped between two uncooperative and inflexible immigration systems, trying to bridge two very different cultures, having lost a reliable income, plus preparing for the unknown of parenting. My child's father couldn't immigrate to or even visit the United States without going through a lengthy and labor intensive visa application process that could easily result in denial. I requested a change to my visa, which had been sponsored by my employer. My passport was stamped with a "LEAVE FOR GOOD" visa and I was instructed to exit the country within 30 days. I couldn't remember ever feeling so frustrated and helpless.

Through our marriage, we were able to get a permanent resident card for me, but I would not be allowed to work in the country. We turned our focus to obtaining a visitor visa for my husband, so that we could both be in the United States when our baby was born. As the stress mounted, the little red flags that I had disregarded earlier in our relationship manifested as frequent conflict. I felt lost without my work, lonely in a new city, worried about money, and uncertain about the future.

My husband's visa request was denied. He was demoralized. I felt powerless. I remember in those most stressful times putting my hands on my belly and assuring (probably more myself than) that little baby inside of me, "We're going to be alright. We're going to be alright."

To my parents' horror, I opted to give birth in Addis Ababa, where my baby's father could be present during the first moments and days of our son's life. It was a different pregnancy and delivery than I am sure I would have had back in my hometown of Los Angeles. It certainly wouldn't have been the right choice for everyone who comes from where I do, but it was the right one for us. I am grateful for my son's uncomplicated birth and the phenomenal midwife who accompanied and supported us through the process.

Sadly, less than ten months later, my son and I were taking the long flights from Addis Ababa to Los Angeles. Just the two of us. Leaving behind my failed marriage, my son's father, and my broken efforts to build a stable, happy, and healthy home for our family. I felt like a zombie following my son as he crawled up and down the plane aisles on those interminable flights. As we flew, my baby became the child of a single mother, which, as a child of divorce myself, was something I never wanted for him.

We arrived and relied on the kindness of friends, family, and the government to start to build another new life. After about two years of settling into 'LA' life, I was working three jobs and just scraping by. I was tired and stressed. My son was in daycare for 10 hours a day. The little time we spent together was overshadowed by the tasks of daily life with fewer and fewer moments of shared joy and play.

With one email, everything changed. I got what seemed like the opportunity of a lifetime…to start a business in London. While it was a risk, if it worked out, it could mean that I could create a different kind of life for us. It would give us the possibility of a future in which I could be the kind of mother that I so badly wanted to be – less stressed and with more time to spend creating happy memories with my son.

It also meant that my little boy would have lived on three continents by the time he turned three. It meant leaving all the comforts of my hometown, home country, and the support and company of family and friends.

I did the cost-benefit analysis and decided I couldn't say no. I forged ahead with the plans to move, telling myself my son was adaptable. He had always been a happy kid who made the best of every situation he was put in. He had amazing qualities that I appreciated, admired and wished I had more of. I was sure that he would do fine.

It never occurred to me how wrong I could be. I often say that I am always learning, and in this case, I learned the hard way. I was focused on all of the tasks that I thought were the difficult ones: settling our affairs, packing, and moving countries. In doing so, I overlooked that I was taking my loving and social little boy away from the people he was used to spending everyday with, the grandparents he loved and respected, and the little home and big city he had grown accustomed to.

We arrived in our new city and for the first time my son was having huge screaming, crying tantrums. It felt constant. He cried and yelled out as I pried his clinging hands off me when I dropped him off at nursery school. He hit and kicked me frequently when he became upset. He approached every stranger he came across, desperate for social connection. If they talked to or played with him for even a moment, he would ask me, "Can they come to our home?" Or, much more disturbingly, "Can I go home with them?"

One dark, cold London night there were kids playing as their father checked out of the grocery store line in front of me. My socially starved son ran over and joined them. After a few minutes their father completed his transaction and started herding his children and groceries towards the door. My son attempted to leave with them. Before he could, I grabbed and held him as I explained that he needed to stay with me. He protested, crying, trying to struggle out of my arms, yelling that he wanted to go with them. I wouldn't let go. He stopped. He looked deep into my eyes. He never took his eyes off mine as he reached over, grabbed a handful of my hair, and pulled it as hard as he could. I grabbed his arm and looked down in horror at his little fist full of the hair that he had just ripped out of my head.

Tears filled my eyes as I carried him home in shock, pushing a stroller full of groceries ahead of us through the cold night to our little flat. I couldn't believe that this was happening. I was terrified that I had broken my 3-year-old child, scarred him for life.

Sometimes there are drawbacks to being a psychotherapist. It's easy to spin out in panic thinking about where I fell short in creating secure attachment during my son's earliest years. Or how I probably endured too much stress during my pregnancy and flooded him with cortisol. Or how damaging the separation from his father was and was going to be.

In that moment, the many parts of my life intersected in a way that felt like it was divinely orchestrated. At work, I had become interested in building the parent-child connection as a way of reducing risk factors throughout the trajectory of a child's life. At the same time I was obsessively doing internet research on how to improve the situation with my own child. I had determined that I needed to change my son from a nursery school near our home to one much closer to my office.

Having worked with juvenile sex offenders and their families as well as children who were victims of crime, I had come to understand that having an experience of the family of origin that felt loving is a huge resilience factor and risk reducer. I had seen many families in which the parents loved their children immensely but didn't have the time, energy, skills, abilities, and/or awareness to have regular interactions with them that felt loving or encouraged communication and affection.

As a result, their children's needs for feeling loved went unmet. As parents, we are often stressed by our efforts to try to provide for the children we love. And that stress makes us less able to show up for our kids in ways that feel loving to them. We have little patience, get easily frustrated, and often turn to yelling or worse to get them to do what we want. I was becoming one of those parents.

In my personal research, I came across an article that talked about making "special time" to spend with our children. This uninterrupted period is when the parents do whatever the children want to do, even if it's not what we want to do. The article said that even starting at five minutes intervals would work, which made the whole concept much less intimidating to me.

Simultaneously, after a string of unfortunate events involving my son's school and precarious babysitter arrangement, I had determined that the best option was to transition him to sharing my daily Tube commute. His transfer to a nursery near my office would enable me to pick him up earlier and allow us to spend evenings together.

Only, there was the issue of that commute. The daily rush hours were already stressful enough for me. I would wait on the platform to see if I could squeeze onto that train or would have to wait for the next one. When I did get a space, I would be pressed up against a bunch of other adults, most of whom were on their way to work, all of whom looked more uncomfortable and stressed than I felt.

The thought of adding a stroller and unpredictable and potentially volatile child to the equation made me very nervous. We had already had one experience where we had ridden the Tube together at rush hour. My son had gotten upset right as we boarded. He proceeded to have an epic crying fit as we went from stop to stop. A woman standing nearby, who could no longer take it, yelled at my son and then turned on me. I knew it would be hard to add him to my commute, but I also knew that this was the right thing to do. I was sure that more togetherness would be good for us.

I had started using special time at home to give my son a sense of real connection. He loved it. And I loved that he loved it. I wish I could say that in those moments my inner child emerged and I reconnected with a wildly imaginative part of myself that had long been in hibernation. Honestly, I often struggled to feel inspired about creating interesting scenarios for his dragons and dinosaurs during those dedicated uninterrupted times. But with practice it became easier.

We began the commuting process, which was predictably quite stressful. The Tube doors would open and already stony-faced Tube riders now looked at us even more unwelcomingly. I would gently push our bulky stroller into the standing room only car, often accidentally pushing people or running over their feet. My son could be quite cute, but his charm, which had rarely failed him before, only worked on a tiny percentage of rush hour Tube riders. Others ignored us completely. A small number of others got huffy, nudged, and even pushed us. As the doors opened and closed around us at each stop, we seemed to be in the way no matter where we were.

As I was stressing over how I was going to continue to commute with a child, I suddenly had an idea. We could have special time together on the commute! I could bring his dinosaurs, cheetahs, or whatever he wanted and spend those long stretches on the Tube as our dedicated, uninterrupted quality time. This idea seemed to tick multiple boxes for us. For one, it would provide a dedicated period for special time, allowing us to enjoy ourselves by playing and pretending. Secondly, it would keep my son entertained and in a good mood. Thirdly, it would create loving, happy memories for us.

Each day my son would choose the toys that he wanted to take. Like before, we would gently push our ways onto those train cars. But once on, our dinosaurs, cheetahs, and dragons would emerge and continue their colorful adventures. As I hunched over his stroller, my son would be comfortably nestled in a cozy, secure, whimsical bubble. All the stony-faced commuters would fade away as our creatures played hide-and-seek or engaged in epic battles or visited the hospital. My son's giggles and joy reduced not only my stress but that of some of the commuters around us. Their stony faces started to melt into smiles and sometimes even giggles of their own.

Other things started to change too. My son's behavior made a noticeable shift, not just on those long commutes but in general. He had less tantrums. When he did tantrum, there was less and less physical aggression. He became more cooperative. Our relationship improved. I had a real sense that I was getting to know and enjoy my son in the ways I had always wanted.

We still have our struggles and I sometimes fall back into stressed single mom mode, but now I'm better at catching myself, stopping, reevaluating the situation. I'm better at determining how I can build the bond of love between myself and my son. I believe we all have opportunities in our lives to make small shifts that can transform our connections. Take the time in your life to find yours. Putting energy into making your interactions with your children into opportunities to make them feel loved will enrich both their experiences of childhood and your experiences of parenting.

Ignite Action Steps

*Start at home when there's little pressure and it's easy. Introduce the concept of uninterrupted play time for you and your child where they get to choose the activities and direct the play. Name it and continue to refer to it by that name. We use "special time," but you can choose whatever fits best for you.

*Notice the experiences that are challenging and take time (i.e. subway or bus rides, airplane trips, drives, waits at doctors' offices). Ask yourself, where are the opportunities where a little bit of creativity could turn these boring or unpleasant activities into fun experiences for your child? Decide to use special time in those moments.

*Prepare your child before you leave by telling them that during that time you will have special time. Have them choose the items they want and bring them with them.

*In those moments, start having special time. While you're doing it, recognize that the reason you are doing it is to protect and create loving experiences for your child.

Sara Feldman - USA
Social Worker, Psychotherapist, and Educator
www.exquisitemess.com

Fitch

My life would not be complete without a few words about my amazing kids!

JBd

HELLE BRODIE

"Treat your kids with honesty, openness, support and trust. Your efforts will come back to you tenfold."

We all learn a lot from our parents: including how to and how NOT to be a parent. I'd like to share parts of my story to empower you to change the parenting template that you grew up repeating.

HONESTY, OPENNESS, SUPPORT AND TRUST

I stepped into parenthood in the same year I became an entrepreneur. Both have been challenging adventures. Though my business provided a roof over our heads, parenting has provided meaning, fulfillment and joy!

Looking back, I realize that I learned how NOT to be a parent from my experiences growing up. Like every parent, I wanted a more empowering experience for my kids than the ones I had.

Like many people, I didn't have a very honest, trusting or supportive relationship with my parents. That's what I wanted to change with my own children.

We have all done things that our parents would not have approved. We have all gone to a lot of places they might not have liked. I recall many conversations with my brother who was always saying "Don't let on to Mom and Dad," or "Mom and Dad can never know that we've been there," or "Don't tell we did that."

My son Erik was born when I was 27. My daughter Megan blessed the world one and a half years later. I had no real experience with babies or children, and I had no idea of the adventure I was about to embark on. My husband wanted to have children early because he wasn't able to relate to his older parents. His father was retired several years before he graduated from University. He wanted to do things differently.

Being in love, I simply agreed, without putting much thought into it. I didn't go into any of this with wisdom. I also didn't realize that these little wonders called children don't come with an instruction manual.

When they were babies, I tried to follow my mother's advice: "Don't spoil them and don't hold them too much. It's OK to let them cry themselves to sleep. Don't be too kind. Don't let them roam around on the floor. Set up that playpen in the living room and keep them in there." That felt more like a prison than a place to play.

When Meagan was three and Erik four years old, we went to visit relatives on my husband's side. Our kids were learning to skate, and we thought it would be fun to take them to Winterlude. Five kilometers of the frozen canal in Ottawa, Canada is cleared and open for skating in the winter. Erik was a strong skater and Megan, though she was only three, had a great sense of balance from her dance lessons, and a free spirit that would allow her to try anything.

Joan and Mike, the warmest, most welcoming and supportive couple you could imagine were with us. They had an incredible relationship with their own three children who were in their early 20's. This was the weekend I would find out that there was a different way to parent that creates an entirely different type of relationship between kids and parents—opposite from the way I grew up. What an eye opener! I learned that some kids actually had honest, open, supportive and trusting relationships with their parents. What a foreign concept *that* was!

We spent the entire Saturday with Joan and Mike: skating on the canal and eating Beaver Tails (sugary deep fried pastries in the shape of a beaver's tail) and going to the ice slides in Quebec city. It was an awesome day! It was every child's dream. As parents, it was an incredible opportunity to play and engage with our kids as if *we* were still kids.

By the end of the day, we all felt that incredible feeling of exhaustion after being outside on a cold crisp day. We had rosy cheeks, smiles on our faces, and contentment in our hearts. We settled into a hot dinner around the fireplace as the perfect ending to our day.

While we were out, two of Mike and Joan's adult children arrived home. What a dream for our kids: their cousins had come home from university to play with them and spoil them. They were at the top of the world!

After our little angels had been put to bed, we all sat around to have some *adult* chat. But it wasn't what I expected. Joan and Mike's kids started to reminisce about some of the things they did when they were growing up. Though they had different interests and extracurricular activities, they spent most of their free time together during their teenage years. They hung out with the same friends, went to the movies together, had the same peer group, and got into mischief together.

They talked about getting fake ID (and who they got it from) to get into bars when they were underage. They talked about bars they frequented regularly, and which bars they could never get into. They talked about life experiences—both good and bad, and some of the trouble that they got into with their friends. The even reminisced about the fun they had engaging others of the opposite sex.

I was shocked by the way they could have these open and honest conversations with their parents. You may recall my brother's voice, "Make sure Mom and Dad never find out that we did this." How could they be so open and honest? How could Joan and Mike just sit and laugh with them about these experiences? This was not my normal! I still had a lot of secrets locked away from my mom and dad!

That week-end was life changing for me as a parent. This was the type of relationship I wanted! I wanted to be a part of their lives and for them to want to include me in their theirs—not to shut me out to what they were doing the way I had done with my parents. I wanted to be supportive of them – not to be critical. I wanted them to be honest with me – not secretive and deceptive. This was what a family could look like. It was up to me to make it happen!

Though I haven't seen Joan or Mike for many years, I will always be grateful to them for helping me to see a better way of parenting!

A few years later, Erik and Megan each received a little money from their grandparents to spend as they pleased. I talked with them about the money for a long time before anything was purchased. Would they spend their money on candy? Would they buy toys? Or would they save some of it for later? It was up to them—not up to me. I wanted to help them make decisions they would not regret.

In the end, each took half of the money to the local store. They had their hearts set on a toy. Erik wanted a Lego set. But that red truck with the oversized wheels and flashing lights was so enticing! Megan wanted a Barbie. Yet that cute little Care Bear was tugging at her emotions. Each time they decided on something, I would ask them to be sure of their decision. I wanted them to think about what they really wanted and could afford. In the end, they proudly purchased the red truck and the Care Bear with no regrets.

It was certainly a test of my patience! It was also a great lesson about choices. They could choose to do whatever they wanted, within their budgets. When I look back, I realize that this was their first introduction to critical thinking: to compare options that they would be happy with; to be responsible for these decisions; to understand the consequences of their choices; to follow their hearts.

As they grew, I learned to encourage and support them in their activities – not just to have them do what we as their parents (or their grandparents) thought they should do. Or to do what was expected of them. As a child, I remember going to piano lessons and hating it every week. I remember my mother nagging me to practice, practice, practice, an hour every day. How I despised that! This was another thing that I wasn't going to do to my kids! They were going to be able to make their own choices about their extracurricular activities.

My husband wanted Erik to play hockey. That's how he became such a good skater and skated the full five kilometre length of the Ottawa canal at the age of four. But he didn't like to go to hockey practice. The hockey pants didn't fit his stocky body and they were uncomfortable; so much so, that it took the pleasure out of being on the ice even though he was good at it. So I stopped signing him up. I remembered the pressures I had to do piano lessons.

My daughter had a passion for dance. We had tried things like soccer and baseball, but she was more interested in picking dandelion flowers than chasing the ball. So ballet it was. Fortunately all the grandparents agreed because it was the "girl" thing to do. At first Megan just loved the tutu, and that's what drove her. But by age five she was so good that she was asked to perform a solo at the ballet recital as the music box dancer. She loved it! So the dance competitions began, and we travelled throughout the province to tap, jazz and ballet competitions.

Erik found his passion in downhill skiing. Now there was something he was motivated to do and excelled at. Over the years, he honed his skills and won many awards and trophies. This passion for what he did led him to racing at the international level (FISC), competing on the same point scale as the World Cup and Olympic skiers. Megan's dance coaches wouldn't allow her to race while she was competing for fear of a ski injury. Yet she was an awesome little skier. Eventually she made a difficult decision between the two. She joined Erik on the racing circuit at the FISC level.

It took great dedication and focus to achieve what they did – for all of us. But it wasn't a free ride. As a single parent, it was challenging to find the money for this competitive level of racing. We had to have rules. They were enrolled in a school program called Interact that catered to kids with extracurricular activities that took them out of school (during the winter months, they were rarely at school more than three days per week). And part of the deal was that they had to maintain their grades in school to continue to have the opportunity to live this wonderful life. The cool thing is that since it was their passion (and not mine) they were willing to do whatever it took to make it all happen. All they needed was some support and encouragement.

As my kids got older, I would drive them to a rented condo at the ski hill so they could train during the week while I went back to the city to work. (Someone had to pay for all this fun.) They had food in the fridge, a few prepared meals in the freezer, rides to the hill, a condo to stay at, and homework to do. I used to tease them about being the youngest kids to have their own condo! I would be back for the week-end to drive them to their races and to support them as their biggest fan. But they had responsibilities if they wanted to make it all happen. They had my trust, support, and encouragement. They knew the rules. They knew what they had to do to succeed in their passion.

At Christmas, their gifts were centered around skiing. They each had several pairs of race stock skis, poles, helmets, shin guards, face guards and tuning equipment. The list went on and on! One year Megan asked if she could also have a new computer for Christmas just like all of her friends. The answer was simple. It was her choice. She could have some of the things that her friends were receiving as gifts if she really wanted them. But she couldn't have the ski equipment too. Megan chose the skis without hesitation. What another great lesson in choices and it was hers alone!

In high school (before Interact), Erik said, "Mom, all of the other kids buy their lunch and I have to brown bag my lunch. Can't I just buy my lunch like all of the other kids?" So we did the math. $10 per day for lunch is $50 per week or $200 per month. Over a period of 10 months, that's $2,000. So if he wanted to buy his lunch every day, he could forfeit a pair of skis. No problem, the choice was his. Again, there was no difficulty in making the choice. Another lesson learned!

At the time I didn't realize what amazing life lessons these were for my kids. I hadn't planned them as lessons. They were just a reality. There was only so much money to go around and I was stretched to the limit already.

I didn't have any kind of hidden agenda with their skiing. It was all about them and their passions. Thinking through these decisions came easily to them. They knew what they wanted. They made the difficult choices without hesitation.

During their time at the condo, Megan and Erik learned to cook (as athletes they were focused on eating the foods that would support them physically). They learned to manage their time (homework still had to be done to maintain their grades). Their skis had to be tuned regularly and, as every parent's dream, they learned to clean up (there were rules about the condo being clean and tidy when I came back for the week-end). They also learned the meaning of responsibility for themselves. They learned resourcefulness to sort out issues that might arise. They learned to work hard and play hard. It's only now that I recognize the multitude of life lessons they learned.

The trust, support and encouragement to excel at their chosen passion has helped to make them the well-adjusted adults that they are today. Neither of them made it to the World Cup, and neither made it to the Olympics. Yet they gained so much more. I'm proud of them for their ability to think through their options, to make their own decisions, and to play full out with passion. I'm grateful that I was able to support them in those defining years.

When it was time to decide what to study in University, I wanted to empower them again, to make their own decisions. Raised by a couple of engineers, I was directed away from the psychology degree that I wanted to pursue because it was a *flaky* career. I was told that I needed something more grounded and realistic. Again, I was determined to break the patterns I had grown up with.

If I had chosen for my kids, Megan would have become a veterinarian (animals are always drawn to her) and Erik would have become a lawyer: he has a sharp mind that can put together a sound argument for almost anything! I'm not sure if it was a coincidence, as we certainly hadn't discussed it, but they both decided on psychology. Megan went to the University of Guelph to study psychology in the arts program. Erik went to McMaster University to study psychology in the science program. Meg went on to teacher's college, and Erik went on to complete an MBA.

Today we live in different cities, so I cherish our time together even more. We now have our own week-ends together where we reminisce about some of those early (and more recent) adventures. The time Megan and I spent three hours putting spikes into Erik's hair. Or the time I rescued Erik and his buddies from the beach before they could be caught drinking in a public place. Or perhaps those adult vacations to the sunny south as a way to spend more time together.

I have managed to shift the template for parenthood from the one I grew up with. It's not perfect, but it's a huge shift, and we are all reaping the benefits!

IGNITE ACTION STEPS

Reflect on your own childhood and decide what worked for you and what didn't. If it didn't work, you have the power to change the template. Love from your heart and give from your soul. Spend the time to raise your kids to be independent, capable, adults. Help them to learn and to think through their life's challenges. Help them learn to have fun! The world will be a better place for it, and you will all reap the benefits!

Helle Brodie - Canada
Entrepreneur, mentor, speaker, coach
Freedomjourneys.ca

TANJA POWELL

"Lead by looking inward."

My intention with this chapter is to help empower Moms. To show how by *not* controlling, yet allowing, enables children to go out into the world and be an empowered individual themselves.

RAISING JADE

My house, my rules. / Do as I say, not as I do. / Children should be seen and not heard. / Money does not grow on trees. / You have to work hard in order to be successful.

This what I heard growing up. This and more, and more.

My parents loved me and did their best given their childhood experiences. However, only after I was pregnant (on the pill – surprise!) did I reflect on how my parents raised me. I considered how this child chose me and wanted to be here. Not planned, not prepared, what the heck? I was never going to have kids. I was going to travel and change the world.

Did you know as of May 2018, 45% of pregnancies in the U.S. are unplanned? They say the pill is 99% effective and often women who get pregnant are blamed for not using it properly. Did you also know antibiotics can negate pregnancy pill effectiveness? Studies show the pill is less effective for women with a particular gene, which can be detected through testing and doctors can advise other contraceptive solutions for these select women! Empowerment.

Back to me being pregnant. This was not the first time. I terminated a pregnancy when I was 17, sadly again at 26. When I became pregnant on the pill, my intuition affirmed, "This child chose you. You have no choice." It turned out to be the best thing that ever happened to me. I have an amazing daughter. I named her Jade.

The following is how a confirmed single person determined to not be a parent survived and even thrived.

Moms, please nap when baby naps! You need to heal and rest to be a better mom. Dishes, laundry, and housekeeping can wait. Better yet ask for help so you don't have to do it ALL. Dad cannot support new babies the same as a mom, but they sure can support you around the house more. One example how to save nap time for self-care: I had plastic containers in a lower drawer; my daughter would pull everything out, then put it all back. It was a game while I was bouncing around doing the kitchen stuff us moms are tempted to do when baby naps.

When Jade was a baby, she was social and not a massive fan of hanging out at home with mom. A cranky baby could be turned around with a walk to the store, a bus ride, a play date, or a trip to the library. She went to part-time daycare at six months and LOVED being with the other children. This also gave me time to work and nurture myself, so when I was with Jade, I could have more energy and be present in the moment. I found a wonderful woman named Judy who was like a mother to me and grandmother to Jade. Judy potty trained Jade, taught Jade her manners and how to share toys. She also managed to get her to nap, so she was always in a good mood.

As Jade progressed to toddlerhood, I would always give her two choices. This allowed her to feel in control, empowered and able to choose her destiny even if it was only cleaning up toys versus folding laundry with mom. Picking her wardrobe, which games to play or food to eat were also choices I offered. Presenting a selection of bath toys and bedtime stories for her decision, all added up to her feeling empowered. We truly only had a few tantrums!

Another habit I developed was to give 15/20 minute heads-up before we left somewhere or time to stop playing. It was critical she knew what's next. We would choose a snack to ease the transition. There was usually a stuffy friend involved or a favorite blanket that provided comfort in changing environments. The best way to avoid power struggles was to let her feel she was in charge.

Routines were a sanity-saving device for us both – meals, bedtime and bath time – do not mess too much with those! In the bath, I don't know how I discovered this, but I learned when I blew on her sweet baby face, she would suck her breath in. I've seen this work with a lot of babies I've known, so it may be worth trying if you are having bath time issues. It's the perfect time to dip them underwater! Today, Jade is still a mermaid, and we even decided to stop swimming lessons as she was so far ahead and preferred to swim in our pool at home.

As adventure is a big part of my life and Jade's, we were bound to have a few tumbles. When she fell, I never ran to her, 'OMG, are you OK?'. Unless I knew it was severe and even then, I would simply hold her and let her feel the love of mom and deal with the next steps. One time she had new shoes on and tripped down the stairs outside dinging her forehead with a tiny rock right to the bone in her forehead – yes, we still see the scar. To the hospital, we went! As they froze her forehead and were stitching her up, Jade saw the needles and thread, "Mom, what was that!?" I calmly replied, "the doctor is making you better."

Raising her this way, meant when something wasn't more than just a bump or scrape it didn't slow her down. When Jade was six, she broke her tibia and fibula during a skiing lesson. She calmly laid in the snow and asked not to be touched, "My mom's snowshoeing, her phone number is…". I got the call. The doctor called and shared, "she won't move and is asking not to be touched." I knew it was serious then. I jogged over in my snowshoes, to find them trying to give her laughing gas, but she refused any and all kinds of medicine, but at that moment, I so wanted to be the recipient. It is amazing how calm a parent can be on the outside but screaming on the inside. I taught Jade my phone number from a young age, so she knew no matter where she was, I had her back.

After she was all healed up, she went back for more skiing. I also empowered her to choose her own activities, especially other athletics. We went from ballet to jazz dance performance to gymnastics to cheerleading. In all these, Jade excelled and did her best, because it was where she wanted to be! Cheerleading ended with a trip to Florida. Being a great tumbler, Jade was an excellent addition to the team. We ended each era with triumph and fantastic life experiences. However, being an empath child, she struggled with taking on too much. I learned being a supportive mom to an empath-child in a super-competitive world did not serve either of us. The cheerleading world, with its frustrations, was easy to leave behind.

As mom and daughter, we coped in the sports world and developed methods to cope at home as well. Often as parents at home alone with our children, we don't have an outlet, especially for single moms. If I became overwhelmed, I would often give myself a time out. If Jade was misbehaving,

I just knew I did not like how I was going to react so, I would go and close my bedroom door. This worked not only for me but also showed her that being upset sometimes meant we just needed quiet time or time out. That and ten deep breaths can help! Getting more air into the bottom of our lungs than the top, breathing deep is relaxing and does wonders for anxiety. Whenever Jade was upset, I would have her copy my deep breathing. I got her to keep her focus on me; it would help her relax along with me. When we had to deal with school and education, I knew we could do it as a team.

There were BIG choices to be made with her schooling. Even there, Jade was the one who directed her own life, and I was her supporting cast. We completed a year in private school, as Jade felt her friends in public school did not treat her like she treated them. According to Jade, public school was a disappointment where she was not taught what she needed to know. After a year of a private school, we discovered they did not teach differently. Despite advertising they had a different approach, it was not apparent. Jade was still just expected to memorize for tests. There was no exploration of aptitudes and encouragement in areas the students excelled. Still, paying for a year of private school let Jade explore her education. Otherwise, she would have always wondered what if?

I've always known Jade is an empath, sensitive to people around her, always caring about others, animals, even insects and bugs as a child. She really picks up on the energy of others and needs to recharge herself like mom, so quiet time is essential to us, especially with how busy our days can be! Our open back-and-forth communication helps in being aware, as the need for downtime arises. Thankfully Jade is heading to a fantastic high school this year and has been creating new relationships in preparation for entering this new arena. I know she will do well!

I always say she is an artistic athlete. When doing homework, she would combine movement with a little homework, movement and then more homework. We can learn so much from our children and what their needs are when we pay attention. I believe I was the same way growing up, but having been raised and disciplined to sit and work longer, expected to be home to babysit my brother, movement or extracurricular activities were not an option. If you, your child or both of you need a time out, we can sit in our rooms and be peaceful, then go do a quick physical activity: run on a treadmill, ride a bike around the block, go for a quick walk... It helps the child and/or the parent to rise above the frustration by locking it to movement. Do you see this as a better option for our children's future? As parents, we have a responsibility to change the school system to enhance education for our children.

Quick story about my childhood, to emphasize why I decided to parent differently: My father was an army brat living all over Canada on different bases and even stationed in Germany once. Rules *ruled* his life; he absorbed this from my grandfather, bringing it into his own parenting style. I don't recall seeing my paternal grandfather smile much. However, I do recall him smoking a lot, and in the end, he was on an oxygen tank. My grandmother mostly just served the family whatever they needed. This is pretty much all I recall her doing, ever! Cooking, cleaning and making sure her husband was happy, and her children were raised to the expected generational standard.

Looking at my childhood, I see that my life was very similar to my father's upbringing since my father would travel all over the province for construction work. Similar to the army brat life, my brother and I were continually meeting new schoolmates and trying to fit in. At the time, I found it hard to read the other kids, and we were lumped in with the "trouble makers" without realizing it. It is hard being a young kid always thrust into new territory, situations and people. These experiences permeated his growing up and I feel my father was always fighting for his life. Because of this, I was raised with this need to prove myself to my parents, to my peers and also to myself.

My mom was raised by her half-sister, Val, as her mom passed when she was only eight. Her dad worked hard to raise both girls and eventually remarried; however, Val was always a mother figure to my mom. Val is now in a care home with dementia. It is sad for me to realize though many work hard, they may not be able to enjoy retirement.

I do have fond memories of driving around with my mom in her red Beetle car, with me joyfully hanging out of the sunroof. (Yup no seat belts then.) The freedom I felt with her at that age was joyful and liberating. It is too bad our children won't be able to experience those moments due to current laws. But it is likely a good thing that safety is a priority these days. (Somedays I wonder how my generation survived, haha.)

My dad and mom met as teenagers, and as my mother tells the story, she loved him before they ever dated. Mom was eighteen and dad twenty when I was born. Far too young to be parents themselves! I wonder if my mom got pregnant to keep dad closer to her? My brother, four and a half years younger, was planned.

When my father passed on, it impacted my mother deeply; it still does to this day. It helped me to understand codependency in relationships and how when one spouse dies suddenly, the other can sometimes no longer know how to exist. It is a mystery to me how she relied so much on my father and still cannot function without him nine years later. Her whole life is TV, adventure books, Sudoku, eating and walking her small dog.

Mom and dad raised my brother and me with the love they knew how to give, making us feel special for birthdays and Christmas. They always wanted to provide us with everything they could afford and perhaps what their parents could not afford, including food, clothing and a healthy dose of "reality" according to them. Lots of rules and required chores around the house. You had to clean your plate even if you did not like something. I recall my brother sitting for over an hour at the dinner table after dinner had finished, and more than once leftovers would be packed up and served for breakfast. Spanking was the norm, and I still recall a wooden spoon being broken. Being grounded was a common occurrence to us both over the years.

When I was thirteen; I rebelled hard – the "my house, my rules" according to my dad, did not seem right! Especially combined with "do as I say, not as I do."

I rebelled in so many ways; sneaking out, older boyfriends, partying and loved every minute of it. Only now as a parent can I look back at teenage me, and look at my daughter, and realize that the reason I acted out the way I did, was because of the way I was raised. This helped me realize how important it is to make conscious parenting choices. I was a lot like Jade when I was 13. I found school boring, and I moved out when I was 16, decided not to go to school, and started work so that I could do what I wanted in life. I knew that I wanted to avoid my fate for Jade, so I aim to give her the freedom that I know every young person craves and create the safety she still needs.

Today, Jade is thirteen, calm, rarely acts out, and is mature beyond her years. What is different and, why? I have to confess I feel she is three to four years ahead of where I was at her age. Most kids are these days, but it made me question if she will want to quit school. Will I be able to keep her engaged enough to attend full-time and graduate?

I had to look back and decipher what I did or did not do differently. Jade is more than happy to spend time with me playing and exploring together. Why do I emphatically trust her despite how I was raised with no trust at her age? Jade and I now live together full-time and the stability has dramatically improved her life. Not bouncing back and forth between mom and dad is the best thing for her as she becomes a young woman.

I have some steadfast rules that I believe have worked over the years. With little ones I find getting down to their level really helps, that way it feels equal when speaking with them instead of talking down to them from above. I always bent down to Jade's level and gave her options to choose from. This empowered her to feel in control. By giving her choices she was able to choose instead of being dictated to, by doing so, I found there were way fewer challenges, and my child felt empowered.

I have learned a lot from my daughter Jade; gifts I didn't know would come into my life until they arrived. There are many unknowns as a parent. Many things we need to learn as we go. If you have learned anything from my story, I hope it is that in allowing your child(ren) to be, you BE-come the parent you were meant to be.

Below are some great tips and action items that will help you change your relationship with your child.

IGNITE ACTION STEPS

*Follow your intuition, you know best, do not follow what your parents did unless it resonates with you.

*Every soul is unique, all deserve empowerment in little decisions and then more significant choices.

*Trust is there already and you can try small tests to see how they handle peer pressure versus doing the right thing.

*Pick a weekly connecting night, one week you choose the activity and the following week child chooses.

*Get out in nature - it is nurturing. Geocaching, scavenger hunts, hikes near water and beauty. Nature is healing.

*Have meal times to share and discuss the day.

*Gratitude moments every morning and night. Get both you and your child to say or list three things you are grateful for.

*Clear your head at night by writing everything down that comes up for you.

*Activate with action - What play does your child truly enjoy?

Tanja Powell - Canada
She.E.O
www.adventuresforconnection.com

ULLA JOVKOVIC

" To be a good parent to my children, I first had to become
a better parent to myself."

My hope for you in reading my story, is you will realize doing your own 'inner child' work paves the way for becoming a loving parent. Additionally, it helps you forgive yourself for not being ready for parenting. It allows you permission to re-parent yourself and to love the way your inner child truly craves.

STAIRWAY TO MY HEART

The phone rang. It was the British embassy calling, "We can't guarantee your safety. We recommend you leave." they reported. This wasn't news to us in Croatia during the war in 1991. By then, my brother, sister, and I weren't going to school because of bomb threats. Men with certain political affiliations in neighboring households were disappearing. By midnight, my parents had made the decision to leave for our safety. It was weirdly silent as Mum, Dad, and we three children packed one suitcase each. The taxi came; I could tell the driver was unnerved, knowing he could be stopped at any moment by the army. When we crossed the border into Italy, I felt my parents uncertain, disbelieving reactions. I remember sensing their vulnerability and it made me feel unsafe.

Leaving that night was viewed as just a safety measure. We thought we'd be back home before long. Returning to the happy surroundings of my childhood, however, was not to be. We went to live with my aunt in northern England. It was a familiar place because I had spent many summer vacations with family there. Although, six months later, we moved eight hours south and the harsh reality struck! "This is it. We're not going back!"

My father fell into a 10-year depression, grieving for his homeland. It was hard to see him in such a state. My mother tried to hold it together, working long hours to feed us, too exhausted to care for us emotionally. One evening when my brain would not switch off, I went to mum's bedroom and told her, "I feel like I'm going to go mad." My life was only school, home, TV, homework, bed, and repeat. I had no friends, no activities. I felt isolated and lonely. She told me to just, "Go back to bed and it will be better tomorrow." It didn't get any better. It was my father who said I should start doing a sport, so my brother and I started playing tennis. Although it did help, I still struggled to integrate and find friends until college, where I made one dear, life-long friend who has become like a sister to me.

Still socially awkward, I found it hard to fit in at university. I retreated to my basement flat for the next four years, stuffing my emotions. I did not know what was wrong with me. I would binge daily on food, vomit, then feel empty and start the whole process over again the next day. It was like I had a need to fill in a huge void. I wanted to feel full inside. Instead of going deeper 'inside ' myself emotionally I ran away, looking for answers on the 'outside'.

After University I took a trip around Asia on my own for a whole year. I had a blast but kept thinking I would find all the answers and instead I only found more questions. I took more trips, made more moves, did more searching for the right place to find my happiness. I got rid of binging, but then started drinking. It seemed like I kept falling down and getting up again. I moved to the south of France, where my parents now resided, to manage a bar. It lasted for 6 months, I went into debt, then paid it off with two new, well-paid jobs. I resigned from the one I hated, and then became redundant at the next. I joined a non-profit organization promoting world peace. I wanted 'world peace' with every cell in my body, but when the organization failed, that was the last straw. At my 33rd birthday party I announced I was leaving. I decided to go back to England. I know I sounded bright about my future, but inside my head I heard I'm 'done', I don't want to try another thing, it always ends up no good... I want to die. To not be alive would be so much easier.

I gave notice on my flat, then found out I was pregnant. I was shocked, but I just knew I had to have this baby. It was what I needed---to take care of someone I could love. Even though I didn't feel stable, I knew I could do it. One day I was walking by the sea thinking, I will never be alone again... but at the same time, I remember feeling like dying might be easier. I was still in so much emotional pain from the past which I had never dealt with. I was tired of trying and then failing.

My baby's father remained a solid presence throughout this time. He helped me move from my flat to my parent's house and was at the birth of our child. He later became my husband and the father of our three brilliant children.

My firstborn shares a birthday with my aunty, who died 3 years before. She was a storyteller with a big imagination and a bit wacky, truly authentic, and we loved her. She drifted through life as an independent soul, found it hard to fit in and be accepted for who she was. Through my own feelings of unhappiness and despair, I felt close to her and so very sad for her passing. She would often drown her sorrows in alcohol, to numb the pain and forget the bad choices she had made and kept making. Her death hit me hard. I had a huge 'ignite' moment when my son was born and I made a promise to never emotionally neglect my child like I thought my grandmother had abandoned my aunty.

I knew I needed to parent differently, but I didn't really know what to do. I wanted my child to be seen and heard; I was going to be present for him. I would be nurturing and caring. I had to gradually sense my way forward, but this in itself, was a "big thing. For the first time ever, I was learning to trust myself and my deeper intuition. I realized I needed to change direction and uncover a new foundation. I started to read books about parenting from a place of greater peace and awareness. I watched videos and signed up for courses to learn I could about parenting and enrolled my son into a Montessori school. I felt focused, with a clear intention to raise my son in a conscious way. I started a networking group for women and, generally, I felt good.

It was then the realization came that I could have ended up like my aunt, harming and destroying myself, if not for my pregnancy and the birth of my child. For my son, a sensitive soul like my aunt and me, I needed to provide safety, love, and belonging from an early age. Those were emotions I had craved since having to abandon the country of my birth at an important developmental time.

With my second son, I focused on having a peaceful pregnancy and a natural birth. During the pregnancy, however, I experienced anxiety symptoms. After the doctor examined me, he concluded, "It is nothing...",

I remember thinking OMG, this is what anxiety feels like – I can't breathe, my chest hurts and feels tight! This was during the time we were renovating our home and although I had a great birth, I found everything very stressful. Nevertheless, I had to get on with it, and become a "Supermom". What this meant for me was 'doing' and not 'being'. With a toddler and a newborn I had to do it all; the cooking, cleaning, shopping and still be there for my kids emotionally. There was no ME time, even though I desperately craved it. It was hard to balance it all. My husband worked long hours. Healthy habits, self-preservation, and personal care were hard to implement when I was responding to what others were expecting of me. However, my understanding of self awareness started to emerge. I knew in theory what self care should look like through reading personal development books. It was just hard to put into practice. Slowly but surely, I realized that self-care manifested in healthy eating, personal prayer, and journaling for myself and my family.

"S**t! It's a girl!" was my first reaction when my daughter was born and we found out she was a girl. I panicked! Darn, I will not be able to fool this one for long. She will 'suss' me out in no time with all my internal chaos and surface attempts to keep myself together.

I felt unprepared for the arrival of my daughter. I consider women as strong, capable and independent, but in my own head, I often still felt like this frightened 14-year old girl who did not belong – scared, unsafe and unloved. It was easy to fake it with the boys (or so I thought), but not with girls, especially a Scorpio girl, who looks at you and sees through you with laser-beam eyes going directly to the soul.

With this pregnancy, I hired a doula to support me emotionally. I was worried about being a good role model for my daughter, which led me to seek professional help from a therapist. From my firstborn when I had thought about taking my own life, to having anxiety with my second child, and in therapy with my third, I knew I had progressed. I saw the journey I was having with every child and what they had taught me. I will always be a 'work in progress' my happiness now comes from the process of internally and spiritually growing. My children inspire me to show up for them, to be the most I can because they deserve the best version of me.

In fact, the foundation of my understanding is that modeling behavior is the most impactful way we can guide our children. By living the best version of ourselves, we are demonstrating to our children they can do the same, too.

New Beginnings: my second chapter – Move to Rural France: We lived in Cote d'Azur, Nice for the next 10 years, but with three kids in tow, living in a city apartment was not my idea of what their childhood should be.

Our move was prompted by my husband's desire to be in a quieter environment. While we searched for our new home and community, it was becoming clear to me what I wanted for my children and for their childhood. I had a desire for them to feel closer to nature, to know the seasons, what the Earth has to offer, as well as a slower pace of life. Also, I wanted for me to not be constantly on their case for being kids – making noise, having a meltdown, shouting, singing because the neighbours might complain.

Some deep, spiritual searching brought me towards a more peaceful, true me and a richer sense of my "heart place". This change and especially living in Nature had a profound effect on my soul and well-being. Our new home is a magical land where time disappears almost completely to give way to all-encompassing stillness and peace. Immersing ourselves in this beautiful landscape where we are using all the senses and, very importantly our hearts, is our everyday job now – a lucky and delightful change from city life and the past.

In our small village in France, my first-born found the transition very difficult with his own emerging anxiety and refused to go to his new school. At the time I did my best to approach the situation in a heartfelt and mindful way. I involved the school, asking them if they could support my son with this transition. They were instrumental in helping him integrate into his new school and take it day by day. I also bought an online course all about childhood anxiety and how the brain works. This is when the breakthrough came and he was able to identify *fight, flight or freeze* and how and why the brain functions when under stress. It was such a relief for me to know I was there for my son when we moved. I was present for him and we took it day by day. It did not occur to me at the same time I was doing what I needed, and should have had when I was a child during the war. I healed the little girl in me. It made me realize I created what I needed in my own childhood experience. Was it easy? Hell NO!!! But we got through it to the other side and now am reaping the rewards of seeing my son open, confident, and free and that is such a delight to watch.

For myself, I felt a huge healing and realizing that for all the time we were not held, heard, or supported and understood I needed healing, too. My gift to my son has become a gift to me. I've heard that when we heal ourselves, we heal seven generations forward and seven generations back. I am happy with three generations in our family!

Our new, more peaceful environment means I have more energy to devote to my own evolution, both as a parent and a person. Remembering my aunty, I feel like a bridge has connected generations of my family and the two very different worlds. One generation being very unhappy and dark, while the other, emerging through me and my struggles, is more open and heartfelt with a firm commitment to this new way forward. The reality which surrounds us now is so much lighter, brighter and more aware.

When I was 14, I used to say, "I want to rewire my brain," to overcome all my disconnection with life. Finally, I was doing just that by taking a 1-year online course with Dr. Shefali, learning meditation, stillness, being aware of my thoughts, and catching and gently reframing them. Now, I observe my emotions and ask myself, "Am I really angry with my son for doing 'x' or is this trigger just the last drop in something that has been going on in me for days, months, or even years?" I am now able to avoid blame, adjust, and take another approach, knowing the answer is always finding a greater connection and compassion with myself, my kids, or my husband.

We all want the best for our children, but how we go about it is shaped by our own childhood experiences with our parents 'parenting' us. We are lucky to live in an age of enlightenment with an array of information and support options available. Only if we are willing to be open to them, we can change the future.

Last year I celebrated my 40th birthday. I really wanted to celebrate me and who I am, which has not always been easy for me. For a split second, I was going to write my achievements; that is what society/culture wants us to believe success is, but I am older and wiser now.

One of my core values is freedom. Staying true to our heart and essence is the only way to navigate through the choices we make in life. Each day I am allowing my authentic self to emerge. It was revealing that two of my friends, including my dear friend from college who has known me for twenty years, came for my birthday party and both said, "This suits you. This is you, the real Ulla".

So, this is me, and there is more to me... I will always travel in my mind, and I never want to feel I have settled. To me life is not for settling, but for exploring – both our inner and outer worlds.

In retrospect, my journey 'back to myself' started with the birth of my son and me feeling my way through, acting intuitively, and finally leaving 'the thinking place' and taking the first steps down the stairway to my heart. Let's face it. I would prefer to take the elevator to get there faster but we all know for things to work better, it takes time. I see myself moving along a staircase comprised of several landings with each of my three children leading me from one landing to the next, deeper and deeper towards my inner heart-place. They say the longest journey you will ever make on this earth is from the head to the heart, and my kids are keeping me firmly on this path. They are my compass, whenever I feel off track or stuck wherever that may be.

I keep going down the stairway to my heart. My children have shown me there is no separation in Love and the only way to loving and accepting my kids for who they truly are, is to accept myself unconditionally. My wish is that you find your own stairway on the journey to your heart-space. See your children as guides which connect you to the truth of who you really are: total and peaceful love!

IGNITE ACTION STEPS

Techniques that could help you on your journey to your heart space:

*Self- acceptance and self-compassion – "Embrace the Chaos" – it all might appear "too much" and "out of control" at times. Our issues often appear unimaginably dark, but they have the purpose of showing us the Light.

*Sensitivity, vulnerability, connection, empathy – all good things. Motherhood issues often turn the volume up on them to an unbearable degree, but address it with boundaries and self-care.

*Embrace the support and resources available – organizational, in person, on-line, there are many different approaches – find the one that truly speaks to you.

*The Nature Path – returning to Presence through Nature, simply "in-tune" to living, Nature is healing, consistent with no expectations which has a profound effect on your soul.

Ulla Jovkovic - France
www.ourfrenchvillagelife.com

URI YESZERSKI

"Dance in the vibration of your creativity. Flow in the creation
of your reality. Grow in quantum leaps."

I share my story with you, unplugged from the depths of my growth, inviting you to meet your soul and come home. On this parenting journey, I hope you find lessons, count your blessings and grow at a quantum leap!

SAY 'YES' TO THE JOURNEY

My name is Uri - Passionate nomadic soul born in Mongolia, lived in India, immigrated to the U.S. as a single mom. Graduated with two master's degrees, MBA, MPA, championed multiple; careers across four countries, TEDxSpeaker on my journey to passion as a headhunter and career coach. Steadfast realtor as a transactional and transitional coach. Self-healer and growth expert as a transformational teacher. Manifested and married my soulmate. Now we create our life between Canada, Mongolia, and Hawaii.

This is my story of growth-hood in motherhood to a teenage girl and a toddler boy. I was that kid who always had a head start. Some was from parenting at its best. Some was the thirst of my nomadic soul to explore and experience life. I started school early and graduated high school at 16. That was my mom's coaching. I met my boyfriend in second-year college, became a mom at 18 and married him. You probably guessed that was *not* my mom's coaching. At 20, I won an MBA scholarship in India, at one of the toughest schools there. As a young Mongolian family of three, we flew to Bangalore and made India home for 2 years. I was the one who supported our family while going to school full-time, working a nightshift call-center job while 'the dad' watched the baby and walked her to Montessori school. That was our arrangement.

While learning to parent and navigating life in a new country, we experienced growth on a separate path. Our marriage grew apart despite our efforts to get to know each other. Upon graduating and return to Mongolia, we kept trying to make it work for the sake of our child. Could staying in an unhappy, incompatible relationship help my daughter grow up happy I asked myself. Does love mean only sacrifice? Deep down, I knew if I am not happy, how am I supposed to model happiness for my daughter? Although taught to never give up, I choose to follow my heart, set myself free and became a single mom with no child support from him. Starting fresh felt scary, yet mostly exciting.

Following dreams to make it in America, I applied for a second master's degree to live as an international student in Washington D.C. Being a single mom, I had to leave my daughter in Mongolia with my parents to get a home ready for us in the USA. With plans to bring my daughter in 3 months, I had no time to waste. Along with a child to care for, school to graduate, my long-term goal was to get employed and be legally sponsored. For the short term, I had no job. No apartment. No one. The best part of this period of my life was I had no fear. In my mind, I had the life experience to prepare me for this. Someone told me, "'If you lived in India, you could make it anywhere." Convinced, I remember singing in my head, "I've done it before, I can do it again." After all, I was an MBA but also what I call 'Master of Being All'.

I was wrong. As an international student without a work permit, I was limited to 20 hour/week on-campus jobs only. It was disappointing but I got a job...Check. Montessori school enrollment...Check. Apartment... Check. "Mom-Daughter Duo" to-do list...Check. I was ready to be reunited with my daughter.

Within the first weeks she struggled to adjust. "Put me in that plane, I wanna go home," my daughter pointed at the airplane in the sky, screaming and crying on the way to her new kindergarten. Thoughts of walking one more block felt so daunting. I was exhausted, helpless and full of guilt. I felt horrible and an unworthy mother to my daughter. How foolish to put her in this situation! How selfish of a mother am I, to separate her from her dad? All the strength I had seemed to disappear, my legs failed me. I managed to sit down grabbing a railing. I don't know for how long I just sat there, with tears in my eyes and tightness in my chest.

Until that moment, I had it all figured out. But what I didn't realize was children mirror our energy, our feelings. I had not allowed myself to feel the emotions of my divorce or any other traumas in my life. No time for that. I was taught to be tough, strong, and just move on. Apparently, I hadn't moved on. I felt such persistence to cope with any challenges yet such resistance to face my fears and feel my emotions. By looking at my daughter's feelings I suddenly saw myself. I paused and slowed down and stopped fighting everything. Her emotion was a reflection of the rage in me. I surrendered to it all and a faith came through for both of us. I **saw** my daughter at that moment and she no longer needed to cry because my grounding, grounded her. I let go of my emotions and so did she. I knew "My baby girl must be terrified of being left with strangers in an unfamiliar place; she doesn't even speak the language." Through compassion for my daughter's feelings, a thread of truth came to me – *I was the one terrified.* Forced to slow down, I surrendered to my feelings of anger, sadness, and grief – I gave them the attention they deserved, and they moved through me. All passed. At a deep level, I knew I was okay in that moment and so was she.

My daughter came into my life when I was not ready for a relationship. So, I made difficult choices to be happy. Twenty-something, young single parent, immigrating with a child – oh yeah, the struggle was real. I was stretched, juggling and struggling to manage it all on my own. Every day I woke up, got her ready, dropped her off, ran back to work the morning shift, attended afternoon classes, then rushed back to pick her up from an extended daycare. As if graduating a 2-year program in one year wasn't enough, I had to find work in the 2008 economic crisis. I found a job with an IT firm where I managed the business. Long hours and low pay earned me my green card. By year 3, I made it in America, my immigration and career goals accomplished. I found success at 27, but not happiness. Sitting in my office, goals achieved, green card in hand, legally and financially secure, now what? I was numb. Shocked how much I had suppressed my feelings while getting to the destination. Along the way, I'd missed the journey of being in the present moment. I lost myself and the parent I wanted to be, in an endless chase for success.

My heart wanted to be truly happy and live in alignment with my truth. What was my truth? Who am I? I really didn't know other than I was a mom and a daughter. I found myself in a rat-race which most consider a successful life. Dissatisfied. Disconnected. Lost. Unfulfilled. Along the way, I saw

I'd become a tiger mom, raising my daughter with high expectations as I was raised. I recognized I grew up not knowing what made me happy, feel 'not good enough' for my parents and for everything in my life.

Now I was doing it to her, making her feel not good enough. My daughter would make the cutest art pieces and show me proudly, " Look, I made this - Mommy." "Oh, that's great! But you can do better," I would respond, I wish I hadn't said that. Believe me, it came from the place of trust in her potential but not from a mean heart. Tough love, that's how I was raised. Just like my parents, I was busy providing, working on my laptop, on some important project. *I wish I could have been a bit more present, kind and encouraging with my compliments.* But that's not how I was conditioned. I felt bad I didn't give her the attention she needed. Despite all we had gone through, my daughter remembered our "Mother-Daugther-Duo" period as her happiest moments. That chapter of our lives when it was just the two of us, doing the best we could; me growing as a parent. I will always cherish her reflection on that time and her words...

Zoe: "Mommy, remember when we were just the two of us?"

Mom: " Yes, Sweetie."

Zoe: "That's when I was the happiest."

My daughter was my priority and an anchor in my life. Making difficult decisions was easy when thinking of her first. She and I grew up together in a way. When I made peace with myself at 31, I met my soulmate and had my son. He gifted me with the most beautiful pregnancy, but quite the challenging motherhood experience. My colicky, gassy, acidic baby showed me resilience. He stretched my emotional bandwidths with his toddler tantrums and filled my heart with love I never imagined. His sweet soft kisses whispering in his toddler voice, "I know, I love you." His little fingers caressing my face "Sun's up - Mommy! Not gonna wake you up; me just gonna snuggle with you." Cute eye contact and thumbs up! "Good job, mommy!." "Night night mommy, I'll take you to the moon."

My kids are my heart, my growth space. I've stepped into seeing them first. When I said yes to conscious parenting, I became a new growth expert. I knew I couldn't parent the same way I had been raised. I had to evolve and grow with my children to become the parent they needed. Today my teenage girl has her own intelligence and wisdom to guide her to explore the unknown. She will always have me to come home to while I too have my own journey to explore. After all, parenting is not the hardest job, but the greatest school of growth. It is a rollercoaster ride which helps parents grow-up. At least I did! To a certain extent. It was quite a task to try to escape myself, it was much easier to embrace myself.

At 35, for the first time in my life, I *met* my soul. Quite It was unlike anything else I've ever experienced. I had tears of joy when I saw my inner self and divine essence. I took four days off from my busy mom/ entrepreneur life for a silent meditation retreat. I observed my usual busy mind as it calmed down. Waves of emotion pass through my body as aches dissolve within hours. I welcomed all my feelings: fear, pain, anger, bliss, sadness, happiness, shame, vulnerability and insecurity---all of it. Then I felt the fuzzy fluffy clouds, the soft sweetness of my inner child appears. I touched her warmth and cuddled her like a baby with so much self-love. I felt peaceful and right at home. My love for me felt so unconditional. I healed my inner child. I felt enough. I hugged my soul. Love felt so infinite. I returned to my kids and husband with so much love to share. My heart was filled with joy, grace, and gratitude. Nothing was left of my usual busy mind. I had to pause and check, to be sure. Really, nothing on my mind? Nope, nothing but peace of mind. I made a self-commitment: *"Make a conscious effort to stop this endless achievement chasing, over-committed life and instead – live in flow. Slow down to speed up growth exponentially. The only growth that matters is inside out. From intention to manifestation. Let the dust settle in stillness, let clarity shine in silence."*

Now, I am learning the art of conscious parenting. I've reflected on my own childhood, young single-motherhood, and then my *growth-hood* in my current parenting experience. Our core values, belief-system and behaviors are conditioned from our childhood, often shape how we show up as parents. My parents did their best with what they knew from their time. Providing safety, security and sacrificing for the family is what love meant to them. But I dare to challenge parents to be selfish about self-love. So we can grow as conscious parents and re-parent ourselves from a place of love, peace, and abundance not from fear of safety, loss, and scarcity.

When it came to parenting, I knew nothing, but still knew it was deeper knowing that "we got this." That day on the stairs, I surrendered to uncertainty and understood, "I am not in control." It is an illusion that anyone has control of what's yet to come. When I lose myself in being "human" again, I just need to be willing and open to what may come. When I had my daughter at 19, I was not ready and knew nothing. When I had my son 13 years later, I thought I was ready and knew quite a lot, but still knew nothing. Today, I am okay not knowing. I dwell in the possibilities of unknowns. I dance with challenges. I welcome difficulty with excitement knowing I am growing. The more we get out of our own way, the stronger our inner intelligence guides us. Trust yourself. Let the miracle happen.

Happiness is not a destination. It is a vibration. I didn't always know that. I did know how to change my radio station and hit my favorite channel. That made me feel happy. It kept me going at times of procrastination, stagnation, and depression. But I never realized that I too am the radio station. My vibrations are the channels. Infinite playlist of energy on demand. If only I can choose to skip the commercial of my stories and remember I can always subscribe to my innate awesomeness. That is who I am.

When I made peace with the fact that the purpose of my life is not happiness, but rather experience and growth, happiness became a natural byproduct. Parenting experience continues to challenge my growth paradigm into a whole new dimension. The joy and happiness of being happy, fulfilled, loved, blessed parents is the epiphany of life.

Dear Parents, in reading my story, my wish is that you say 'yes' to your own powerful growth-hood journey. I welcome you to this sacred space, where it is safe to show up as messy, real and big as you are. Are you ready? To shift to a creation mindset? To claim your highest self? To live your dream life? To re-birth through your story? To create your new reality? These are my gifts to you.

Be fearless. If you feel naive know that growth is right around the corner. Determination create destiny and the foundation of parenthood.

Think about all the hard times, you could not see beyond the thought. But you did. Deep down in your heart, in your gut, you know you are okay. There is something soothing about that. Gift yourself time to surrender to those emotions.

Have you ever asked what does my heart want? How often do you find yourself missing something when you think you're doing everything you're supposed to?

It is my sincere wish that you let go of your stories, heal your inner child and carry less-judgement and guilt towards your parents. Hopefully less self-doubt of who you are as a parent and who you are deep within. Let us heal our stories one child, one parent, one inner child at a time. Let us parent from a place of peace within.

Does your face light up when your children walk into the room?

Ignite Action Steps

Dear parents, Destroy the idea that you have to be constantly working or grinding in order to be successful. Stop hustling and start aligning. .Embrace the concept that rest, recovery and reflection are the essential parts of the progress towards a successful and ultimately happy life.. Life is a dance not a hustle. You have the power to create your reality and live in-flow everyday.

*Unapologetically be selfish about your growth space. Growth happens only when you are conscious of your energy and space. Listen to your body. Let the mind slow down to let your own insight come up. Intentionally center yourself. Ground yourself – connect deeply to your truth. That's how you refill your energy. It is the love that flows out of your full heart which is the purest and magical.

*Uplift your energy. Raise your vibration. Ignite your soul. Raise your vibration by simply changing the frequency of your radio channel. Interesting enough, you'll change the negative chatter to positive praise instantly. Ignite your soul and shine your light.

*Unleash your passion and hearts desires. Peace of mind. Listen to your inner voice, your unique invitation to own your stars. No excuse. Show up. Be you. Play big. Be fearless. Come home. Learn to meditate. Get a coach. Write your story.

Uri Yeszerski - USA
Transformational Coach
www.GrowthSpace.ca

YENDRE SHEN

"You can't plan for what life brings you,
but you can embrace it gracefully."

My wish for you, the reader, is that when you find yourself in the worst possible place in your life and you think you're lost... trust that you are not. When things you didn't prepare for happen, or when you think you've taken a wrong turn, embrace it, for in that moment you don't yet know where it'll take you.

UNEXPECTED

My children are beautiful surprises, both figuratively and literally. They taught me to love and to know how they each needed to be parented. Before they came, I was waiting for my former self to return. Instead, they helped me transform into someone new.

Grief and deep depression settled upon me after my father's death, which I did not fully understand. We were not close. In private moments, my sense of despair would bring me to tears. Inner anguish made life feel hard and 'not living' was sometimes a comforting thought. On the outside, no one would imagine this was my internal struggle. My life looked good. I started a naturopathic practice, found a new passion in rock climbing, traveled, and did my first marathon in Iceland. Looking back, I'm amazed at all the things I was doing. Regardless, I felt my life had no meaning and I felt unclear about my life's purpose.

A year and a half later, I met the man who would be the father of my children. It was exciting at the beginning and we explored the possibility of being a couple. He was open to trying new things I shared with him. He even took a self-development course with me. We decided to attend the next one in Los Angeles. Some weeks before our trip, I broached the subject of going as friends and he disagreed with me. He didn't acknowledge our incompatibilities. We differed in how we communicated. In fact, our first child was the result of a lack of communication.

We made love on the morning of the second day of our course. When it happened and in the moments that followed, I felt time slowed down for me. Later I told him, "I think it's my fertile time of the month." He looked at me and said, "I guess we'll figure it out." We didn't speak of it again until the inevitable became apparent. I missed my period. I bought a pregnancy test and called him. He was away on business.

"I got the kit," I told him.

He laughed, "You couldn't wait."

"I want to know. I'm a few days late." I explained, then paused, "Whatever the result, let's see it as a blessing. Okay, here goes."

We waited. "I think there are two lines showing up. That means I'm pregnant."

"Wow, I'm numb, speechless, wow," he babbled.

"I think you're in shock."

"I guess we'll have to talk when I come back," he responded.

I don't think pregnancy was in either one of our plans. I remembered his mother playfully scolding us, "Don't you two know better? You're not kids, you should know how to prevent this sort of thing." There was some irony to the situation. After all, I am a medical professional.

I was ambivalent about having children, perhaps due to growing up without a mother. She died when I was one and a half. As a child, I was told a story that she wanted to give me away. That story comforted me. Having a mother who was alive and didn't want me would have been terrible. Still, a part of me wanted to know her; perhaps being a mother would help me know her.

The choice to have a baby or not would have been easier if we were confident about our relationship and not wondering whether it'd work out. The responsibilities that come with raising a child are immense and foreign. It would be a permanent change to my life as I presently knew it. I was aware that life is precious, that there was a future human being growing inside me. It became clear; I would feel more regret giving up the baby than having it.

With that decision our lives were forever changed. On the morning of January 2nd, our daughter came into our world with the help of midwives. The coziness of our home birth was interrupted when I had difficulty nursing and her jaundice became serious enough to require hospitalization. It's painful as a parent to watch your child suffer. We had to stay overnight as they needed to do tests. I had tears streaming down my face as I helped to hold her down so vials of blood were drawn from her little body as she wailed.

My daughter was a colicky baby. Her crying at night would drive her father crazy. He sometimes wished it wasn't criminal to chuck her out the window. When she finally fell asleep, I'd stare at her for a long time. In that stillness, I realized that only in the face of great hardship would a mother choose to give away her child. I recalled a memory from when I was studying naturopathic medicine. I attended an aboriginal healing ceremony because I wanted to know if my mother loved me. I came from a culture that valued boys more than girls and I was the third girl. Women are blamed or praised for the gender of their children. It must have been hard to endure the criticism of having only girls.

At three months old, my daughter started to develop severe eczema. Her skin was dry and she would itch, causing bleeding. As a parent you tend to feel it's your fault when your child is sick or has a condition. I felt responsible and helpless. I was fortunate to be able to find homeopathic medicines that managed the flare-ups.

The strain of being new parents and sleep deprived by a colicky baby with eczema, further eroded our relationship. We were unable to communicate our feelings. Never having learned to connect compassionately with one another, many of our responses were reactive. Being a team in difficult moments was not our forte. We fought instead. To avoid arguing, we spoke less and less to each other.

I began to feel very alone in my relationship. My tendency to do too much and not ask for help left me feeling even more alone. How we managed to make the same mistake a second time is a mystery to me as we had stopped sleeping together. Our son was somehow conceived 'immaculately'. His father would joke it wasn't him. Seeing their similar mannerisms and walk is uncanny; it's undeniable that father and son are cut from the same genetic fabric.

I had asked for a separation long before the second pregnancy and he'd been looking for a place to move. "Do I have this second child or not?" was again a choice I had to face. It was obvious now we didn't know how to be a healthy couple. Our families expressed their worries of having another child if we're breaking up. I felt I could live with myself more easily preserving life than destroying it.

When children are involved in a deteriorating relationship, it's difficult to determine whether it's harder to be together or apart. It's a heart-wrenching choice for a parent to leave their children. I know he tried to stay after our son was born. He didn't want to leave and be separated from his kids. Even after he bought his condo and it was ready to move in, he didn't. Until one night when he left hastily in a fit of anger. We were all overtired from being out late; he could not deal with getting the children ready for bed.

He slammed the door and wasn't aware it didn't close properly. In the middle of the night, I awoke with cold air blowing through the house. As I closed the door and felt the cool fresh air, it hit me. "I'm alone with a four month old baby and a two and a half year old toddler." It wasn't something I wanted or planned for. I had three lives to care for – How am I going to do that? I wasn't even sure I knew how to take care of my own life.

When my father died I had silently said to myself, "I'm an orphan now," which is a strange thought as I was not a child. I had felt alone most of my life. I sensed these emotions were not only mine but they were my father's and mother's, too. This time, however, I felt the strength in me that I'll do whatever it takes to be there for my kids.

I knew he left that night to avoid inflicting harm to those he loved, to protect us from himself. Not knowing any other way, we used anger to channel our unpleasant emotions. He had so much pain which he directed towards me, in corrosive words and actions. If our communication was difficult before, it became even more challenging with the separation. I knew if I fought with him, our children would be the casualties. There was no winning. If I let winning become important to me, then our children would lose. I can walk away from someone who's being unpleasant but I couldn't do that here. I wanted my children to grow up with their father in their lives. I thought it was especially important for my son. I felt boys needed their fathers as strong role models.

I grew up without my father until we were united when I was almost five. My father also grew up without his father until he was eleven years old. My grandfather left to escape being drafted in World War II. My father didn't meet him until some years after the war ended. I sensed his childhood left him feeling scared and alone most of his life. Growing up without my mother or father around, I felt disconnected. I didn't quite know who I was or where I came from. For a while, I didn't understand how some of my relatives were related to me. I was like a frail thread pulled apart from the whole. Even today I'm confused. I didn't want that to be my children's experience.

Looking back, I see we were two hurt people in our own worlds of pain and depression, somehow thinking being in a relationship with another would help us find our salvation. That's not how it works—no one can save us. We can only save ourselves with love, acceptance and forgiveness. I applied these like medicines to the open, painful wounds. I would love. I would accept. I would forgive. Whatever he threw at me, I would remain loving. I would accept that was where we were and I would forgive. I practiced patience. I would be kind in return, when he was being hurtful. It felt like swallowing acid sometimes, but I tried my best to let it course through me and not react.

It took time, but eventually we were able to work together. A daycare worker who had been through divorce herself, praised the emotional well-being of our children, knowing we were separated. As for my concern for my son, he came back from his father's one day and said to me, "When I grow up I want to be a daddy."

The invisible work that no one sees, paid off. Last year, when my daughter was in grade three, I felt proud as a parent. From kindergarten to grade three, my daughter required an Individual Education Plan to get the support she needed to learn to self-regulate her emotions. When it started, I was called to school about once a week to take her home as she was being disruptive in the classroom. My daughter has a strong and willful personality. She can be oppositional, defiant, and behave in ways impossible to reason with. When she didn't get what she wanted, she would have tantrums and cry for over an hour. This deeply concerned me and I sought counseling to work on myself. I was afraid I would end up having a contentious daughter-mother relationship.

Fortunately, the right actions were taken and we are able to have wonderful, interesting conversations. Being a bright, curious child, she asked me one day, "Did you want to have kids, Mommy?" I paused, wondering where would this lead? Will I reveal the truth of how she came to be? Then I told her, "I wasn't sure, but I'm happy that I have you."

She pressed for more, "You didn't plan to have us?"

I decided to just tell her the truth. "You were surprises."

Then she casually shared, "My friends Jackie and May were surprises too." She pondered, "How many people do you think are surprises, Mommy?"

I thought for a bit. It dawned on me that my daughter didn't see unplanned things as unwanted things. I replied, "I don't know. It's possible there are a lot."

I see my children, purposely or not, test the limits to find out if I'm willing to love and accept them. It's like a dare. They want to see I can love them no matter what. They want to know they can be redeemed, no matter what they've done and how badly they have behaved. My most important task is knowing how to separate the child from the behaviour. These challenges have taught me I have infinite capacity to love. No matter what the situation, there's always the choice to love, including loving myself. My older sister said my childhood tantrums were worse than my daughter's. I wore out the heels of all my socks and cried until I lost my voice. There is a blessing in getting my children: they have taught me how to become the right mother for them and how to be the parent I missed having for myself.

For my son, I see him in me too. He's a sensitive child, hard on himself, anxious and worried about making mistakes. His father would sometimes call him soft and weak. Knowing I'm here to help, he doesn't need to harden his tenderness and sensitivity. I want him to learn it's a strength to have those qualities as a man. He's a thoughtful child; he asked me the other day, "Momma are you happy?" I answered, "Yes."

Recently, in cleaning out some things, I found the notebook I used for that course in Los Angeles when I got pregnant. One question I wrote down was what do I want to get out of the course? I had said, "Something that gives my life a purpose worth living for." I gasped as tears welled up in my eyes and tears fell on the page. I realized having my children saved me from my depression. It demanded from me something greater than what I thought I could be.

Being a parent became my spiritual journey and it helped heal wounds I didn't know I had. It allowed me to see I'm a bridge between the past and future. It helped me understand my parents and how our lives were woven into each other's. The memories of the past when not healed, carry residues into the future. My work to heal the past has the power to alter the future patterns of my children. There are hidden gifts from the unexpected things that happen to us. Embrace the unexpected with grace. Only in looking back, can you see how everything was there to help you arrive at where you are now. You'll come to know you haven't been alone. You've been held in an embrace by the Divine all along.

IGNITE ACTION STEPS

We have the life that's meant for us to learn. Similar things will keep recurring until we learn the lessons. Letting go of needing things to be a certain way has been a challenge for me. Life is unpredictable. Kids make it even more so. Having children provided me with opportunities to practice **embracing the unexpected with grace:**

*Turn a mistake into a masterpiece. Be willing to make mistakes and not get upset about it. It will help you and your children to keep trying at the things that are important.

*See the beauty in flaws and imperfections. Being yelled at as a child, I find myself quick to yell at my kids. I work to correct this everyday and I ask my children to help me.

*Be open to seeing surprises and accidents as adventures.

*Disappointments are blessings in disguise.

*Welcome unexpected outcomes.

*Balance expectations and standards.

Differentiate what needs to be corrected and what can be let go. This helps children see there is more than one way to do things and respect each other's differences and styles.

Embracing the unexpected with grace allowed me to look forward from where I was and not look backward staring at my mistakes and being unhappy about them. I learned to focus on what's good about the situation and what I would like it to be. Keep practicing. If you don't give up, you'll get better and closer to what you want. Be open to unexpected possibilities as you never know where life will take you.

Yendre W. Shen - Canada
Naturopathic Doctor and Bowen Therapist
Innerguidance.ca

ANA SOFIA OROZCO

"Good parents understand they are chosen by the Universe to facilitate another human being's life and purpose."

Through four brief stories describing some of my personal experiences, I want to inspire better parenting by understanding that our children do not belong to us; by letting go of the ego; by learning to relate with children from a place of Empathy; and by acknowledging and embracing Diversity.

PARENTING FROM LOVE AND EMPATHY

Being a mother has been without any doubt the biggest project I have undertaken in my life. Early on in this journey, I realized I had been assigned a mission with a higher purpose. I believe this is the first step for conscious and meaningful parenting.

Understanding Parenting as a Higher Mission – After waiting four years for this miracle to happen, I was lying down on a bed at Nuestra Señora del Rosario Hospital in Madrid, Spain. It was 4:00 AM, one summer day, in 2004. Suddenly the commotion of labor stopped. I wasn't sure if everything was all right; I do not recall what the doctor and nurses said and just remember a bloody blob being put on my stomach. I was shocked. I had seen so many TV commercials of beautiful scenes with moms carrying cute calm babies. That's what motherhood looked and felt like to me before this moment. Of course, I knew that parenting involved a lot more but nevertheless, those romantic images were a more subconscious idea of mothers with their newborns. But there I was lying down, feeling the most primitive, raw, and vulnerable ever and this purple, pink, bloody creature was on my stomach. I remember telling myself, "This is your baby. You must hold her, kiss her, and love her." This was actually a very profound moment and at the same time, it seems quite comic today. It was all quite a shock! I doubtfully put my fingers on her. As soon as I touched her body, a nurse took her away and I was left there with my hands all bloody. This is how my parenting started.

Moments later, my baby was brought back to me, all cleaned up and nicely swaddled in a little cozy white bassinet. I was now responsible for protecting her, feeding her, changing her diapers and educating her. I was submerged in feelings of awe, joy, and absolute devotion to this stranger, although nothing felt idyllic. Instead, it felt more primitive. I did not yet know how to take good care of her but I did feel that I would give up my life to protect her. I fell asleep. My baby next to me.

Giving birth had revealed me as being part of a bigger purpose and paradoxically, it had made me the most vulnerable ever. I was oblivious to the fact that conceiving a child is one of the biggest manifestations of real human power: that of being part of this Universe, of existing, of perpetuating it. This vulnerability transformed me forever. I was brought down to reality, away from the domains of individuality, ego and pride. It was humbling to understand myself as one part of this Universe and its transcendent rules and unknown motives.

After this profound inner transformation, life went by between the happenings of my ordinary life, the new demands of parenting, and the great wonders of seeing my baby girl laugh, feel, learn and develop. I had become a transformed Being who intuitively knew parenting should come from a place of humbleness over ego.

Parenting is about the child; let go of your Ego – Four years later, another transforming moment happened. My baby had become a smart, sweet little girl, full of curiosity, enthusiasm and will. In the month of October, the school had organized a costume parade and competition. One day at home, having a casual conversation, I asked my daughter: "So what would you like to dress up as for Halloween?" She looked at me with her exotic vivid eyes, "I want to be a tea party…" What? Had she really said 'a tea party'? Where was I supposed to get such a costume? I was tempted to tell her that wasn't possible, then I thought: *'My daughter can learn creativity has no limits… if we can pull off a tea party costume!'*. We headed to Michaels and bought a two-inch thick square of foam and a piece of fabric to make a tablecloth.

I converted the foam into a table board to sit around my daughter's waist. I stuck toy plates and tea cups on the table with cookies and pastries. I had created an extraordinary costume!

Halloween arrived and we headed to school, all proud. Suddenly the kids and parents headed to the auditorium and my daughter was called on stage as one of the best costume finalists. She looked at me and said: "I don't want to go." I thought to myself, yes she was, and we were winning that prize. Tears started forming in her eyes. "No, mommy, no!" The teachers said we had already won. We just had to go on stage. My daughter kept refusing and started crying. She did not move and we did not win.

I was very annoyed. She was very anxious. It was supposed to be a happy moment. Suddenly, I realized. What was the point? My daughter wanted to look like her friends, she wanted to play, not to win. The process of creating the costume had happened and we had succeeded. I also realized this was her Halloween party and it was becoming a celebration of my pride. I understood my child's life was not supposed to happen according to my wishes and expectations, but to hers... I was meant to facilitate a path on which she could become the best version of her true self.

Letting go of my ego is still one of my biggest challenges as a parent; letting go of my expectations, ignoring useless social demands, and allowing my kids' authenticity to show up. I still find myself demanding from my children certain attitudes, choices and behaviors that respond to my wishes and not theirs. I often share with them my struggle to let go of my futile beliefs and open space to co-create something which serves us better. I am fortunate when they resist and challenge me, blessed with their fierce drive to be themselves.

Empathy and Compassion to Raise an Extraordinary Being – Along came my second child November, 2007. The doctor was concerned about my baby's growth and induced birth. I did not have good memories about labor; pushing without understanding what was happening felt useless and long. My new doctor surprised me by offering a mirror to project the reflection of my son's birth. This was an extraordinary experience! It allowed me to push more effectively and I am immensely grateful for one of the most exquisite moments of my life. This time, I was aware that babies are not born that cute.

In the following months, my charming boy gave us some trouble because he was so thin it made the pediatrician wonder about his health. We worried and tested him for this and for that, but finally, with time, we started understanding that he just had a fast metabolism. He was constantly moving and touching to decipher his environment. He would crawl up the stairs, then roll down, followed by going up and down from the outside of the banister! He would put his fingers inside wheels to see how they worked, or throw things at a fan! He would play with the bees, get under the backyard's deck (habitat for snakes, rats and spiders in Texas) and shut himself inside a box not thinking he could suffocate. I knew he would be the one to jump in a pool, so I had to put him in a baby swimming program. He would try out knives and tools and run away with them! And… he did not like food…

It was not long after he started moving independently that others started to call him a 'naughty' boy. But that sparkle in his eyes told me otherwise. He was curious, not misbehaved or bad. I started realizing that whenever he was interested in something, he would hear, "Stop", "Be careful", "Do not touch", "You are so naughty". I could see how this might affect his self esteem. One day he was at the table and grabbed a pair of forks and started making an X with them. He held the center and start moving his hand trying to build a fan with the forks; he tried to hold a spaghetti noodle in that hand, as if it were the string to turn the fan on and off. I suddenly grew aware of the beauty and potency in his curiosity and interest. I knew I had to allow him to explore, learn and create – and to protect him from those who did not see his interest as a gift to himself and to our world.

Today, he is a happy boy who spends his days marveling, creating and enjoying. Sometimes when he makes a mistake, he still will say, "I am stupid." And I know it came from those times when he heard he was a bad boy. I'm grateful I had enough consciousness to redirect my feedback to, "You are smart. That is interesting. Make sure you do not get hurt." I took the time to be there to make sure he was encouraged and supported. I understood that being mischievous was the thing a smart, curious boy is supposed to do.

I feel he is different in many ways and this makes him unique. I really hope that every child and every person is given the right to be who they are, acknowledging that this is what makes them special. This is a big portion of what parenting is about. I feel conscious parenting invites us to look beyond what seems like inappropriate behavior and refrain from judging.

Promoting Diversity and Inclusion to generate Happiness – I was a busy mom with a lovely strong-willed girl and a rambunctious boy when a new member of the family was due to be born. A friend of mine told me that given it was my third baby and my body already knew what to do, it was likely that he would be born before I could get to a hospital. (It had happened to her.) Her third baby was born in the street in the hands of a fireman. My mom and I were out shopping when something made us laugh. Oh no! I could feel my baby ready to come out. I felt really nervous and could not stop laughing.

My mom started to freak out. She got so stressed that she forced me to leave the mall, drop her off at home, and head to the hospital. That saved me from giving birth to my child at a shopping center. When I got to the hospital, I was soon pushing and moments later, my beautiful boy was sleeping next to me.

This one had to grow up more quickly. He had to keep up with an older sister who was more and more graceful each day and a brother who was constantly living risky adventures and desperately wanted a pal to wrestle and play ball with. He also had very busy parents. Nature was very generous with this baby and gave him useful tools to deal with these life challenges. He was a strong-built boy who soon became a fairly decent contender to his older brother. He had the most beautiful expressive brown eyes, and he was so loving and attentive that anyone who met him would succumb to his tender heart. He had a genuine interest in people and their stories and an extraordinary ability to understand and connect with emotions.

With time, my kids started to show the most fascinating differences. My girl had an inspiring sense of ethics and stern determination. Teachers would notice her incredible ability to lead and organize, showing no tolerance for nonsense. Such good qualities also implied conflict with her brothers, who turned our house into a hectic space. My older boy lived in his particular and exciting world of action. He played with cars, trucks, spaceships and Legos; he drew battles and designed robot and transformer factories. My younger one, on the other hand, would play with animals, figures, music and stories, while looking for opportunities to please and get lots of attention.

Little by little, these differences led to conflict and frustration when they realized that in our shared space it wasn't always easy to get what they wanted. I started to hear sarcastic and impolite conversations. "That is not cool." "You are weird." "You are such a loser." "I don't like you." These hostilities became another big challenge in my parenting life. I taught my kids to respect others and I was astonished with such intolerance in my own household. I wanted them to build a lifelong strong, solid connection.

One day, trying to find a way to make them acknowledge that we needed each other and should respect our differences, I decided to tell them a story. I still recall the moment in which they understood the importance of every person's strength.

This is the story:

"There was once a community of soldiers and warriors. They were strong and smart and no other community around them could compete with their military force and technological power. They were always tired because they had to be constantly alert and trusted no one. Their life was a continuous

power struggle and so they would frequently kill each other.

There was another community of generous and sweet people who showed no interest in being better than the rest. They supported and helped each other, particularly disliking competition and fearing conflict. Caregivers, artists, poets and musicians, lived in beautiful houses and fruitful gardens. One day, a foreign tribe, looking for food, came to their village. The generous people welcomed them and fed them... A few weeks later, the outsiders started to take advantage, they stole food, wrecked the place and abused the people.

Miles away, another community of thinkers, smart and organized people, would spend their days studying and trying to explain the world around them. They overanalyzed things striving for perfect theories, and with time, afraid of making mistakes, they began to have difficulty making decisions and taking action. Their evolution and progress started to slow down."

After telling them the story, I asked my kids what community seemed better than the other. Their faces showed that they had realized there was no objective true answer. I asked them what community would be better at protecting their territory and keeping them safe; which one would be better at nurturing each other; and which one would most likely produce the smartest inventions and would be best at solving problems. My kids realized they all had different strengths and weaknesses. This was a very profound and inspiring moment. A conversation about the greater power of a community that includes and respects different types of people, followed. I pointed out that I had a new expectation, "To acknowledge each other's individual traits and interests and to have respect for each other's personality".

Such a lesson did not have an immediate and drastic effect in our family's lives. Nevertheless, I felt I had found a way to make my kids understand the importance of diversity. Every time I would notice disrespect, I would come back to the story. Gradually I started to see a shift in my kids' attitude towards each other. I started to notice the beginning of an appreciation of them being wired differently. I now can see them being more empathetic, and I enjoy witnessing how this has improved their ability to connect with others. As a famous Harvard study points out, being able to establish a connection with other people, is the main pillar of our personal fulfillment and happiness.

My four stories wish to inspire parents and caregivers to become facilitators of the child, educating them from a place of Humbleness, Love, and the embracement of Diversity. My Ignite moments created an awareness for the importance of parenting from a place of appreciation and inspired me to support my children to become the greatest version of themselves. My action steps intend to be exercises that help you accomplish this in your family.

IGNITE ACTION STEPS

*To develop Humbleness: Look for a beautiful space. Get in a comfortable position or just go for a walk. Turn off cell phones or any distractions and put your focus in feeling with all your senses. Notice what you are surrounded with: Images, sounds, smells, textures, shades, air quality, temperature, tastes, colors. Breathe in and out with awareness. Give yourself enough time to enjoy this experience, then try to make the following reflections: Is everything around connected? What place are you occupying in this bigger picture? Do you feel you are more relevant as an individual, or as a part of this Universe?

*To develop Love, Empathy and Compassion: Reflect upon the following: What is the biggest gift you have ever received? People commonly state 'Love' and their ability to feel and connect with others (especially family and friends), is one of their biggest gifts. Reflect upon whether you spend enough time and energy taking advantage of your ability to love and be loved. Become aware of how much you devote to loving and being loved by your children. Are you embracing love and receiving it generously and openly? Are you expressing and showing them your love?

Make a plan to give more relevance to Love and Empathy in your life, especially in your Parenting. Put it into practice and find a way to keep yourself accountable for this.

*Embrace Diversity – Think about your family, your kids. Write down a description of their personalities, their biggest strengths and what their true individual talents are, even if you do not understand them or like them. Find different ways in which they can contribute to your community, to our world. Make a plan to help your children become the best version of themselves, facilitating the development of those very special talents, and supporting them to overcome their challenges. Let this plan be thorough and committed. Look for accountability.

Fulfillment can only come when you are empowered and free to be yourself; there is no better feeling in this world, than to be YOU.

Ana Sofia Orozco - Canada
Empathy and Conciliation Coach
www.planandthrive.com

§

Please know that every word written in this book, and every letter on the pages has been meticulously crafted with fondness, encouragement and a clarity to not just inspire you but to transform you. Many individuals in this book stepped up to share their stories for the very first time. They courageously revealed the many layers of themselves and exposed their weaknesses like few leaders do. Additionally, they spoke authentically from the heart and wrote what was true for them. We could have taken their stories and made them perfect, following every editing rule, but instead, we chose to leave their unique and honest voice intact. We overlooked exactness to foster individual expression. These are their words, their sentiments and explanations. We let their personalities shine in their writing so you would get the true sense of who each one of them is completely. That is what makes IGNITE so unique. Authors serving others, stories igniting humanity. No filters.

A tremendous thank you goes to those who are working in the background, editing, supporting, and encouraging the authors. They are some of most genuine and heart-centered people I know. Their devotion to the vision of IGNITE, their integrity and the message they aspire to convey, is at the highest caliber possible. They too want you to find your ignite moment and flourish. They each believe in you and that's what makes them so outstanding. Their dream is for your dreams to come true.

§

BOOKS AND RESOURCES MEANINGFUL TO THE IGNITE YOUR PARENTING AUTHORS

Ashley Avinashi ~ Visit www.raisinghumanity.com

Bippan Dhillon ~ *Transforming the Difficult Child: The Nurtured Heart Approach* by Howard Glasser and Jennifer Easley.

Catherine Malli-Dawson ~ *Optimum Nutrition for the Mind* by Patrick Holford. *The Inflammation Solution* by William Sears, MD. *A Mind of Your Own* by Kelly Brogan, MD.

Michaela De Sapio-Yazar ~ *Raising Your Spirited Child* by Mary Sheedy Kurcinka. *You can't say you can't play* by Vivian Gussin Paley. *Multisensory Teaching Of Basic Language Skills* by Judith R. Birsh. *The Magic Years* by Selma Fraiberg. *Positive Discipline: The Classic Guide to Helping Children Develop Self-Discipline, Responsibility, Cooperation, and Problem-Solving Skills* by Nelsen Ed.D., Jane.

Parth Nilawar ~ *Brain Rules for Baby: How to Raise a Smart and Happy Child from Zero - Five* by John Medina. *Play: the Foundation of Children's Learning* by Lisa Murphy. *Thirty Million Words: Building a Child's Brain* by Dana Suskin, MD.

Sara Feldman ~ Visit http://DrMarcie.com/IgniteYourParenting.

Virginia L Lehay ~ *The Secret Life of the Unborn Child*, Thomas Verny, MD. *Tomorrow's Baby: The Art and Science of Parenting from Conception through Infancy* by Thomas R. Verny, Pamela Weintraub.

Upcoming Books in THE IGNITE SERIES

If you feel you have had an IGNITE moment and a story you would like to share, please apply at www.igniteyou.life/apply. We look forward to all the applications.

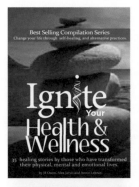

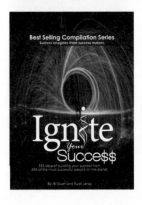

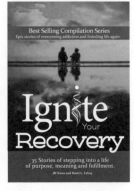